Through the Eyes
of
Mary Magdalene

BOOK I
Early Years & Soul Awakening

Magdalene Weeping at the Feet of Jesus

ESTELLE ISAACSON

Through the Eyes
of
Mary Magdalene

BOOK I
Early Years & Soul Awakening

LOGO*S*OPHIA

First published in the USA
by LogoSophia
© Estelle Isaacson 2012

For information, address:
LogoSophia, 36 Tom Holder Rd.
Ranchos de Taos, NM 87557, USA
logosophia.com

Library of Congress Cataloging-in-Publication Data

Isaacson, Estelle
Through the eyes of Mary Magdalene — 1st edition.

p. cm.

ISBN 978-1-59731-504-3 (pbk: alk. paper)
1. Mary Magdalene, Saint—Legends.
2. Mary Magdalene, Saint—Cult.
BS2485.T 493 2012
226'.092—dc23   2012009883

Cover Image: James J. Tissot (1836–1902)
Mary Magdalene at the Feet of Jesus, Detail.
Brooklyn Museum of Art, acc. no. 00.159.164
Cover Design: Cristy Deming

CONTENTS

Part One
Magdalene's Early Years & Conversion

Part Two
Magdalene Becomes a Disciple

Part Three
The Raising of Lazarus

Part Four
Appendices

ILLUSTRATIONS

Part Three
The Raising of Lazarus

Part Four
Appendices

Acknowledgments

HEARTFELT THANKS go to the publisher, James Wetmore, for his careful attention to every detail, his generosity of spirit, and his publishing expertise. To Bill and Arla Trusiewicz: I thank you for scribing dozens of visions, and for all the assistance you gave me at the beginning of this remarkable journey, and for supporting me in countless ways. I gratefully acknowledge my editors, especially Richard Bloedon, for the many hours spent preparing this book for publication, and for faith in this work and sensitivity in maintaining the integrity of what came through me. And of course I thank Robert Powell and Claudia McLaren Lainson for their introductory words.

I would be remiss if I did not also thank all my dear friends near and far who are lovers and friends of Christ and Sophia, and who are each a miracle in my life through the many ways they supported the process of bringing this book forth: scribing, proofreading, mentoring, healing, advising—and in so many other ways! I am eternally grateful for each one of you!

My utmost gratitude goes to my noble father, who dwells just beyond the veil and is a guiding star for me, and to my wonderful mother, who has always been a calming, stable influence in my life. And to my husband and children: I am so grateful to you for your unwavering love and support and for being so understanding throughout this publication process.

Finally, eternal gratitude to our Heavenly Father and Divine Mother, who guide us and constantly behold us with their loving gaze. It is only because of them that I am able to do this work.

ESTELLE ISAACSON

Dedicated to Divine Sophia
and to Her
Coming World Culture

The Rose of the World

Preface

IN THIS FIRST book of a trilogy on the life of Mary Magdalene, Estelle Isaacson presents her visions of the life of "the Apostle to the Apostles" as seen through Magdalene's own eyes. She begins with Magdalene's birth and follows her through the years leading to the raising of her brother Lazarus from the dead. Estelle presents these visions as her own experiences,[†] and makes no further claims regarding them. She herself selected the visions presented here, setting them in the chronological order of the events depicted.

The reader will find that there are sometimes substantial gaps between events, so that questions arise which may not yet be answered. It should be said also that many visions regarding the life of Christ Jesus and those around him have been, and continue to be, recorded—so that, when published, these may serve to at least partially fill in such gaps. However, for the present purpose, only those visions that feature Mary Magdalene have been gathered together here (and in the two volumes to follow).

Following a Prologue "in the starry heavens," Part One encompasses Magdalene's childhood, her journeys and education in Egypt, her struggle with temptations, and her conversion. Part Two takes the reader through some of Magdalene's experiences as she lays down her former life and follows Jesus as his disciple. Part Three visits the Lazarus mysteries and includes revelations concerning his initiation, death, and resurrection. The book proper ends just after the raising of Lazarus. Part Four comprises five appendices presenting subsidiary visions. Among these are a vision regarding the holy women and a message from them, as well as two visions of Magdalene's mysterious sister Silent Mary,

---

† In March of 2008, Estelle had a profound experience of the wounds of Christ, and thereafter began receiving (mostly on Fridays) continuing visions from the life of Christ.

i

a figure otherwise unknown except through the earlier visions of the Catholic stigmatist Anne Catherine Emmerich.† Estelle has said that Silent Mary is now, and has ever been, a special guide in this work of beholding the Mystery of Golgotha.

The book is graced with many illustrations by James J. Tissot (1836–1902), whose work, largely inspired by the visions of Anne Catherine Emmerich, resonates also with Estelle in a very special way, the artist's depictions being so very close to what she herself witnesses in vision.

Estelle hopes that this trilogy on the life of Mary Magdalene will inspire many to seek for and find the Christ. Magdalene's story is the story of humanity: each of us has laid down our own divinity and willingly descended to this world to gain wisdom by passing through the refining fires of opposition and duality. It is through Christ's redeeming sacrifice that we may find our true selves, and Mary Magdalene can be our guide in this quest. It is no mistake, Estelle has said, that this first volume of the trilogy both opens and closes "among the stars."

Those who find this book valuable and inspiring will be glad to know that the two subsequent volumes of the trilogy are also nearing completion, and that further volumes on other subjects drawn from the ongoing wellspring of Estelle's visions will follow those. Book II of the Magdalene trilogy is subtitled *From Initiation to the Passion*, and Book III is subtitled *From the Ascension to Journeys in Gaul*. Each volume will comprise thirty-three visions, as well as appendices.

JAMES RICHARD WETMORE

---

† See Foreword, p. v, notes.

Foreword

IN THE PAST, seers and prophets were acknowledged and valued for their contributions to society. In the Old Testament, for
example, one of the twelve patriarchs of ancient Israel, Joseph,
while still a mere youth, was acknowledged as a seer by his father
Jacob, who gave Joseph the wondrous "coat of many colors,"
symbolizing his highly developed faculty of "spiritual beholding,"
a faculty linked to the gift of prophecy. Such "spiritual beholding" is known also as *clairvoyance* ("clear-seeing"). Later, while in
Egypt, Joseph foresaw the future, and on the basis of his vision
acted wisely on behalf of the Egyptians by making provision for
what the future held in store. At that time, the ability to see spiritually was highly honored—in Joseph's case by no less a person-
age than the pharaoh of Egypt, who, acknowledging and trusting
Joseph's seership, appointed him vizier over all his lands.

In more recent times, seers have for the most part ceased to be
honored as contributors to culture and society, other than by way
of poetry and literature—with a few notable exceptions, such as
Joan of Arc (1412–1431), whose prophetic ability led her to the
heights of political influence in the early fifteenth century, and
the German Romantic poet Novalis (1772–1801), a gifted visionary
who ascertained profound truths relevant to every human being,
truths of a significance reaching far beyond the literary realm.
Here is what another such seer of our own epoch, Rudolf Steiner
(1861–1925), had to say about Novalis:

> From time to time there appear in the world individuals who
> are able to see *in direct vision* . . . the effects on evolution of
> the event known as the Mystery of Golgotha. The entire spir-
> itual sphere of the Earth was changed through what took
> place with the event of Christ's sacrifice on Golgotha. And
> ever since then, if the "eye of the soul" has been opened
> through contemplation of this event, the seer beholds the

presence of the everlasting power of the Christ in the spiritual sphere of the Earth. [To] a seer, this is *perceptible reality.*

The young German poet Novalis became [such] a seer . . . through a deeply shattering event that made him aware . . . of the connection between life and death. His "eyes of spirit" were opened and a great vista of past ages of the Earth and of the Cosmos, and then also of Christ himself, appeared before him. Novalis was . . . one who with the eyes of spirit had actually seen what is revealed when "the stone is rolled aside" and the One becomes visible who furnishes earthly existence with the proof that *life in the spirit will forever overcome death.* . . .

Because Novalis looked back through the ages with his own awakened eyes of spirit, he was able to affirm that nothing in his life was comparable in importance to the experience of having discovered Christ as a living reality. Such an experience is like a repetition of what happened at Damascus when Paul, who had hitherto persecuted the followers of Christ Jesus and rejected their proclamations, received in higher vision direct proof that Christ lives, that he is present, and that the event of Golgotha is unique in the whole process of the evolution of humanity. . . .

Novalis also speaks of the revelation that came to him as "unique," and maintains that only those who with their whole soul are willing to associate themselves with this event are in the true sense human beings. [He] says that the Christ whom he has seen with eyes of spirit is a power pervading all beings. This power can be recognized by the eye in which this same power is working. The eye that beholds the Christ has itself been formed by the Christ-Power. The Christ-Power within the eye beholds the Christ outside the eye.[†]

This lengthy quote regarding Novalis is relevant to the visions of the contemporary seer Estelle Isaacson (b. 1968), whose visionary power has also been honed through her experience of repeated

---

[†] Rudolf Steiner, *The Christmas Mystery: Novalis, the Seer*—a lecture given in Berlin on December 22, 1908 (CW 108).

immersion in the life of Christ, culminating with the event of the Mystery of Golgotha. She is living testimony to the reality of Rudolf Steiner's words that "those whose eyes of spirit are open can themselves behold this event." In her case it is true to say, in relation to her visions, that "the Christ-Power within the eye beholds the Christ outside the eye." This is the key to entering into the visions of Estelle Isaacson.

Estelle's visions are varied and far-reaching in scope. The present volume is the first of three in which her visions relating to the life of Mary Magdalene are being published. In these volumes the extraordinary life of Mary Magdalene—known, on account of her experience of the Risen Christ in the Garden of Gethsemane on Easter Sunday morning, as the "apostle to the apostles"—is described "from within." For it is characteristic of Estelle's visions that she beholds the Christ events *through the eyes of* Mary Magdalene. In other words, there is a special resonance between the spiritual vision of Estelle Isaacson and the inner life of Mary Magdalene.

Not only do Estelle's visions furnish us with a wealth of otherwise largely unknown details concerning Mary Magdalene, but they also—as in the case of the inspired works of Novalis—communicate profound moral and spiritual truths stemming from the living Christ impulse.

Estelle Isaacson's visions may be compared with those of Anne Catherine Emmerich, the Augustinian nun (1774–1824) who received the *stigmata* (the visible wounds of Christ) at the age of 38, and who devoted the remaining years of her life to communicating her visions of the life of Christ.[†] Anne Catherine Emmerich's visions, at least in terms of the chronology of the life of Christ they furnish, have been conclusively established as authentic.[‡] But apart from this, the validity of Anne Catherine's visions is revealed through their moral effect, when read with open mind

---

[†] Anne Catherine Emmerich, *Visions of the Life of Christ* (San Rafael, CA: LogoSophia Press, 2012).

[‡] Robert Powell, *The Mystery, Biography, and Destiny of Mary Magdalene*, "About Anne Catherine Emmerich's Visions," (Great Barrington, MA: Steinerbooks, 2008).

and heart. The same may be said of the visions of Estelle Isaacson, whom we might well regard as "spiritual sister"—some two hundred years later—to Anne Catherine Emmerich. This connection can provide the reader a context within which Estelle's visions may be better grasped in our materialistic age, when true seers are not esteemed, but are generally ignored.

As also in the case of Anne Catherine Emmerich's visions, many find that these accounts by Estelle are best read aloud—and better still, in a group, in the spirit of Christ's words, "Where two or three are gathered in my name, there am I in your midst" (Matt. 18:20). In such settings the visions have special power to evoke in a living way that which they are describing.

Estelle Isaacson's visions are a remarkable contribution to humanity's spiritual life. Not only do they open up—from within—the life of Mary Magdalene in relation both to Christ and to her brother Lazarus, but they also offer spiritual and moral insights of a far-reaching nature. This volume is a treasure-trove of contemporary spiritual wisdom, and paves the way for the volumes to come, leading ever deeper into the all-encompassing Christ Mystery.

ROBERT POWELL, PH.D.

Introduction

Witnessing the Witness

NOTHING IN these pages is trivial! Seeing "through the eyes of Mary Magdalene," our author raises up a spiritual beacon sorely needed in our time—for we have lost our way. Indeed, we have forgotten who we are. Wherever we look we see that humanity has lost something that formerly gave dignity to the Earth and to civilization. So silently has decency crept out from our culture that we scarcely noticed its passing! In truth we are spiritual beings seeking a human experience, and the greatest model for this fulfillment can be found in the Son of God, who came to Earth to manifest the radiant glory of the fullness of human potential, and thereby to redeem the world.

Having met with the author of this book many times, I can testify to her expansive generosity of soul. Reading her visions, I find myself bathed in goodness, gentleness, and purity. There is a force at work in our world that bears contempt for just these qualities, and Estelle's visions offer an antidote, for they are a spiritual calling. Their light beckons us to turn away from the perilous slopes of materialism in order to walk upon a path of service that the turmoil of divisiveness, and even war, cannot obscure.

Over two thousand years have passed since the turning-point in time when Christ, the Logos, became a human being and walked among us. Our author is a witness of this event in our own pivotal time, telling of things never before spoken. She opens to us the spiritual archives of history, where the greatest deed of earthly evolution is recorded—the life and death, the resurrection and ascension, of the one known as the redeemer of humanity. She invites us into conversations, joys and sorrows great and small, anguish and tragedies. She opens sweeping new perspectives on the events that accompanied the destiny of Jesus and affected life on Earth for all time to come. These spiritual-historical truths had lain dormant until a time came when they could be received by a new level of wakefulness called forth by the second coming of Christ.

For we are living now in the season of Christ's second coming. This second coming is not a physical incarnation, as was his first coming, but is as was decreed at his ascension: he returns to us "in the clouds." What does this mean? It means that he is manifesting in the vital periphery, the etheric sphere of formative forces that surrounds the Earth. Indeed, he is already present in this form. Christ in his second coming will not be seen with physical eyes. Neither will he be heard with physical ears. Estelle tells us he will come to each of us in a way perfectly suited to our own, personal nature. We must first turn to him, however; we must seek him, and listen for him.

But there is something more, something whose time has come: the mysteries of the Divine Feminine. These mysteries have suffered greatly upon the steel anvil of pragmatism, and in consequence, Wisdom, the embodiment of the Divine Feminine (among whose many names is that of *Sophia*), has been silenced. The search for wisdom has been a signature of philosophies and theologies since Isis lost her beloved Osiris in the ancient times of Egypt. The Magdalene mysteries revealed by Estelle thus serve to lift a veil.

Magdalene offers us a golden key to the manifold workings of the Divine Feminine in our time, inspirations that kindle inner striving and call for spiritual vigilance. This book invites us to participate freely in what we may call the new Sophianic community, where all the 'petals' of the Rose of the World may open together in harmony with world evolution. This key is essential for our passage through the crisis currently facing us all.

More immediately, the visions recorded in this book bear witness to the personal experiences of Mary Magdalene—sister of Lazarus, and *spiritual* sister of Jesus. New revelations call out to us as these scenes are brought to life. Seeing through the eyes of

Magdalene, our author sounds a dawn-bell of inspiration an octave above what humanity has hitherto been able to receive.

Jesus brought Magdalene twice through a conversion of her soul. Twice did he cast out her demons. Following the second conversion she joined the holy women, later to become one of those closest to Jesus. She was an intimate witness to the momentous trials he endured during the last years of his life. Through her soul's conversion, Magdalene was filled with a wisdom that uniquely prepared her to understand the mission and the teachings of Jesus Christ. The depth of this wisdom is revealed through these visions. As our author brings to light the unfathomable spiritual love between Jesus and Magdalene, we begin to truly understand why she is called "the apostle to the apostles."

Ours is a time of the descending revelation of Sophia, and the rising revelation of the Divine Mother. As the Proverbs of King Solomon so inspiringly reveal, Wisdom *is* Sophia. There it is stated that the Lord created her at the beginning of his work. She is honored and recognized as the ruler of all cycles of time—ever delighting in the human race. It is her veil that our author is lifting, for it was the Sophia mysteries that streamed into Magdalene. These mysteries, concealed until their destined moment had come, stream now through all of creation. Together, the Lamb (Christ) and his Bride (Sophia) permeate the content of these visions. Their presence becomes so tangible that we can experience them with our entire being.

Estelle reads from the Book of Life, the Eternal Gospel. In this Book, every moment in time has been preserved, chronicled for eternity, awaiting those individuals appointed to turn its pages. In the usual course of life this Book is read as one crosses the threshold of death and enters into the ocean of timelessness. There, angels read and reveal its secrets. But we are all meant to read in this Book during earthly life also, and in times to come this will hold true for a growing number of human souls. For now, however, let us be grateful that some go before us as our guides, bringing to us stories that inspire us to be more of who we surely are.

The visions in this first volume thus invite us into a community of spirits who long to assist us. They ask that we take courage to open ourselves to the power of truth; for when we stand before the mysteries of abiding certainty, we are brought to our knees. We weep, and the Mother takes us in. To stand before these mysteries pierces the heart, just as it pierced the heart of Mary Magdalene so long ago. Such a heart becomes an organ of perception, weeping "tears of grace." These also are the tears of our time.

Our author was not yet 33 years of age when Christ, radiating love and clothed in pure light, first called her. While seeing through the eyes of another, she fell as if struck—for in the brilliance and purity of the eyes through which she gazed, the darkness within her soul howled in stark contrast. She gave up her darkness to Christ in order to become transparent, and this darkness he willingly received. She urges us to understand that he does this not for her alone, but for you and me also.

She has suffered the isolation and loneliness of the "dark night of the soul" that accompanies such changes in consciousness. This is part of the path of preparation. Her trials brought further testing as she struggled to feel at home with her awakening gifts. Prudence required that she keep these things close in her heart, letting her gifts painstakingly mature. Her journey continued in alternating currents of spiritual experience followed by apparent setbacks, leading her again into the dark night of the soul and thereby into ever-deeper stages of inner preparation. This pattern continued until spiritual poverty finally emptied her heart. To the silence and emptiness she surrendered. Thus in inward poverty of spirit, she has come also to feel in her own person, and in ever-increasing measure, the pains of the wounds of Christ.

Estelle was an unusually sensitive child. She was raised in a deeply religious family, shielded from influences that bring harm to the heart. This was a blessing that sustained her and preserved her ability to see deeply, with spiritual sight, into the world that surrounds and penetrates all of nature. This gift of childlike innocence radiates from her. Through her meditative life she has also been led to various religions, finding in each both beauty and truth. This has made her a weaver of peace on the loom of diversity.

Now a mature woman, Estelle is still learning how to live with her gifts. She does not claim that what she sees is perfect. She experiences her visions in layers, sometimes visiting the same scene several times. Each time she sees a new element or hears something that did not come forward the time before. She trusts that what is given in each vision is the best possible presentation for her understanding and for the understanding of those who feel called to read her visions.

Many have experienced the healing power that courses through these visions. Estelle reminds us that Christ himself is present in them, and that it is his desire to touch the reader through them. She asks us to forgive the inevitable imperfections in her documentation of these experiences. She knows that Christ dwells in them and hopes that we will feel the great love of our Redeemer.

We are called here to remember what lives deep in our own hearts. These pictures from the tableau of Magdalene's life carry the magical power to release us from the transfixing illusions of materialism—for we children of Earth do truly long to hear what can free us from the deadening deceptions that surround us. Then we shall no longer feel alone, or hopeless, in a world whose tangled complexities seem so daunting. We shall know that Christ speaks to us, is with us, and sends to us the Comforter. Estelle invites us to stand witness by her side, in community with the Logos and with Sophia. She tells us we need not wait until we are perfect, for Christ comes to us now!

CLAUDIA McLAREN LAINSON

Prologue

I WAS TRAVELING swiftly through space, guided by my heart. A tremendous feeling of love was drawing me to some other place and time. Soon I saw beautifully colored rays streaming toward me in shafts of rose and green. Then I passed through many veils of light, until I came to a star system that I knew was in fact the *Being of Mary Magdalene*. Indescribable harmonies resounded around and within me. In awe, I went back to the beginning of time and witnessed the creation of that being who would later be known as Mary Magdalene. I could hear the "voice" of the soul of Mary Magdalene singing its harmonies.

The Cosmic Creation
of the Being of Mary Magdalene

AS I was drawn into the streaming harmonies, traveling toward their source, I saw that these harmonies and the colored rays were emanating from the Christ Being. Christ was "singing the being of Mary Magdalene into form." There is no other way to describe this! She *was* his voice—the veils of harmonies and color-tones emanating from him *were* her being.

Christ was radiating from the Central Sun, the realm of the Father. I felt throughout my whole being the *perfection* of the highest Father Principle, which was embodied and brought to Earth by Jesus Christ. And as the Father's love permeated my soul, I rejoiced!

I saw a seed of light emanate from the Central Sun, through the Son; and it was through the Son's harmonies that Mary Magdalene was birthed into existence. Out of the harmonies of her birth, stars were born. I heard the harmonies all around me and was surrounded by the stars of her being. I felt the Divine Breath moving upon her. I felt the utter holiness of new creation, along with the undeniable recognition of Christ as Creator. I was humbled to witness such a holy event: *to experience the creation of the being that would eventually become Mary Magdalene!*

I was then outside this star system, beholding it as though from afar. Out of this star system emanated the *spirit* of Mary Magdalene, who then appeared before me. I understood that she was present at the beginning of Creation, that she is a part of Sophia; and that she elected to sacrifice herself and descend—in order to go through the Fall, and thereby separate herself from All That Is. Thus was the work of Mary Magdalene pre-ordained: through her incarnations she would descend to the depths. She would take upon herself the task of entering into that which was *unknowable* to the Father: darkness, sin, disease, and death. She said, *I will go down and I will know the unknowable, and I will know it to the depths of my being.*

And the Mother said in answer to her:

I shall send the Son to be your Savior, and to be the Savior of the World—so that when you have reached the depths of the unknowable, Christ shall descend after you and find you in your depths and raise you up; and you shall do this for humanity, as their representative.

You shall guide humanity as it lays down its divinity and descends into the unknowable. By thus descending into the dark abyss of separation from All That Is, you shall walk with human beings and suffer all that they shall suffer in the abyss of their own souls—in the abyss of the World Soul. And you shall continue to suffer with humanity until the unknowable has been known.

Then you shall guide them to Christ, who is the Knower of All Souls, the Knower of the Unknowable. It is he who shall lead the soul out of its own abyss to restore it to All That Is, in the realm of the Father. Christ shall receive all souls who come to him, and they shall be known by him. Thus shall he then present these souls as a gift to the Father—for they shall be victors over sin, disease, and death.

You shall go down to Earth; and the further you descend, the more shall you forget your divinity and seem to lose your power—until you reach the depths. I shall be in the depths. Have no fear, for you shall be victorious!

Her Birth in Bethany

JUST MOMENTS before the birth of Mary Magdalene at her family's homestead in Bethany I beheld her soul descending through the spheres toward the Earth. She arrived finally at the bridge of rainbow light, which leads down into a mother's womb just before a soul incarnates.

The bridge of rainbow light *is* Christ! Accompanied by his angels, he ushers in the souls as they incarnate. I saw that it is through the light of Christ that we come to Earth, that out of our love for him, and his love for us, we agree to incarnate in order to serve the Earth's evolution. I saw Mary Magdalene's soul passing through Christ's light, condensing and contracting into physical form as she entered her mother's womb. I then experienced the birth—from both her mother's perspective and from Mary's simultaneously.

So fiery and strong was the being of Mary Magdalene that her mother's womb was burning like the sun. The birth was arduous. Mary's mother found herself at death's door, for it seemed that her own being had to expand to receive the being of this child.

I experienced likewise the contraction of Mary's soul as she descended toward the Earth. This transition from a state of spiritual expansion to a state of dense physicality felt like a profound soul pain within me, perhaps because she was descending from so high a state. The mother's labor contractions seemed to directly accompany the pain of this extreme contraction of Mary's soul, mirroring that pain in the world of incarnated life. As Mary's soul passed through the womb, I saw her descend through the crown of stars, the "veil" that separates the spiritual realm from the physical realm.

The first to greet her on this side of the veil was Naomi, her mother's pious elder sister. As Naomi beheld the little one's sweet face, she noticed that her hair was a striking shade of golden-red. The newborn immediately let out a cry that seemed to speak of her soul's grief over the fallen world. It was as if she were weeping for the Earth, as if she were crying out: *What a world! I am now here in this fallen world! Oh, what a world!*

To make the transition easier for Mary, Naomi was embraced at the portal of birth by Mary's angel, so that the tiny infant in Naomi's arms was in turn embraced by her angel. This opened Naomi's heart to the spiritual world; and as she held the swaddled infant to her cheek, she experienced a vision.

Naomi's Vision

NAOMI saw a star cast itself from the heavens and fall to Earth, becoming a little babe. She saw the infant grow into the most beautiful woman she had ever seen. But her joy turned to sorrow when she beheld this child, her red-haired niece, overtaken by forces of darkness. In subtle ways, little by little, the girl grew vain and prideful—and was trapped in the world.

Naomi watched her struggle to find her way through the darkness, at times in great anguish, and plagued with illnesses brought on by evil forces. She held the newborn to her breast and cried, *O, Almighty God! Let this not be! But if it is Thy will that she be tried in these fires, then set Thy hand upon her and save her in the end!*

She wept in sorrow and rocked the child while the other midwife worked to stanch the blood hemorrhaging from the mother's womb. Mary's mother had fainted and was losing blood quickly. Filled with anxiety over her sister's condition, and over what she had seen in vision, Naomi prayed for strength, both for herself and for her sister.

Then she entered into vision again and saw the sun descending toward Mary just at her darkest moment, illuminating her. She saw Mary freed, rising up victorious over the darkness, and giving her life to God. Upon seeing this, Naomi praised God in exultation:

> *Blessed be the name of the Most High God,*
> *Who sets His hand against all evil,*
> *And redeems our souls!*
> *And bless us, O Almighty God, each and every one*
> *Who suffer like vagabonds in the wilderness—*
> *Who have fallen so far away from Thee.*
> *Deliver us and encircle us with Thine angels*
> *And restore us to our former habitation.*

As Naomi prayed and rocked little Mary in her arms, a beautiful rosy light formed a sheath around the sweet infant. The rosy light was the gift of the Divine Mother's love, which would forever abide in her soul. This gift of the Mother's love descended with Mary. It was the flicker of light that would one day lead Mary to seek redemption. It would lead her to Christ.

Mary's mother, Jezebel, returned to herself after Naomi's prayer. The bleeding slowed, and her strength began to return. Naomi placed the infant in Jezebel's arms; and as Mary began to nurse, Naomi stroked Jezebel's hair and kissed her face several times, praising her for bringing to Earth so special a child.

Several days later Naomi went to the Temple in Jerusalem to make an offering on behalf of her newborn niece. She offered prayers for Mary and requested blessings for her, knowing the challenges she would face. These prayers became angelic beings with wings of light that remained in the greater spiritual atmosphere of the Temple as gifts and blessings for her, accompanying and watching over her throughout her life.

I was then given a message for all who receive this vision:

Pray for each other. For your prayers are angels, and can save souls. Your prayers can bring souls to Christ. The prayers of Mary Magdalene are angels who surround you now, for after the Resurrection she spent thirty years or more praying continuously for the redemption of humanity. You have claim on the prayers that she spoke on your behalf—for she saw you, and prayed for you! As you ask, so shall you receive. She will guide you to the Shepherd's Fold; she will present your soul as a gift to the Father.

O Divine Human! No longer think that you are nothing! For you are a jewel in the Father's crown! The jewel that you are lies in the depths of your soul. As you descend into your depths, you will find the jewel that you are. Do not fear your own depths, but ask for the Comforter to be with you. The only way to know your Self is to pass through your depths.

Be at peace. There is time enough for you to do your work. And the blessing of Mary Magdalene is upon your head forever!

Amen.

Rural Manor in Galilean Hills near Magdala

PART ONE

Magdalene's Early Years & Conversion

Sea of Galilee Near Magdala

I

Secret Meetings Between
a Young Girl and an Egyptian

I FOUND MYSELF standing in a deserted road. Perhaps it was a holy day. It was almost midday, and I wondered why all was so quiet. I saw a young girl, eleven or twelve years of age, dressed in a striped robe. A natural-colored mantle was wrapped around her head and shoulders; her tunic was beige with purplish-blue vertical stripes. She was excited, and was having difficulty containing her elation.

She walked along a path in front of a building, then down some steps to its left. To her right was a little area below the level of the street, surrounded by a low stone wall. In that place a woman named Tara was preparing large flat oval-shaped breads. She smiled at the girl and continued her work, as the warm scent of baking bread hung on the air. The girl nodded her head at Tara and kept walking, coming to a back alleyway where the path narrowed. On the side of the building to her right was a door.

As she opened the door, sunlight penetrated the small room, which was otherwise only dimly lit by a narrow window. Inside sat a handsome, olive-skinned man with mesmerizing eyes of golden amber. It was clear that the young girl loved him. Around his neck hung an amulet—its center stone an opalescent green color with a yellow cast, encased in gold. "Horns" surrounded either side of the round stone. She wanted to touch it, but dared not ask. The man had procured it while journeying in Egypt.

There was a small recess in the room, where he had built into the wall a wooden grid of boxes, each holding a scroll. He took one of the scrolls down, along with a small vial of fragrant oil about three inches in length. The vial was rounded and broader at the bottom, with a cork stopper in the top. As he unrolled the scroll and showed it to the girl, she noticed that it was covered with hieroglyphs and colorful drawings. It captivated her.

I understood that this man, whose name was something like "Heoman," had been telling the girl magical tales of Egypt, and of the powers Egyptians possessed. I was wondering how she had come to know him, when, suddenly, the answer came.

I saw an episode from her past, when she had done something quite magical. Heoman had been there and witnessed it. It happened at a holiday gathering when she was about seven years old. A celebration was in progress. The girl's family and guests were feasting outside on the grounds. Garlands of boughs and flowers adorned the tables and trellises. A lamb was roasting on a spit, the smoke rising in wisps.

The girl wandered into a nearby grove and sat beneath a large olive tree, telling herself a long, fanciful story about a maiden possessed of magical abilities. Acting as though she were that maiden, she tilted her face upward and gazed into the sky, crying earnestly, "O, gentle Wind, bring my little bird to me." She threw her arms wide open—and just then a small bird settled on her wrist.

Heoman stood nearby, and had been watching and listening in amusement. But when he saw the bird alight upon her wrist, he realized that she had a gift. Later that day he spoke with her privately, wanting to hear her ideas about the world, and found that she possessed unusual wisdom for her age. That was how they became friends. I saw then that this little girl was Mary, later to be known as Mary Magdalene.†

I returned now to the little room where I had seen them meeting in secret over Egyptian scrolls. Heoman was teaching Magdalene what the symbols meant. She was not supposed to be visiting him, especially alone. But she was enthralled with him, and fascinated with the Egyptians and their death rituals, especially their practices of burial and embalming. She was also intrigued with their views of life after death. Heoman, who was not Jewish, told her that he found the ideas of Judaism limiting—especially

---

† We use the name "Magdalene" to refer to the individual later known as Mary Magdalene. She was called "Magdalene," by her peers or family. Her castle was on the shore of the Sea of Galilee, near a city later called "Magdala."

their beliefs regarding life after death. This brought on for Magdalene an inner struggle: a path was opening to her, yet at the same time she felt constrained in her present life.

From time to time Heoman gave her small vials of oil and lent her some of the smaller scrolls to study. Magdalene began to feel "homesick" for Egypt. Every time Heoman journeyed there, she would tearfully beg him to take her along. Sometimes he brought back fabrics—rich linens in bright colors, as soft as silk. I saw her fondling one of the fabrics. It had been dyed with the rind of an exotic fruit to a beautiful shade of maroon, embroidered throughout in a tiny palm leaf motif, and finished with borders of straight lines with leaves in between—all done in a silvery thread. Magdalene thought it the most beautiful thing she had ever seen.

With such beauty available to her, Magdalene came to reject the dowdy dust-colored linen fabrics of Judea. The older she grew, the more outlandish did her clothing become. But to wear such bright colors, she had to seek out places where people of the right sort were present. And so, over time, she found her way into circles where such fashion was expected and desired, for example among groups of wealthy Egyptians.

At this time I saw her still meeting with Heoman, and for the most part living apart from her family. She was growing more and more displeased with life in Judea, which she regarded—for women—as that of "sheep" obliged to do whatever they were bid. Although she came from a wealthy family and had finer things than most in the region where she dwelt, life was still too dull for her—she could no longer endure the drab colors, the modest architecture, or the staid philosophies of her culture. Magdalene wanted the best of everything, and to be surrounded by beauty.

From an early age Magdalene had lived in a castle that had been bequeathed to her. She was attended by a governess commissioned by her mother, shortly before her death, to watch over her until she came of age. The young Magdalene was willful and precocious. She was belligerent and resentful toward the governess.

Magdalene's mother had been unable to exercise much influence over her as a child, and she died when Magdalene was still young. Her old servant, the governess, was pious to a fault and very strict. But she could barely tolerate the young Magdalene.

Lazarus Attempts to
Arrange a Marriage for Magdalene

I SAW Magdalene hiding behind an arch inside a stone building. She was thirteen or fourteen years of age. From time to time she peered out from behind the arch, spying on a gathering of men in the dining hall. These men were feasting together at tables arranged in a great U-shape. Furniture resembling chaise lounges was pulled up at either end, upon which the more important men reclined as they dined.

Magdalene scanned the hall for someone in particular, but did not find him. She crossed the hall with quick, light movements and stood among some shadows, sweeping the room again with her eyes. Then she saw him: a thin-faced youth with thick, curly, dark hair, seated in such a way that she was able to attract his attention with a wave of her hand. He smiled at her, his eyes brightening. She slipped silently out of the hall into the dark garden. Understanding her cue, the young man arose from the table, adjusted his brown and red striped robe, excused himself, and ventured into the garden to find Magdalene. As he walked through the flowers and shrubs looking furtively from side to side, Magdalene emerged suddenly from a shadowy corner and they giggled mischievously together.

It seemed at first that she might be in love with the youth, but I soon discovered otherwise. In reality, Magdalene was on the verge of betrothal to a certain man whom she did not wish to marry, and so had chosen this youth as her way out—for if she were found to be untrue, the other suitor would want nothing further to do with her. Her sole intention with this youth was to befriend him in order to sabotage the impending betrothal. At her tender age she was quite willful and rebellious, wanting to have her own way even if it might cause others pain.

Lazarus, Magdalene's elder brother, was greatly concerned for her well-being, and had been working with a patriarchal relative (I believe their father's brother) to find her a husband. He wanted her to marry young, for fear her unruly nature might otherwise prevent her ever being married. The sooner she was betrothed, the better! Lazarus had decided upon a certain man who was outgoing, quite agreeable and witty, as well as quite pious—and the uncle agreed he would make a fine husband for Magdalene. But Magdalene did not like him. He was wealthy enough, and intelligent, but his personality did not suit her. And so she had schemed to evade this arrangement by plotting secret trysts with the youth.

When the relationship with the youth was discovered, Magdalene's old servant-woman broke into a tirade. She reprimanded her for thinking she had any ability to choose for herself a husband. "What you are doing is unsafe—sneaking around with that young boy! The only sensible thing is to allow your family to make you a good match!" Magdalene was taken aback by the words of her governess, but did not fuss over her outburst. It merely strengthened her resolve to advance her schemes.

Meanwhile, as Lazarus pressed forward with arrangements for the betrothal, the time approached when Magdalene was to pledge her agreement. This was to take place at a family dinner. The family was of course anxious to have the matter settled. An intimate dinner was prepared. All were at table, waiting for Magdalene, when finally she emerged from her quarters.

Lazarus, waiting in the main hall, was the first to glimpse her. He knew at once that she was up to something, for she was not dressed in her usual finery. Instead, she wore traveling clothes—a dark blue dress and veil, and hardly any jewelry. She breezed past the startled Lazarus, leaving by the front entrance, where a small caravan was drawn up, awaiting her. Lazarus followed, not believing his eyes! *What on earth was she doing?* The suitor came out and stood beside him, watching Magdalene hoist herself into the chariot. "What is the meaning of this, Lazarus?" he asked in a strained voice.

Magdalene turned and coyly smiled. "I am leaving, and I am *not* giving my consent to this betrothal today." She spoke matter-of-factly, daring Lazarus to contradict her.

With these words, she sped away like a bird set free, giving not a moment's thought to the fact that she had humiliated her brother and the suitor. It mattered not to her; she was not going to marry someone she did not know or love, just to please others! She did think for a moment of the young man—the one with whom she had been dallying—but only to shrug her shoulders and send him an inner farewell. She had no use for him now. Tantalizing adventures lay before her, and soon she was plotting how she might spend her time with friends on the coast of the Mediterranean Sea.

The two men stood at the entrance of the estate. They were confounded, unable to speak. Then, Lazarus turned his face heavenward and said something like "Well, I did try!"

Magdalene stayed for a time in a portside village with two girlfriends who had been to Egypt and who entertained her with their stories. It seemed that no matter where Magdalene went, Egypt always beckoned her. She decided she would go to Heoman when she returned, and beg him to take her to Egypt.

Egypt Calls

I WAS taken ahead in time. Magdalene was about sixteen years old. Her relationship with Martha, her sister, was growing more and more strained. The sisters were so different, and Martha felt it her duty to see that Magdalene remained pure and followed the cultural standards of the time. She kept herself abreast of Magdalene's doings, much as a mother would, except that there was not much feeling of nurturing love in her concern; rather, Martha fretted incessantly over Magdalene and resented her for causing such worry.

Magdalene's family had grown increasingly worried about her involvement with Heoman and his Egyptian enticements. At a small family gathering that year I saw Magdalene speaking with Heoman (she must have invited him), and again she seemed charmed by him—his light amber eyes were so engaging. As she spoke with him, her governess grabbed her harshly by the arm and pulled her away, creating a scene. It became rather ugly— Magdalene was humiliated in front of family and friends.

Later, she locked herself in her room. The governess stood outside, yelling at her, saying she was becoming loose and wild, and that her bad reputation was so unbecoming that she might never find a righteous husband. But Magdalene did not care. Instead, through the servant's ranting, she heard Egypt calling to her. She threw a tantrum in her room, tearing apart her bedding and overturning the furniture. She hated her life—she did not belong with her family!

I found myself then following a caravan, and saw that Magdalene was a little older—evidently I had again gone forward in time. Camels and donkeys were making their usual sounds. When the caravan stopped for the night, Heoman performed an evening ritual that had to do with the moon and the stars.

At this time Magdalene was unsure what she thought about God. She was not inclined to worship Egyptian gods, but she did feel they embodied her notions of the divine more than the Jewish concept of God. She was traveling to Egypt to find her lost self—it was something she had to do. She knew that this was a matter between her and the stars.

In Egypt she stayed at the home of a woman who, although of advanced age, was very beautiful. This woman's house, with its clean lines and elegant details, appealed to Magdalene. It was a long, narrow home, open to the air and situated adjacent to a tributary of the Nile. White linen draperies separated the living spaces. The elderly woman had long, straight, silvery hair and wore a simple, sheer dress. She was an acquaintance of Heoman.

Magdalene was taken to a Mystery school, where there were only a few students, all of them female. The teacher was a woman as well. They met in an underground chamber, a stone room with hieroglyphs covering the walls and an altar at one end. Above the altar, a hole in the ceiling let in a dim light.

At first, Mary felt like an outsider. She was unsure of herself, wondering whether she was doing the right thing, and whether her choices might hurt others, especially her family. It was as if she stood at a precipice, about to fall away from the life she had hitherto known into unfamiliar territory. Furthermore, as the only non-Egyptian in the school, she felt overwhelmed.

What she really wanted was a sign from God that she was doing the right thing, but she lacked faith—not only in herself, but also in God.

The teacher was detached and cold. The students were not allowed to have relationships with her or with each other, and so Magdalene felt completely alone. The teacher impressed upon the students that once they took this first step, they could never turn back—for they would be entrusted with deep mysteries that might never be divulged. Magdalene took this step, but she did it not from a sense of certainty; rather, it was from a feeling of constraint: she had come all that way in a defiant manner, and it was pride—more than purity of intent—that kept her from leaving.

And so a new phase in Magdalene's life began. From the outset she was attacked by demons feeding upon her fear of leaving the old behind. She knew she had come to a place of higher knowledge, but these demons aimed to prevent her going forward. Two demons in particular attacked her with great vigor.

The teacher knew of this but chose not to address it with Magdalene directly; instead, she told the neophytes a lengthy story intended to initiate them into an understanding of evil. The teaching was given so that the students might learn what to do when encountering the "dark side."

Magdalene felt unsure, however, whether this teaching truly derived from "the light," for she had been raised believing that evil was to be avoided at all costs. *We do not touch anything that is unclean; we do not intermingle with those who are not consecrated to God,* was the teaching she had always heard.

And yet this woman was trying to bring Magdalene to an understanding that evil had a place, that it served a purpose. With this idea she did not at first feel comfortable, but she resolved, nevertheless, to continue on her path of learning. She knew she was there for a reason, even if she did not yet fully understand what that reason was.

She tried to accept the new teachings as well as she might, letting go of what did not yet feel right while clinging to her original impressions of Heoman—remembering how she had felt so drawn to Egypt. Aware that her heart beat in harmony with what she knew of Egyptian life and ideas, she felt she should trust in the flow of these events and see where they might lead her.

As the vision was closing, I saw Christ in the spiritual realm. I felt the weight of my path, and of my own uncertainty. I had so many unanswered questions. He handed me a scroll of light and said, *The Truth will set you free.* He told me also that greater understanding and wisdom would in due course come.

Egyptian Temple Garden

II

Magdalene and the
Hierophant of the Death Mysteries

I STOOD at the head of a series of stone steps. They smelled dry and musty. To my left rose a wall of massive square stones, set one atop the other, fitted perfectly together without mortar. Spare, dusty vines grew up part of the wall. I looked down the steps and saw that they led to an underground chamber. I looked behind me and saw a desert landscape. I knew I was in Egypt.

I saw Magdalene. She was dressed in the Egyptian style, her hair beautifully arranged with small golden adornments. I was unsure of her age, but she seemed young—certainly less than twenty years old. Leaving the bright sunlight behind, she descended the steps into a torch-lit passageway. In the flickering light, hieroglyphs were visible on the walls. I understood that this was not Magdalene's first visit to this place. The passageway ended in a square room with a rectangular altar at its center. On the left wall were depictions of Isis holding a child, as well as other scenes from the legend of Isis. Behind the altar was a scene of the death of Osiris, surrounded by hieroglyphs that I could not so clearly make out.

This room was dedicated to the enactment of the Death Mysteries, the "temple sleep" initiation, a ritual in which the initiate was led into a kind of sleeping death for three days, in hope of uniting thereby with Osiris, who would then bestow upon the initiate important esoteric truths. The initiate would in this way become a "child of Osiris," born anew as he or she re-entered the body, bearing the imprint of all that Osiris had taught. Such an initiate was referred to as a "Son of Osiris," or a "Daughter of Osiris."

In this way were the Great Mysteries taught to some few chosen individuals prepared to receive the training from established initiates. After their initiation they would be able to recall their experiences from the time of the temple sleep. There were in fact various classes of initiates, those at a lower level in their training receiving instruction from those at higher levels.

Magdalene loved the paintings on the walls. She was fascinated by the familiar stories of the mystical love between Isis and Osiris, tales that lived in her heart. She knew that Isis and Osiris were eternally in the stars and that their love was everlasting.

Presently a man emerged from a chamber to the left of the room. Magdalene felt some anxiety at being in this hierophant's presence, especially alone. His role was to guard the Death Mysteries, to facilitate the initiatory work of the temple sleep. He had been brought up for this task and dedicated to it, even set apart, and had never known an ordinary life among the common people. For all his life he had been a temple initiate, and now he was a high initiate of the Death Mysteries. He had passed through many levels of the Mysteries and acquired great wisdom, far beyond most others living in this time and place. Because of his spiritual background, it was not easy to relate to him according to usual social customs. This made Magdalene uneasy, for she was quite identified with her social gifts—gifts that had no relevance, however, to such a man as this.

The hierophant was dressed in a short tunic and bore a breastplate and headdress resembling a dog-like creature, which I understood to be a symbol of the guardian of Osiris. Just the sight of him, as he entered the room, sufficed to put Magdalene into an enhanced state of awareness.

On this occasion she had come to him to be prepared as his handmaiden, or assistant, in certain initiations. After greeting her, he showed her where to position herself during a particular ritual. This was to be at the foot of the altar, which was long enough for a person to lie upon. She had witnessed such rituals several times before in connection with her preparation for this role.

While she was standing next to the altar, I looked up and noted in more detail the scenes depicted in the hieroglyphs: the rows of pictures portrayed what happens to the soul as it crosses the threshold into the spiritual realms during the temple sleep. These were vivid imaginations for Magdalene. She was very drawn to these pictures and spent much time meditating upon them.

Looking more closely, I saw three primary horizontal rows of images. Each row was divided into a further three rows, giving nine rows in all. The drawings were quite intricate. They illustrated the nine paths the soul can take during its spiritual sojourn. I received the understanding that initiates were taught and carefully prepared before crossing into the sleeping death, and that they had *always* to remain in the Middle Way, that is, on the middle paths, of which three were here portrayed. The three paths Above and the three paths Below were heavily guarded. The paths Above were obstructed by angelic beings, and those Below by evil beings. These beings barred most souls from entering into the Mysteries of these two levels, whereas the middle three paths were open to all undergoing initiation. Only highly seasoned initiates might experience the Above or the Below, and only after having first received much wisdom from traveling the Middle Way.

Because the present hierophant had gained considerable experience in the Middle Way, he had been able to venture also into the other two realms. Upon the walls, the Middle Way was depicted in great detail, whereas the paths of the Above and Below were only sketches, works in progress. This man was adding further wisdom, as he acquired it, bringing more details to the older hieroglyphs. Very few had dared venture into the "catacombs" of the Below. And the lofty heights of the Above were even less known.

While being instructed in these Mysteries, Magdalene had expressed an avid interest in both the Above and the Below. This caused the initiate great concern, for this interest of hers would not be appeased. These two paths enticed Magdalene, and throughout her training she wrestled often against her obsession with them.

At the time of this vision Magdalene was still young and wealthy, vain and beautiful, living a life of luxury. Even so, this was well before the debauchery into which she would fall a decade or more later, after which she would finally go to Jesus for spiritual help. But at this stage of her youth she had an insatiable curiosity, coupled with a desire to rise to the loftiest heights in whatever pursuit she chose. This pursuit of excellence derived, however, not from a healthy spiritual maturity, but from the kind of vanity that had driven her to seek ever-higher social status.

During her time as the hierophant's apprentice she struggled with these desires within herself. She had been taught that desires such as these posed great danger to the soul undergoing temple sleep, and that they must be mitigated or subdued. All focus was to be on remaining in the Middle Way. There were even certain practices the neophyte underwent precisely for the purpose of cleansing and purifying the soul of such desires. Indeed, instructions for this purification were laid out in pictures on the right-hand wall.

Having completed their passage through the temple sleep, successful initiates would return bearing wisdom. This wisdom was carefully recorded, adding thereby to the accumulated body of knowledge. Priests of varying vocations could then draw from this knowledge what they required in their work among the people. Such knowledge was of course not accessible to all. Only those who gave evidence of certain gifts, and whose times of birth fulfilled particular astrological requirements, were permitted to enter the path of initiation. They were trained for this from an early age. This was indeed a serious matter on account of the dangers inherent in this path, including that of death. If after crossing over the threshold in the temple sleep a soul wandered from the Middle Path into the Above or the Below, it was quite likely its bodily vehicle would perish in consequence of its difficulty finding the way back.

The man now teaching Magdalene was called a "Son of God," a name given him because of his high initiation. Only those able to go where he had gone and then *return* were accorded this title, for they were regarded as having been "born" directly from the gods. They were thus honored for having undergone a literal death, from which God had decreed that they should be delivered back to the body to continue in life. This was seen as a new birth, for these initiates were forever changed by their experience in the spiritual realm. There were very few such "Sons of God."

As part of her training, Magdalene would lay herself down upon the altar, and her teacher would then facilitate her passing into a trance-like state. He would instruct her, step-by-step, regarding everything her soul would undergo in its journey into the spiritual realm. Each time, various obstacles would arise in her—and these would require of her some sort of work. These obstacles were primarily negative emotions, such as anger or fear, associated with events from her past.

Certain rituals of preparation had to be celebrated before anyone could be taken into a temple sleep. One who had passed through the first levels of temple sleep could then serve others preparing for initiation. Magdalene had experienced the preliminary initiations; thus she was deemed ready to prepare to assist others. She was taught how to prepare the body, a task that required lengthy ministrations. The temple of the body had to be cleansed, purified, strengthened, and consecrated—so that the soul, returning from higher realms, would find its body a suitable temple to reinhabit. Herbs and oils were employed, and rich foods avoided. There was also a period of fasting.

In these places of initiation, certain rooms were set aside for cleansing the body. They were built over energy meridians in the Earth, which would cleanse the body in a special way. The Egyptians knew of a vertical stream of energy that rises up through the center of the body. They knew also that in most people this stream of energy is inhibited by many factors. In the body of an initiate undergoing temple sleep it was very important that the vertical stream of energy flow uninhibited. Thus there were places in the preparation rooms where the candidate was directed to stand and connect to the Earth in such a way that the vertical energy stream would be strengthened. Such standing-places were referred to as "pillars of the temple," for standing at them enabled the vertical energy to stream in, upholding the body in firm rectitude, bringing all the meridians into alignment with the Earth. Most often these places also had pyramids built over them, centered over the energy stream.

As was noted earlier, Magdalene had first come into contact with the Mysteries of Egypt through Heoman, a friend of her family. It was he who had recommended her for this work because of her gifts. Her teachers in Egypt recognized her gifts as well. I understood also that Magdalene's father had had some connections with Egyptian initiates. He was himself of Egyptian descent and had taken this wisdom into himself—although for the most part had hidden it away. But what he had thus received nevertheless influenced Magdalene on a certain level, even when she was a young girl. She had inherited some of her father's Egyptian writings after his death and had kept these in her castle; many years later, after having attended the mystery schools in Egypt, she was able to study them. Only then did she realize that her father had understood something of these Mysteries.

Magdalene's teacher, the one called the "Son of God," admonished her many times regarding her vanity and pride. He warned her that this delusive aspect of her nature might prove her downfall, and that on the other side of the veil it would rise like a great demon—if she did not overcome it. But she was not swayed by his warnings. She thought she had the right to be proud of who she was: beautiful, wealthy, admired of many, and also quite clever. She did not see how admiring her own qualities could pose so great a threat. And yet her teacher's warnings did instill in her some fear, for she wondered whether he might after all be right. Perhaps if she did go too deeply into the temple sleep she would indeed be greeted by the terrible demon he spoke of. This was a frightening thought, and she did not want to put his warning to the test.

And so, to avoid having to face the demon of her own vanity by practicing the temple sleep herself, she had pretended to take an even greater interest in assisting at the initiations of others. She put on a façade of piety and humility whenever she was around her teacher, pressing her vanity down into the depths of her soul, pretending she had overcome it, though knowing all the while that it lurked just beneath the surface.

Eventually, as we shall see, this vanity would rear its head and threaten to destroy her—not just in some spiritual realm, but also in her life as the charming, vivacious Magdalene.

III

MAGDALENE WAS SLEEPING soundly in her bed. She was awakened abruptly by a young man urgently shaking her. Though I saw him only from behind, I thought it must be her brother Lazarus. She jumped up from the bed, threw a tunic quickly over her nightdress, and tied a sash around her waist. After wrapping herself in a mantle, she said a breathless, careless, morning prayer. Clearly she was in a great hurry, and excited about what the day would bring.

All around Magdalene's castle the land was quick with spring. Day was just breaking, its rosy light touching the dew on the ground, lending everything an expectant sparkle. Magdalene fairly flew through the castle, calling out disjointed orders to servants left and right as she grabbed something to eat from the pantry. Her young face was vibrant with the promise of adventure.

Outside the front entrance stood a few camels and a chariot, or some kind of large cart. Behind the camels and the cart four young, dark-skinned servants stood at attention, awaiting further orders. Each wore a tunic of the same color, with a striped shawl draped across the left shoulder and belted. Some held parcels tied tightly with rope. I understood that the servants had been brought from Egypt. One of the camels was for Magdalene and the other for the man who had awakened her—whose face I had yet to see. Everyone in the caravan awaited Magdalene. And as soon as she emerged, the journey to Egypt commenced.

Magdalene and Lazarus in Egypt

I WAS then taken ahead in time. The caravan had arrived at the mouth of the Nile delta, gateway to a sprawling megalopolis comprised of four great cities of Egypt: Cairo, Giza, Heliopolis, and Memphis. The pyramids of these cities were a remarkable sight, for some had not yet been much worn by time. One of the pyramids indeed looked almost new, while the two largest ones were perhaps a few hundred years old. The cities were spectacular! I looked down upon them for quite some time, taking it all in.

Again I followed Magdalene's caravan, and saw that she and Lazarus (for it was indeed he) were staying at an inn southwest of the largest pyramids, in what I think was Memphis. It was a long narrow building of many rooms with a large yard or pen for the animals behind.

Then something strange occurred. I felt a strong pull drawing me toward the largest pyramid of the city. I could not stop hovering high above the pyramid's center, even as I willed myself to descend.

The energy of this place was so strange—it seemed as though the pyramid were piercing into the spiritual realm in order to provide an opening. All around the pyramid the veil between the earthly realm and the spiritual realm seemed extraordinarily thin.

Because of my state, I was aware of the spiritual activity around the pyramid. My desire was to go inside it and to explore its spiritual aspects, but I was not directed to do so. I was given only a more general awareness of how this pyramid was creating an opening through which the people in the region might experience the spiritual world. I saw that the people of the Nile delta were a visionary people: they dreamed in lucid pictures, and were in touch with the spiritual world more than other people I have experienced from this time.

I saw that there were two general classes of people living in and around these cities: those of the laborer caste, who were earthy, simple in their lifestyle, and rather superstitious in their beliefs; and those of the nobility, who were highly educated and more in harmony with the spiritual realm (or at least they had a deep interest in spiritual matters, wanting to interact with the gods, and so forth). These two classes were for the most part segregated, which was entirely natural for them and in no way the result of any antipathy toward each other. They did not often intermarry, but remained within their respective castes.

The laboring caste seemed unaffected by the energy of the pyramid in any direct way. Their religion was simple, although it was probably disseminated from the upper caste. They kept their focus mostly upon the Earth, taking care of the temporal aspects of life—which was good, for it seemed to help balance out the intense energy of the area. For the most part they inhabited the outskirts. I could see that the closer to the pyramids one approached, the stronger the spiritual energy became. All the people in the Nile delta seemed to have more of the ancient form of clairvoyance, and by comparison were less "incarnated" than the people of Judea.

Magdalene felt as though in heaven while in Egypt. She frequented the markets, purchasing textiles, exotic spices, and trinkets of all sorts. Although she seemed so taken with the finer things of life and was quite materialistic and pleasure-seeking, still she harbored a deep and genuine interest in the Mysteries of Egypt. Her dual nature was torn between the material and the spiritual.

At night, however, she was often attacked by a demon that looked like an evil Egyptian god. It so frightened her that she felt she was struggling all night for her very life. But when dawn broke she soon forgot the torments of the night and returned to the enticements of the day, procuring treasures and pursuing the Mysteries. She was somehow able to keep her night and day experiences separate. Her overall attitude was one of complacency: her sense of self would not allow her to ponder the reasons why she was being attacked—she could not fathom what might be the cause. Instead, she chose to ignore her fears and to carry on through the day as though nothing were amiss.

Magdalene in the Palace of Women

I SAW then some young Egyptian women of high standing with whom Magdalene was acquainted. Finely dressed and haughty, these women were sequestered in a small palace with beautiful rooftop gardens. Magdalene felt a sense of belonging with them and enjoyed their company. I am not sure how she had come to know these women, but they liked her very much—they thought her red hair particularly exotic and admired her strong presence. These women were considered "works of living art," and were pampered and provided whatever they desired. Venerated as objects of beauty, they made special appearances at certain celebrations and other events. Like geishas of Japan, they had always to maintain their beauty, knowing little else than being admired and worshipped.

Magdalene was as intrigued with them as were they with her. They seemed about the same age as Magdalene—twenty or so. Magdalene's infatuation with them grew into a veritable distraction, leading her astray from the work she had undertaken in the temple initiations.

Her desire for all things spiritually mysterious began to give way to a hankering after worldly power. At the outset of her initiatory training she had truly desired wisdom, but at the same time she had struggled with aspirations for high social standing and wealth. These two tendencies fought for precedence in her soul until finally materialism won the field. And so the trip to Egypt, intended as a deepening study of the Mysteries, became instead a playground for cavorting with other young women equally enraptured by the frivolities of outward beauty.

Meanwhile, Lazarus busied himself with meetings of city officials, agricultural specialists, and other important authorities. He was following in the footsteps of his father—not so much from the military standpoint on this particular trip, but more in a civil capacity. I understood that his father had visited this great city also.

Lazarus had an interest in the Mysteries also, but I did not see whether he was pursuing such studies at this time. He spent hardly any time with his sister Magdalene. It seemed to him that she had been pulled away, and had become dull or numb. It was almost as if she had been served a strange concoction that led her to squander her time.

Sometimes, when the two were alone together, Lazarus would speak to her of her training in the Mysteries. He knew it was a serious thing to be allowed into a Mystery School, and thought that Magdalene's initiatory training should be important to her. She seemed not to be taking it seriously, however, and he knew well where her heart stood in the world. He had tried to hide his chagrin, his annoyance, with her flippancy and her vanity; and he entered into these conversations hoping to encourage her to return to her studies. But his efforts were in vain.

Magdalene tried at first to interest the young ladies in the Mysteries, but they only stared at her with wide dark eyes full of amusement. Why would they want anything else? They had everything they could wish for and were perfectly content. They cared nothing for a world beyond what they knew. Nevertheless, Magdalene began staying with them in their palace for longer and longer periods and was even offered a place among them. As time went by, she was losing touch with reality.

At the back of the palace where the Egyptian women dwelt, a staircase led down to a private lower garden. One day, Magdalene and the others were amusing themselves with rich food and drink while some musicians played. A servant of Lazarus appeared suddenly at the garden gate. His eyes opened wide at the sight of the garden full of women delighting themselves in the sun. He requested a moment with Magdalene and delivered to her a message from Lazarus: *Return at once to the inn!* Magdalene laughed and had the servant promptly cast out, telling him to inform Lazarus that if he wanted her to return to the inn, he should come and attempt it for himself!

An evil intention arose in her heart: a hope that he also might find her new life attractive and join her. She wanted Lazarus to behold her in all her glory, holding court with the most beautiful women in all of Egypt. It was sickening to see her in such a state.

Lazarus was so incensed by her treatment of his servant that he did indeed come without delay. He stormed into the garden and demanded that she return with him at once. He hardly noticed the coy looks cast in his direction by the other women. He had eyes only for his sister, who looked so pretentious in her Egyptian attire—ostentatiously bedecked with gold, eyes blackened with heavy kohl. She was not acting at all like herself.

He grasped her by the arm, commanding her to leave with him. She resisted with boisterous laughter. Through sheer physical strength he finally removed her from the garden, fuming within as they walked. Something inside told him to calm down, however, for she would not respond if he lashed out at her in this way. The further they distanced themselves from the palace of women, the more Magdalene seemed to come to herself. Embarrassment set in. She had always admired Lazarus and was ashamed that he had seen her in such a state.

Having recollected himself during the walk, Lazarus began to speak with Magdalene about her initial intention in coming to Egypt. *What had she wanted to accomplish?* He was trying to search her soul, to awaken her to her original purpose. She could not answer him. She burst into tears and hid her face with her arm, the kohl running in little rivulets down her face.

Thankfully, the inn was just a block away, so she broke away and hastened there. Once in her room, she fell into despair. She did not emerge for days. She was attacked again and again by demons. But the attacks came now during the day as well as by night. She had for a long time been able to distract herself with frivolities, managing in this way to resist the daytime attacks. But now at times she seemed to be throwing fits. Finally, she succumbed to an illness in which her body was racked with fevers and her mind plagued with hallucinations. Servants waved palm fronds over her sweaty skin and tended her in whatever ways they could.

A Harsh Confrontation with the Teacher

LAZARUS did not know what to do with Magdalene, and so sought out her teacher, the hierophant I had seen earlier. He asked the teacher for advice on Magdalene's behalf, fearing she was losing her desire to live and might not recover from her malady. Lazarus was not aware of the demonic attacks, or of what was raging in her soul.

When Magdalene learned of Lazarus's meeting with her teacher, she flew into a rage. She had not wanted the hierophant to know of her struggle with the darkness. When the teacher learned of this, he requested that Magdalene be brought to him.

Too weak to walk, or even to stand—and also too feeble to protest—Magdalene was carried to him on a litter in a chariot. Near the pyramid where he worked was a secluded veranda, hedged round with foliage. Magdalene was taken there and laid upon a woven mat at her teacher's feet—her long hair unkempt, her face peakèd, her body thin.

The teacher did nothing to conceal his wrath. He railed at her for having concealed her dark nature, for having pretended she was in a state of purity when she was not. He told her he was going to shut her out, thus threatening to bar her from advancing further in the Mysteries. She groveled in her weakened state, begging and pleading, until finally he relented—saying he would put her through three tests of character, and that if she passed these three tests he would admit her once again. She complied with his terms. With this, he dismissed her, letting her know that her tests would commence once she was returned to health.

Magdalene was carried back to the inn to rest, but her illness and depression continued for some time. She had not divulged to her teacher that she was under attack by evil beings, because this was such a source of shame to her. She had hoped these beings would just go away. And although the daytime attacks lessened as she regained her strength, they did continue.

Sequestered in her quarters, Magdalene busied herself sewing dresses and embroidering with a servant girl who came to assist her. She set to work on a special dress for use in the rituals, but wondered whether she would ever have occasion to wear it. Still, something inside her remained hopeful, and she was able to finish the dress.

She wondered how she could ever withstand the world's temptations. Was it just presumption that led her to hope she could return to her initiatic work? *Would she be able to pass the tests of character?* She was plagued with doubts that shook her to her very core.

The Three Tests

This vision was received in response to a request that the nature of the three tests set Magdalene by the hierophant be further described.

WHEN in vision I arrived in Egypt, I saw a tree with oval-shaped fruits and thick leaves. The tree grew alongside a wide canal leading from a tributary of the Nile into a city I recognized as the place where Magdalene had been a student of the Mysteries. I was excited to be back here as I gazed at the beautiful architecture.

I was in Magdalene's quarters just after she had been taken to see her teacher, who had stipulated that she pass three tests of character before being allowed to resume her training in the Mystery School. Magdalene was just recovering from a life-threatening illness. Her hair was unkempt, and she was only just beginning to eat again. Although she had little appetite, she knew she must regain her strength in order to face the coming trials. Filled with anxiety, she picked at the food before her. The confrontation had caused her such humiliation that she had kept to herself and avoided socializing ever since. From time to time, however, she had taken short walks in the gardens.

As her strength returned, Magdalene dispatched a servant to the teacher to notify him that she was now well enough to begin the tests. Several days later she received a message that these would shortly commence. She was instructed to bring her personal effects—clothing, jewelry, perfumes, and anything else with which she adorned herself—to a certain structure built to accommodate burnt offerings.

There was a name for this place, but I cannot remember it. It was not a temple, but was in close proximity to a temple. Within was a square room with soot-covered stone walls. In its center a deep iron receptacle was elevated on supports. I understood that this was a place designated for the lower class to make burnt offerings, and that the upper classes had far finer places to offer theirs. The door was guarded by two men dressed in religious garb. They were not priests, however, but of a much lower station, and had been given directives as to what Magdalene was required to do upon her arrival.

Timidly, Magdalene entered the room. She surveyed the premises with disdain. She was told that she must burn her clothing, jewelry, ointments, and everything else she had brought with her—even the tunic she was wearing! Feeling sick with shame, she briefly entertained the thought that following her trials she could, after all, go and purchase whatever she needed to replace what she might lose in this way. But despite her love for beautiful things she cast the thought aside, as she was preoccupied now with wondering what would happen next. One thing was certain: Magdalene would be allowed no further contact with her teacher until she had passed the tests—that is, *if* she passed the tests.

Magdalene wept silently as she threw her dresses and robes upon the fire, crimson and green surrendering to charcoal black. Intricate embroidery, the work of many years, succumbed to the flames. She was then given a pauper's sackcloth sheath to wear. "You must wear this until you are told otherwise," she was told. She winced as the coarse cloth chafed her skin.

In the course of her initiatic studies, Magdalene had learned of the Middle Way—that is, of the region in which one might safely travel while out of the body. She had been taught also that there was such a "middle way" on the *physical* plane, that of living a life of moderation, balance, and harmony—of abstaining from intemperate pleasures. Initiates were taught the pivotal importance of this way of life, a way a life from which Magdalene had so often fallen away.

The three tests she was required to undertake had to do with purging desires—not only desires for sensory pleasures and self-aggrandizement, but also the desire to abase oneself. The teacher knew that Magdalene's soul was not yet in a fit state to travel in spiritual worlds, and that it was possible she might even lose herself either in the Above or the Below. It was precisely because she did not yet exhibit the necessary purity for such spiritual travel that her teacher had assigned her these tests.

The first test had to do with what Christians later would call "taking a vow of poverty," which meant emptying oneself of material possessions and worldly identity. With no personal property but for the sackcloth she wore, Magdalene was sent to live among the poorest of the poor.

She was lodged with a large family in a shack crammed into a row of boxlike structures leading down to the banks of the canal. She was stripped of her identity: she could share no personal information with the people in the "industrial district" where she was to live and work. Indeed, she was to have no name at all.

Of course, this made her an anomaly in the slums at the swampy end of the canal, with her long fiery hair and pale skin. Nor could she make out their dialect.

I saw her working in a place where meats were prepared and cured for the wealthy caste, her fingers going raw from stuffing intestines and then sewing them up. She was humiliated at having to work in such a place, but her pride was so overweening that she managed to preserve her dignity despite these circumstances. Thus did she remain there, unruffled and biding her time, enduring everything in a detached way as she went mechanically through the motions required of her present status and duties.

Magdalene was exposed during this time to many unseemly things, for these people did not esteem or value life in the way her own people did. They were more animalistic, we could say, following instinctual urges in the coarsest of ways. Nor did they have any direct control over their lives, or any voice in how their daily affairs were ordained by higher authorities. Frequently some among them would be rounded up and jailed for the most trivial infractions—and such detainees were seldom seen again.

Their ways of worship and sacrifice were also distasteful to Magdalene. Her feelings toward them were more of pity than of compassion. Never for a moment did she allow herself to consider herself one of them.

I noticed that Magdalene felt some attraction toward one of the young men engaged at the end of the canal. His job was to keep the channels clear of the sludge that would accumulate there, and to assist with the smaller boats plying the waters in the vicinity. Sometimes Magdalene would wait for him at the end of the alley and they would speak together in broken sentences. But she could not be truly open with him, for she was under a strict injunction to be no more than a nameless pauper to these people. She was to be totally reliant upon them for every morsel of food, for any little comfort or kindness that might be shown her, no matter how middling.

At length Magdalene was deemed ready to proceed from this place to her second phase of testing.

She was sent to live as a slave in the palace of a certain ruler. In this setting her humiliation was intensified. She was now surrounded by more finery that even she had ever before seen. Yet it would have to remain forever beyond her reach. She ate what the slaves ate and slept in a tiny cell where the slaves were kept. Again, she could reveal nothing about herself to anyone.

One day, as she was standing at service in one of the palace halls, Magdalene was startled to see one of her former friends from the "palace of women" gracing the social gathering that was underway. The girl was dressed as a goddess in a beautiful costume and stood statuesquely in the center of the room, surrounded by flowers. Magdalene quickly dropped her eyes and edged away, hoping she hadn't been recognized.

The ruler was a large man who lounged upon an ornate throne as he was entertained by various performers and sampled foods from small dishes brought him from time to time by servants. He noticed Magdalene standing in the corner and wanted to know where this unusual slave had come from. Since her identity had to be kept secret in his house, Magdalene kept her eyes downcast and acted as though she was unable to answer, no matter how many questions he asked. So beautiful was she, however, that he could not refrain from finding some way to speak with her, and so requested that she be moved to a higher position, from that of "slave" to that of "servant." But Magdalene made it clear that she could be no more than a slave.

Temptations and tests of her humility continued. Her desires for power and beauty were put to the test. She had never been the sort who would steal or commit a real crime to satisfy her desires, but she did enjoy employing her charms to get what she wanted. The ruler kept augmenting his offers, but through sheer force of will Magdalene remained true to the station she had been assigned. She was careful not to assert herself.

Finally, the ruler offered her a place among his mistresses. Magdalene knew that if she said yes to this offer, any desire she might have would be fulfilled. She even allowed herself to imagine leaving both the Mystery School and her harsh teacher behind. *I may be ruined socially if I continue longer in this way as a slave! I will surely be found out, and then my humiliation will be complete. Perhaps the Mysteries are not for me; no, I belong with the upper class!*

But when that night she lay exhausted on the straw in her cell, she ached to return to the school. It was the only place where she had felt life had a deeper meaning, and she wanted to know the secrets that had brought the other initiates such great peace. She felt sure the ruler had the power to request that the teacher re-admit her to the school, but she knew that if he did so, she would have lost the teacher's trust forever. Then she mulled over the likelihood that the teacher was perhaps so highly respected anyway that even the ruler would not be willing to risk such a plot.

It must be said that not everything Magdalene endured was orchestrated directly by the teacher. The teacher knew a way to call forth tests for Magdalene through the use of magic. In other words, he did not ask the ruler to tempt her, but rather set the tests into motion through the use of magic by framing the intention that whatever her soul may need in the way of testing would come forward to meet her in a natural way.

After her time as a palace slave, Magdalene was shifted to her final period of testing. She had now to show that she could be completely obedient, that she would not waver even one iota from what was required of her, and that her obedience could be immediate.

She was given a variety of tasks to accomplish, most of them centered on denying sensory pleasures—tasks such as fasting, or abiding alone in the wilderness. Some of these tasks were tedious, requiring great concentration and focus. She could not allow her mind to wander even for a moment from the task. One such task was reciting text for long periods of time, standing alone at a lectern while a hidden observer kept close watch. In all these things she persevered, as she had done when facing the first two tests. She was indeed much humbled by the time she completed her series of tests. She felt a sense of relief, so greatly had her vanity and her obsession with material goods diminished.

At the end of her time of testing she was required to go before her teacher to defend herself. This was a lengthy process akin to defending oneself in a court of law. Again she stood at a lectern, but this time to deliver a speech in her own defense. From time to time the teacher would interrupt and ask probing questions. Some of his questions were meant to trip her up. If there was any character defect left, it was his goal to bring it out of hiding. It was better for her to answer "I do not know," than to give an answer she thought would please him.

As the final test of her character, the teacher praised her performance with a lofty speech. Then he offered her a much higher position in the School than she could ever have hoped to achieve.

But she was sharp-witted enough to realize that he was trying to entrap her. Kneeling on the floor in her sackcloth dress, head bowed, she murmured: "I cannot accept your offer. I am worthy only to enter as a novice, Most Venerable Teacher."

It was this, in the end, that saved her from being cast out. Had she accepted his offer, the teacher would have known her heart was not truly changed. He would have cast her out forever. But her answer was to him a sign that she was now ready to return to the Mystery School. And so he granted her immediate entrance.

Magdalene was relieved, even though she understood that this meant she would have to start all over again as one of the young girls who acted as servants, replenishing water vessels, cleaning, acting as silent witnesses, and so forth. She was determined this time to prove her worth, and to keep any remaining inner darkness in check, hidden from the view of others. She felt certain this was the only path for her. Although to some extent still vacillating and unsure, she continued onward in her studies of the Mysteries, making even more rapid progress now than she had before her time of testing.

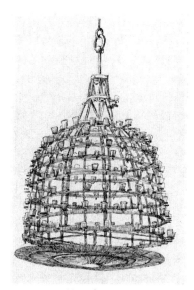

Temple Lamp

36

IV

I FOUND MYSELF inside a beautiful, domed building. The architecture reminded me of Greek-inspired buildings I have seen in vision of Alexandria, in the Egypt of the same period; but I knew I was not now in Egypt. Through a wide opening at the top of the dome I could see blue sky. I was in a single room, quite large—perhaps as large as a small theater, and oval-shaped. The ceiling was covered with mosaic tiles in beautiful patterns of maroon, lapis, and gold. The walls were painted with many scenes, mostly in the same colors as the tiles. Pillars divided the painted scenes from each other, and the floor was covered with smooth, flat stones. I could tell that the style of painting was Greek.

In one scene I saw a bare-chested man standing under a tree holding fruit up in one hand—just beyond the reach of a faun-like creature, half-man, half-animal. The faun was craning its head, mouth open, reaching for the fruit, while the man seemed to laugh in jest.

Other than the pillars, beautiful paintings, and mosaic designs, the room was empty save for a pool of water at its center. The pool was surrounded by a low stone wall, perhaps a foot and a half high. One could sit at the edge of the pool and see the sky reflected in its waters.

Magdalene in Greece

MAGDALENE sat at the pool's edge, wearing a Greek dress, white with gold borders, and fastened at the shoulders with ornate golden pins. She appeared to be about twenty-two years old. Her lovely face was framed with small, tight curls. She was in a pensive mood, gazing up at the entrance to the temple, wondering if she should leave. Nothing had yet happened in the temple, and she did not know how long she should wait there.

After saying the prescribed prayer, and stirring the waters with her hand as instructed, she had waited in silence, feeling as if she were on display for some invisible watchers. As she gazed into the deep waters, waiting for them to still, there was only silence... and more silence. No message came to her.

Finally, she stood and shook the dust from her fine linen dress. She did not know what she was expecting, but she had expected *something*. She did not even know what she was hoping would happen. All she knew was that she had felt compelled to come to this place, and had done so.

Once outside the temple, she was greeted by two of her servants. They had brought fans to keep her shaded as they made their way down the hill.

The temple was isolated from the city, protected by a forest, and some effort was required to scale the hill upon which it stood. Magdalene faced the city beyond the hill and took in the landscape, with its green trees and grasses that had turned to late-summer gold. In the distance the cerulean sea glinted in the afternoon sun. The wind seemed to whisper around her, tugging gently at her hair. She felt peace hovering in the air all about this place, a peace left behind by other visitors who had been able to commune with the goddess. She wondered why she had not been successful in this. What was holding her back?

Her mind returned to the conversation she had had with the old priestess who lived in the hut at the base of the hill. She had followed the priestess's rather jaded instructions: *The temple is the sacred sanctuary of Demeter and Persephone. Remove your sandals when entering. Circle the pool three times. Think of your heart's question as you connect to the love between mother and daughter, and gaze into the pool—the waters are the place where mother and daughter meet. Stir the waters to bring the mother to the daughter. As the waters still, receive your answer.* She had followed these instructions, except that she had not been able to think of a question. Perhaps that was why she had received nothing.

Feeling her emptiness, she gazed down at the city, hoping the evening's activities would be filled with something to satisfy her desire for communion—and not just communion with the divine, since the divine did not seem to want to commune with her! She turned her back on the temple and proceeded down the hill. A tight frown pinched her face as her servants did their best to shield her from the sun.

Later that evening Magdalene attended a party held outdoors, next to an inn situated at the port where her ship lay at anchor. Lanterns dangled from trellises and musicians played while guests danced, drank to Bacchus, and laughed.

Magdalene sat at a table off to one side, surrounded by men, most of them Greek. They were trading stories of the interesting people they had met upon their journeys—and Magdalene had plenty of such stories to relate, for she was almost as well-traveled as they.

As the night wore on, the conversation became more philosophical, centering upon the politics of certain city-states—and Magdalene was reminded that the Greeks thought quite differently from the rest of the world. Although she admired their way of thinking, she did not try to meet them on their own ground in their philosophies, nor did she much care for the dispassionate, unemotional way in which they analyzed everything. Instead, she used her wit and humor to try to present herself as exceedingly clever. She wished to gain their attention, hoping she might utilize their assistance in future business ventures.

It worked—they were completely taken by her charm. Throughout the conversation, however, her thoughts would often wander back to the temple of the goddess, leading her there wistfully—but she would then quickly cast it off. *Nothing happened, so why should I go back there?*

A Vision in the Temple

MAGDALENE awoke the next morning feeling rather bored. The previous night's conversation and company had not been all that captivating. But at least she had new friends in this country. To her, this meant greater opportunities for expanding her social circle. Perhaps she would meet a man of high status.

But then, once again, she found herself thinking of the temple on the hill. No matter how she tried to tell herself there was nothing special about that place, her sense of intrigue grew until finally she decided to again seek out the elderly temple priestess. After all, there was nothing else of much interest for her in this place.

Her servants went on ahead to set up a resting place in the woods near the temple. Again, the premises were vacant—it seemed that the temple rarely received visitors these days. The Greeks of this island were clearly losing interest in the Temple Mysteries.

Magdalene, however, had still the echoes of Isis resounding within her from her sojourns in Egypt. In fact, she had a whole repertoire of memories of the goddess, which she had collected from her journeys to Egypt as well as from her own Judaic heritage and education.

"What is your purpose in coming here?" The priestess asked, amused by Magdalene's sudden, colorful reappearance in her solitary world.

"I want to know about the paintings inside the temple..." Magdalene did not really know how to answer the woman's question, for in truth a part of her wanted to *worship* in the temple.

"The temple is calling to you," was the reply, but Magdalene shrugged it off, saying she was only visiting the area and was interested in the architecture. In reply to Magdalene's response, the priestess provided a few facts about the temple's history, including a brief account of the story of Demeter and Persephone—as the light of her hope that this visitor might prove someone special flickered out from her eyes.

Magdalene left the old woman's hut and walked up the hill. Again she entered the temple. She truly wanted to find a connection with the goddess this time, but did not know just what she sought. She followed the instructions again, kneeling finally at the pool's edge to gaze into its depths and stir its waters.

At this point I received knowledge of the significance of the sacred pool: the surface of the water was the place where Demeter could touch Persephone, and it so happened that now was precisely the moment when that touch took place each year—the first day of spring. Demeter was Persephone's mother, and she had lost Persephone to Hades, the god of the underworld. While Persephone resided in the underworld, it was winter upon the face of the Earth—for Demeter, the Earth goddess, would mourn for Persephone, and this caused the Earth also to go into a time of mourning. But at springtime, Persephone was allowed to reunite with her mother—and the Earth would renew itself as Demeter rejoiced. The stirring of the waters signified the change that would take place when Demeter touched Persephone. It was believed that within one's soul it was possible to replicate the bringing together of Demeter and Persephone—with all the auspicious effects of their reunion—by stirring the waters of the sacred pool.

The experience of the temple could be approached in various ways. One way was to reflect upon Persephone in the depths, reaching up for her mother. Another was to connect with Demeter, feeling her descent toward Persephone, looking for the joyous reunion.

As for Magdalene, she identified with Persephone in the depths. She was not able to see that it was her materialistic and vain nature that caused her to feel this connection with the depths. She was plagued with anxiety and emptiness, but did not know why. It was this anxiety that rose up in her as she sought out Persephone, all the while feeling deeply the loss of her own mother, and estrangement from the Divine Feminine.

She had very few female friends; and for all her undeniable beauty, she lived her life in a masculine way, for example in the way she took charge of her business. She had need of bringing Persephone and Demeter together in her soul as a means of connecting with her own feminine nature. All this had been at work within her since she arrived in Greece a few weeks earlier.

There she sat by the pool, poised to stir the waters again, gazing into the depths, thinking of Persephone. Then, looking up, she noticed the painting on the wall to her right, depicting Persephone with long flowing hair and a star over her head. In her left hand, she held what appeared to be a pomegranate, while next to her feet ran a river full of skeletons. In the background lurked a dark dragon.

Magdalene shuddered as she recalled her own battles with evil, especially the challenges she had undergone in Egypt. It had been quite some time now since she had last suffered such attacks. The demons were apparently satisfied that she was being led deeper and deeper into her materialistic life, so that they no longer saw any need to press their advantage. She was indeed deeply entrenched in her chaotic high life, following the ways of the world. For vain as she was, she was still charming and warm and optimistic. This made her very popular with all sorts of people and beloved wherever she went, despite the many painful dramas played out in her relationships.

Magdalene reflected upon Persephone, feeling heavy-hearted and empty. Many images arose in her mind, until at last a question did pose itself: *Was she following her true path?* She did not know what other path she might follow; she felt like a rudderless ship. She identified with Persephone in feeling herself to be in a darkened place, uncertain of her path.

Holding all this in her mind, she put her hand into the water to stir it, whereupon she felt suddenly dizzy. Tingling sensations came upon her, along with the feeling that she might faint. As everything whirled around her, she knelt down and rested her head on the stones at the edge of the pool.

Suddenly it was as though she were in a dream. She found herself walking down a path through a misty garden, dressed in a simple sheath. Her hair was much longer. Up ahead she saw a shimmering light. It was like a mirage. Within the light was a man, visible only from the side, his head surrounded with rays of light. She could not see his face, but watched as he broke bread and handed it to someone invisible to her. The bread seemed to multiply in his hands, for it was never depleted even as he continued to feed unseen people.

With great curiosity she tried to go to him, but invisible walls prevented her. The feeling that she must meet this man intensified, so that with all her strength she strove to reach him. But then she noticed that a deep chasm, filled with all manner of evil creatures, opened between them.

She was at a loss for what to do next, when the man turned suddenly and looked straight at her, the mist clearing for a moment so that she could see his eyes. In that brief instant she felt he knew her. The light around his head seemed then to gather into itself, until he was changed into a star, rising up and disappearing into the sky.

Magdalene came to herself. She felt a great pain in her heart, and held her hand over it as she opened her eyes. The first thing she saw was the painting of Persephone with the star above her head, and she wondered to herself whether the star was Persephone's way out of Hades. *Maybe the way out had always been there, but she had not known it.*

Magdalene knew that if this man were real, she must find him. As soon as she regained her strength, she ran down the hill to the hut of the priestess and told her what had happened.

"You must follow your star—look for your star and follow it." The priestess could barely conceal her joy upon hearing of Magdalene's experience. It had become rare that someone would have so profound an experience in the temple. "The gods are in the stars, dear one. Find your star and follow that star."

"But who is this man I see becoming the star, the one who will feed the hungry?"

"Child, you will know. You will know when the time is right. This vision is a great gift. You have a gift for seeing. But do not abandon your heart. I fear you are already running from your heart."

Her words brought to Magdalene a feeling of shame. She was selective in accepting the words of the priestess. She loved hearing that she had the gift of sight, but did not want to think there might be something amiss in her character.

"The chasm represents what in your soul prevents your finding this holy man. Search yourself to know what stands in the way of your reaching the true light of love." Magdalene winced at the woman's words.

For some time following this visit to the temple, Magdalene felt she needed to find this remarkable man. She knew she had experienced something profound and incomprehensible, and wondered often about its meaning. But as time passed she came to shrug it off as a dream of Persephone rather than as a personal message to her from the spiritual world.

V

I SAW MAGDALENE in the dressing room of her quarters in her castle at Magdala. She was anxious and restless. She was running her fingers over her many gowns, trying to decide which to wear, while mentally reviewing her most recent activities. I saw that she had been at some kind of soiree the preceding evening, where she had been, as usual, the center of attention.

A large group had gathered around her to hear a gossipy tale. They had laughed raucously and praised her for her entertaining stories. Several men had vied for her affections, their advances returned with flirtatious eyes and coy murmurs as she held court, worshipped for her wealth and beauty. At the time she had reveled in the attention; but now, as she reviewed this memory, she felt suddenly outside herself, observing what she had become. And she did not like what she saw.

Anxiety gnawed at her. This new way of seeing herself, as an observer, was unsettling. Her vanity and pride were now reflected back to her in such a way that she could stand apart as judge of what she had always known to be her life. In this moment of clarity, she could see herself rising above the vain and prideful person she had been. But this flash of lucidity was to prove short-lived. She looked around her quarters: everything was a mess.

The castle and its outlying buildings were surrounded by swathes of land bordered with flowers and foliage that showed signs of care and pruning. But as one passed through the outer gates into the castle's inner gardens, all was in a state of neglect. These inner gardens had not been properly cultivated. Weeds choked out the fine shrubberies and exotic plants. The gardeners of the outer fields seemed to be doing some work, but those caring for the inner gardens were lackadaisical.

Magdalene had no real power over her servants. For the most part she allowed them to do as they pleased. From miles away it appeared that Magdalene's castle was the finest in the region, but inside its gates chaos reigned. And within the castle itself all was in disarray as well: tapestries clung haphazardly to the walls, goblets and plates were strewn about, veils and shawls and hats belonging to unknown guests were flung everywhere. There was no rhythm to the lives of the inhabitants: they ate whenever they pleased and slept at odd hours.

Magdalene on the Road to Conversion

MAGDALENE started to hunger for a closer relationship with her brother Lazarus and sister Martha, from whom she had for some time been estranged. As her soul began to stir and awaken, she felt the need to connect with others spiritually—and Lazarus and Martha were the only truly spiritual people she knew. She was, of course, acquainted with others who pretended to be spiritual, but she was so gifted at "reading" people that she could see through such pretense.

Lazarus and Martha had been hoping all along to reach Magdalene, for they worried about her way of life, and had offered many prayers on her behalf. And so they were pleased when she invited them to her castle for dinner one evening.

As they sat at dinner, Magdalene was at first apprehensive, feeling that Martha was judging her; but she tried to lay this fear aside as they spoke of the more trivial details of life. It was amusing to observe how Magdalene sat herself at some distance from Lazarus and Martha, leaving ample space between them at the table. It was obvious that she was not fully receiving them, or what they might have to say. She struggled, vacillating between wanting them to be there and wishing they would go away.

The conversation was for the most part light and uneventful until Lazarus began speaking of Jesus. In the end, he divulged to Magdalene that he was financially assisting Jesus with his ministry.

Magdalene had been acquainted with Jesus and his family as a child, but had had little interaction with them since that time, although she did know of his more recent activities through the reports of others. She laughed in a haughty way, saying she thought Jesus a very odd person, a bit "off," and that she could not imagine how he might have a ministry. She commented that she had heard he was traveling around, speaking to people, and performing healing miracles. "And I have also heard that he has lived among the Essenes. Surely he must be preaching the doctrines of the Essenes?" she asked.

At this Lazarus shook his head, saying, "He does not preach the doctrine of the Essenes. They would not allow him to reveal their ways and their teachings. His doctrine comes to him from God; God has opened his mouth and he speaks words of great wisdom. He has also the gift of healing."

Magdalene could not fathom what Lazarus was saying—that Jesus was gaining audience among the people and garnering followers. "I do not know how anyone in Judea can associate with him—he is so strange," she said. She looked at Martha, whose face appeared like one in love. At this Magdalene grinned, thinking her sister had fallen under some kind of silly spell. Martha truly stood in awe of Jesus, and loved to hear Lazarus speak of him. She also had for many months been following Jesus.

Despite her vanity and her effort to keep Lazarus and Martha at a distance throughout this discussion, something was at work in Magdalene's heart. Her conscience was pricked by what they said. Her soul was stirred up, and her feeling of unease increased till she felt ill and wished to leave the table. But she remained, and the conversation went on late into the night. Little by little, Magdalene's heart softened. Eventually, Martha suggested that Magdalene accompany her to hear Jesus speak in a nearby town—and surprisingly, Magdalene accepted the invitation.

I went forward in time and saw the two of them walking toward the town. Magdalene felt from her heart a tremendous attraction toward Jesus. This surprised her. Although she was feeling adventurous, her anxiety and unrest remained. As they walked along, she chattered incessantly of trivialities. When they arrived at the town, they went straightaway to the small synagogue where Jesus was to speak, but found only a few men milling about outside, among them an elderly priest. Martha's brow furrowed as she asked the priest, "Where is Jesus? Is he speaking here today?"

The priest answered, "I am sorry. He has spoken and left."

Martha looked at Magdalene, who had bowed her head. It was clear to Magdalene that she was not worthy to see Jesus. She thought it must be an act of God that he was thus hidden from her, that no matter how she might search him out, she would not find him, because she was so sinful a woman. Throughout her life she had gotten what she desired: riches, and attention from all. Had she wanted any man, she could have him. Now, suddenly, she wanted to hear Jesus speak, and he was not there. A feeling of great unworthiness rose up within her, clashing against her usual vain, self-centered approach: *If I want to see him, I will see him!* She looked away from Martha for fear that she would detect her feeling of unworthiness.

Martha knew Jesus's traveling schedule and said there would soon be another opportunity to hear him speak in a nearby town. She knew he would spend a few days there. This town was larger, and the inhabitants knew of him already. Martha told Magdalene that there was an inn there where she could stay, and that she and some of her friends would be staying there also.

Pierced by the Master's Gaze

MOVING ahead in time again, I saw Magdalene arrive at the inn with an entourage of servants and a cart of gifts for Jesus. She requested the largest room at the inn and ordered her servants to set up a temporary household. Just outside her quarters was a balcony with a view of the town, including its entry gate. She stood on the balcony anxiously searching the road from time to time for Jesus's traveling party. She was quite a spectacle, dressed as she was in all her fancy clothes. She had taken great care to arrive well before Jesus, so as not to miss him this time. Beneath her anxiety and feeling of unworthiness, however, her vanity struggled for survival.

At last she saw the procession approach. It was early evening and the streets were wrapped in shadowy shades of blue. Several dozen men walked up the street, surrounding Jesus. Behind Jesus walked several women and a few adolescents. Magdalene recognized the women, but did not have warm feelings toward them— they were Martha's friends. Jesus was very thin and had a serious look upon his face. As he drew nearer the inn she felt his approaching presence; something welled up within her. Her eyes filled with tears. She did not know what was coming over her. She had a grievous feeling in her heart. Rosy light from the setting sun rested momentarily upon Jesus's face as he walked closer. Just as he reached the place below which she stood, he looked up at her. His eyes seemed to pierce her to the core. She raised a clenched fist to her mouth, trying to fight back the tears. And then he passed by, swallowed up among the shadows and the small throng of followers.

Magdalene grew almost frantic. She was beside herself. Where could she go? What could she do? How could she remain in her room and await the coming day to see him? It was as if she were going mad, unable to think clearly. Her servants could not understand what was happening to her; she was making no sense—so full of grief was her heart. She decided, finally, to go out and search for him, as her fierce hunger to see him could not be denied. She told her servants that they need not accompany her, and with these words ventured forth alone into the dim light of dusk. As she walked along she kept her hands over her heart, as if it were in great pain.

Outside the inn loitered a small gathering of people. They eyed her mockingly. Near the group stood an immoral man, who was up to no good. He looked at Magdalene with lust as she asked, "Did you see the teacher pass by? Do you know where he went?" The man answered, "I heard he is going to heal the lepers." She thanked him for the information and walked quickly past him.

Magdalene came in due course to a long, low-lying building, from which a horrible stench issued. The building stood a short space removed from the rest of the town. A small crowd of raggedly-clothed people hung about its door. They all seemed to be talking at once, and in excited tones. As Magdalene approached, the crowd fell silent. Her attire did not allow her to go unnoticed. She was enveloped in yards of reddish-coral colored silk. And as she tightened her mantle protectively around herself, I could see small golden adornments along its fringes. Gathering courage, she cried, "Is Jesus here?"

The crowd parted. No one answered. They were shocked by

her presence. She decided to take matters into her own hands and bolted into the building, into the miserable odor of sickness. People were lying about on pallets. On one side of the room lay lepers in various stages of their disease; on the other lay women outcast because of certain infirmities. Between the two sides hung a shabby drape separating the women from the lepers. There was very little light inside, for only a few small windows opened along the side where the women lay, and the lepers suffered in almost complete darkness. The sick moaned and thrashed about.

Magdalene was in a state of such grief and confusion that she did not have her wits about her. She moved in the darkness to the right, toward the dim light coming in through the windows. "Jesus?"

One of the women nearest the separating curtain answered, "He is not here. Who are you?"

Fear overcame Magdalene then as a small crowd thronged the door, watching her. They began to laugh at the obviously wealthy woman traveling on foot alone at such an hour—they thought she must be crazy. Magdalene called out, "Has Jesus been here?"

"God have mercy on us!" cried someone from the darkness. The crowd outside began to taunt Magdalene, causing her to run for the door. As she emerged from the filth and din she saw that the crowd had grown in size. Many had been attracted by the strange spectacle of Magdalene in such a place. Some had even followed her from the inn.

Voices from the crowd spewed vile words at her. Some of the sick were possessed by demons, and these demons used the voices of their hosts to utter terrible things—sometimes also very personal things—about her. Magdalene did not know that these words came from demons, wondering instead how the crowd could have recognized her and perceived her unworthiness so well as to say such things to her. She felt as though stabbed to the heart as she heard her own sins called out by these lunatic people! It was all so frightening that she took off running for the inn.

When she reached her room she threw herself upon her bed. She suffered a spell of panic. A fever overtook her. She shuddered and shook and sobbed all night long as the voices in her head tormented her without reprieve.

At the first light of dawn, Magdalene directed her servants to pack everything up; she knew she must return home. She was grief-stricken that she would not see Jesus again, for by now she felt he was her only hope. But in such a state she could not see him.

So she returned to Magdala, where she fell into a malaise and spent the next few days thinking only of Jesus. She knew he had seen into her soul, and wondered whether he had seen all the sin that the lunatic people had seen; she wanted to be free of her darkness, but did not know how.

Later, when Martha went to see Jesus, she told him of her grief that Magdalene had tried twice to see him but had failed. She was sure Magdalene would give up. She had felt that Magdalene's heart was changing, and was so sorrowful that she had been unable to hear him teach. Jesus consoled her, saying, "All is well with your sister. She will see me soon, and will eventually be made well. Continue to pray for her."

Martha gathered several of her friends to pray for Magdalene. One of these was Joanna Chusa.† It was Martha's prayers that sustained Magdalene through the darkness she then faced. And it was her prayers that eventually led Magdalene to seek out Jesus, on her own, for healing.

---

† Joanna Chusa was a niece of the prophetess Anna, who was in the temple when Simeon blessed the child Jesus (Luke 2:36–38). She is described by St. Luke as the wife of Chusa, head steward in the household of Herod Antipas (Luke 8:2–3). Joanna's son had already made the acquaintance of the 12-year old Jesus when he (Jesus) remained behind in the temple and later was one of Jesus's secret disciples in Jerusalem. Joanna was frequently at the home of Lazarus and Martha in Bethany and was one of Martha's most industrious helpers. Jesus often dined with his disciples at Joanna's home. It was Joanna Chusa who, together with Veronica and Mary of Hebron, a niece of Elizabeth, went to Herod's castle at Machaerus to retrieve the head of Elizabeth's son, John the Baptist. She was also one of the four holy women to bear witness to the Risen Christ in the garden of the holy sepulcher on Easter Sunday morning.

VI

Magdalene Secretly Attends A Teaching

MAGDALENE WALKED with quick, mincing steps along an unpaved road in the dim light of early evening. Her restrictive, high-fashion dress was overlaid with a voluminous robe in a dark color. She was able to step only in short strides, out of concern for her dress. Up ahead stood a building at the foot of a small hill. As she approached this low-lying building, with its short, narrow doorway, Magdalene could see light glowing from within and hear the drone of male voices. She looked furtively from side to side, worried that someone might notice her, and then slipped inside the main room, which was filled beyond normal capacity with many men and a few women. Some of them had never heard Jesus and wanted to satisfy their curiosity. But most in the crowd were disciples of John the Baptist. They had come to hear Jesus speak, for John had pointed to Jesus as the one for whom they had been waiting. Magdalene discreetly took a place in the shadows at the back of the room.

Jesus stood before the gathering and began to speak, saying that his gospel was the gospel of Love. As he continued his discourse, most of the men in the audience grew restive. He was speaking of love in a radical way, teaching that God wanted all people to love one another, that not only should there be familial love—such as the love between parents and children, and among brothers and sisters—but that humankind must learn also to love outside of racial, cultural, and family boundaries. This was a difficult idea for the time, an almost unfathomable notion.

Jesus stretched out his hand, beckoning to a young Samaritan lad embedded in the crowd. "Come to me, my young friend."

The boy had been so determined to gain audience with Jesus that he had endured the blatant disregard of the others present. Somehow he had avoided being cast out. He came forward, as he had been bidden, and Jesus put his arm reassuringly about the boy's shoulders while the men in the room shifted awkwardly.

Addressing the crowd, he said: "It is easy to accept those who are like you, and for this you shall indeed be rewarded. But a greater reward shall come to those who love all, regardless of differences." He then turned to the boy. "Tell us what it is like to be a Samaritan youth."

The boy spoke first of general things regarding the ways of the Samaritans, things everyone knew; but as he grew more confident, he revealed his sadness that Samaritans and Jews could not get along with one another, and that he could thus not be accepted, simply because he was Samaritan. This conversation between the boy and Jesus caused the men to examine their hearts. They thought to themselves: "How can he place as much importance upon a Samaritan youth as he would place upon a Jewish nobleman?" Jesus continued to speak of God's love—that God sees the heart, not the skin color or tribal affiliation.

Jesus's eyes remained on the youth's face. "And what else is causing your sadness?"

"My mother, who lives near Sychar, is very close to death." His lips trembled as he said this, his eyes turned to the ground. "For this reason have I followed you here," he added, his voice betraying his embarrassment at having sought out the Master in such an unwelcoming setting.

Jesus was moved with compassion. He held his left hand to his heart while placing his right hand on the boy's shoulder. All present were moved from discomfort to compassion and empathy for this boy and his mother as they watched how Jesus treated him. The estrangement and hatred between the two cultures had been so great for so long that it would have been very difficult, if not impossible, for a person of Judea to think outside his or her customary thoughts, to move beyond the accepted cultural boundaries. But as Jesus showed them how it could be done, light filled the room and illuminated their minds.

When Jesus told the young boy that he would himself travel with him to see his mother, murmurs rippled through the crowd. All marveled that Jesus would go to Samaria. But they could no longer object, after having been touched by the compassion he demonstrated. Jesus said to them: "The kingdom of God is within you. It is not within the walls of the synagogue, but is within you. Remember this as you greet one another." He wished them to understand that God could visit the Samaritans in their places, just as he could the Jews in their synagogues.

This was a important moment for Magdalene. As she witnessed this event, she felt a glimmer of hope that she also might cross her own boundaries to accept others, and that others might accept her. She wondered if it would ever be possible that she could become a disciple of Jesus. She had been very hesitant to come to this meeting, but something within had urged her on. Feeling uneasy, and knowing she needed help and healing, she kept to the back of the room. She did not speak to Jesus, for she did not want to call attention to herself in such a setting. I understood that she was acquainted with a few of John the Baptist's disciples who were present, but she did not converse with them either. She wanted only to hear Jesus speak and did not want to be noticed.

VII

An Invitation to Hear Jesus Teach

I WAS TAKEN into a warm kitchen in the Holy Land. I saw Martha working with Joanna Chusa, preparing a delicious-looking dish consisting of leaves (perhaps grape leaves) with soft cheeses and herbs, together with something I could not identify. All of this was layered in a deep earthenware dish to be baked in a kiln. They were preparing supper for when Jesus, accompanied by the twelve disciples and the holy women, would return for the evening. As I focused on Joanna's face I thought how much I liked her—she was strong, reliable, and level-headed. Her husband was an important man—Herod's steward—and she was a most fitting wife. I hope someday to receive more of her story.

The kitchen was part of a family-owned inn not often accessible to the general public. It was more a place for family members of the owners to stay while journeying between Jerusalem and Galilee. The inn was situated on the western side of the Sea of Galilee, between Tiberius and a much larger city. As they worked together, the two women spoke of the coming day, sharing their hope that it might be a blessed one: Jesus was to speak on the mountain nearby, and it was said that some of those expected to attend were Roman officials who had heard of Jesus's great healing abilities from one of their military leaders and were curious to see the teacher for themselves. Martha hoped this might encourage greater peace between the Romans and Jews in Galilee. She mused to Joanna that it would be so wonderful if the Romans could accept Jesus's message of peace. For several decades, Galileans had felt it was only a matter of time before the Romans took full possession of Galilee. Martha and Joanna were anxious about the coming meeting, but also excited about its prospects.

Martha finished the dish she was preparing and set it into the kiln to slowly bake for the balance of the day. Her thoughts turned to her sister Magdalene. She mused that Magdalene would perhaps be more inclined to hear Jesus speak if she knew that Roman officials would be present. Martha knew that Magdalene loved to mix with anyone deemed important. She decided to make another attempt to arrange for Magdalene a chance to hear Jesus speak. They were not too far from where Magdalene lived— perhaps an hour's walk. The invitation might not be well received, but Martha hoped nonetheless that Magdalene would try one more time to see Jesus. With this hope in their hearts, the two women set off for Magdala.

As they arrived at Magdalene's castle, lively music could be heard from within the garden walls. Joanna and Martha looked at each other and smiled at the audacity of Magdalene putting on such rowdy merry-making at midday. Tightening their veils around their faces, they passed through the gates and followed the music to the main garden. They stepped around the corner, and there she was: the centerpiece of the party, bedecked in jewelry and red veils, dancing in the heart of the garden, fully enjoying herself. The moment Magdalene saw Martha and Joanna, she abruptly stopped the dancing, wrapped her veil around her head, and sauntered over to them. "What brings you here?"

Martha knew she had not much time, as Magdalene was busy celebrating with her friends. So she was quick to answer: "Jesus is speaking tomorrow on the mount, and they say some important Roman officials will be there." Above the shining red veil wrapped around the lower part of her face, Magdalene's eyes widened. Martha found it amusing that Magdalene feigned modesty thus with her gold-ornamented veil. She continued, "We would love for you to come."

Magdalene shifted her feet, mulling the invitation over. She had made such a scene the last time she had attempted to see Jesus with Martha, and felt still some humiliation. Nonetheless, she was keen to meet him. Finally she said, "Yes, I will come. Would you like to dance with us?"

Martha and Joanna declined, saying they must return to finish supper preparations for the disciples. They were invited to take some refreshment before returning to the inn; after this they left Magdalene, feeling very encouraged.

Later that evening Magdalene was at work making plans for the morrow, wondering what to wear—after all, there was always someone to impress!

Back at the inn, as the disciples and holy women gathered together with Jesus for the evening meal, Martha told Jesus the good news—that Magdalene was going to come hear him speak. He smiled. I could see how Jesus's thoughts toward Magdalene were loving and compassionate. He did not hold in his mind an image of her as the overdressed, willful, ostentatious woman of ill repute. The image he held was beautiful. He saw her enveloped in white light, like an angel, appearing almost as though she could be his sister. He loved her. Martha was nervous about her coming, but also optimistic.

The First Conversion of Magdalene

THE NEXT DAY, the disciples and other followers met on the nearby mountain. It was a perfect location to address a gathering, for it offered a place like an amphitheater, with very good acoustics, so that the teacher's voice carried easily. A few dozen people had come to hear Jesus—but only a small contingent of Romans. One important Roman official was there, however, with several high-ranking officers and their wives. Although the day was not very bright, the wives sat in little tent-like structures to shield themselves from the sun. I thought how different the Jews and Romans were, each with their own customs, despite living side by side in their towns.

Magdalene arrived somewhat late, again making a spectacle of herself. Dressed in the Canaanite style, which was quite colorful—and with many tinkling little ornaments—she sat toward the back of the crowd. On her head was a sort of diadem with dangling golden charms, and around her neck she wore a collar of hammered gold along with several longer necklaces, and on her arms and hands bracelets and rings shone. She wore something called a "girdle" just under her breasts, embroidered in gold and decorated with yet more trinkets. Below, a lavishly embroidered sash was slung across her hips. She clearly loved her jewelry. Though her face had been coarsened to a degree by her

Magdalene Before Her Conversion

worldly life, she appeared to be softening around the edges, and a certain eagerness showed in her countenance. I thought she looked beautiful. There was a new light about her face. She permitted everyone to stare at her, inwardly gloating over the attention. Several times she looked over at the Romans, but I never saw her make eye contact with anyone. Martha and Joanna sat off to the side with the other women.

Jesus began to speak. I watched in wonder as he communed with the crowd of people, most of whom he knew. His heart reached out to every heart in the throng, giving to each whatever light he or she could receive.

He spoke of the Fall, especially the fall into sin, and how sin hinders people from knowing the Father. As he spoke, he could see each of their souls in its fallen state. But he saw at the same time their divine natures. His words and his love were beginning to heal these divisions. The people began to receive the light of understanding, and to realize that they were not just the fallen selves they had always known.

The words of Jesus were without judgment. Because he had never fallen, he was able to enter easily into the non-fallen aspects of their spirits. He was able to awaken this part of them so that they could experience their true selves. They were in awe, many of them with hands over their hearts, as they began to see all they had done against their own divine natures—an awareness they gained because they were in the presence of Jesus. Many felt great remorse and wanted to be released from their darkness. Jesus was showing them the way out.

Magdalene on the other hand, although she also heard his words, understood them only in her mind: she was so busy justifying her privileged life that she could not take his words to heart.

Finally, Jesus stood and opened his arms wide, as if to embrace the crowd. He looked at Magdalene and began to speak. Magdalene looked up and saw his intense gaze turned in her direction, and was both puzzled and captivated. It was as if every part of her suddenly turned toward him to hear what he had to say. With a powerful voice that penetrated her heart, he said, "No longer forsake yourself for the things of the world, for you are a child of your Father in heaven, and He calls you out from the world to come to

Him. Return to Him! You cannot return to your loving Father if you are weighed down by the things of the world. Turn away, lest the evil one—the prince of this world—take hold of your heart!"

Magdalene did indeed feel a tremendous force weighing upon her heart. It clutched at her breast. She burst into tears, feeling the encumbrance of her worldly life all around her. She wanted to be free of it at once. Jesus sat down and resumed teaching. He had spoken those words for her personally and she knew it. She wept and hung her head and could not hear the rest of what he said. With her arms around her knees she gathered into herself and sobbed. Then, suddenly, she felt someone beside her, looking at her—and raising her eyes, she saw Jesus's feet.

"Magdalene, arise." He held out his hand to her.

She stood up weakly. Jesus put his hands upon her head, and speaking to her higher self, he said: "In the name of my Father who sent me, let go of the evil that has you bound."

He was asking her higher self to expel the demon that her lower self had allowed to inhabit her soul. The demon came out with a repelling force and she gasped and fell to the ground. Light filled her soul and she felt peace and clarity. The sickening guilt and shame were gone, and in their place flourished love.

Jesus said, "Your sins are forgiven you, but see that you do not return to them." Magdalene looked up at Jesus, seeing him with new eyes. He was radiant, and she wept tears of joy because of the beauty she saw in him.

A remarkable change came over Magdalene's countenance and demeanor. Although still clothed in her finery, she emanated true humility—and all who witnessed this healing wondered at the change. Many then cried out to be healed also, asking for Jesus's blessing.

Magdalene felt profound gratitude and peace. She looked at Martha and saw the unbounded joy in her face.

Some in the crowd, however, were not so convinced that Jesus had the authority to forgive sins. These were Pharisees, and later they questioned Jesus. But Jesus paid them no heed. He worked his way through the crowd, touching some and blessing others, while Magdalene joined the other women—who received her with compassion and joy.

As I was returning from the state of vision, I received the following words:

The Pharisees Question Jesus

Christ beholds us and all that we are. He knows who we truly are. We are not in truth the person who sins. He has faith in us because he can see who we are. It is by him and through him that we may know ourselves. It is by him and through him that we can be healed of what stands in the way of knowing our true selves. He offers us his sacred heart so that we may find peace and rest for our souls!

Supper with Simon the Pharisee

I SAW Magdalene in the bedroom suite of her castle, pacing back and forth before the window. She had been exceedingly restless since hearing Jesus speak upon the mountain. She was so grateful for what he had done that she felt she must again go to him. She could not be still, nor could she eat or concentrate on anything. Her need to see him was all-consuming. She perceived him to be her only source of hope—her only way of escape from the evil that threatened to destroy her.

Jesus had been invited to have dinner in the home of a certain Pharisee by the name of Simon. Simon had invited Jesus to his house in part because he sought release from his rigid beliefs. He wished to be cured of his closed-mindedness, and of his hardened heart. But he also felt protective toward Jesus, worrying that he was in danger on account of his radical teachings. He thought he could perhaps advise Jesus to make a few changes in the way he taught. Feeling oppressed by his conundrum, he sought out a deeper friendship with Jesus, although he knew doing so exposed him to certain risks.

The first few times Simon went to hear Jesus speak, he had been resistant to what he heard. Afterward, he would run to his scrolls and pore over them, trying to disprove the words of Jesus. He looked to the law to find support for himself in face of such revolutionary ideas, devoting much time to this effort. After awhile he would resume feeling comfortable with his accustomed dogmas. But another opportunity would then arise to hear Jesus speak, and he would again feel impelled to go hear him.

Several times this happened, until he felt as though something inside him was dying, as though he was standing in darkness, not knowing what to hold fast to. Often he told himself that he would not listen to Jesus again. But then he would find himself once again in a synagogue, or on a hillside, listening in rapt attention to the Master.

His inner struggle led him finally to the decision that he needed private counsel with Jesus, so that he could pour out his soul and tell him of his conflict. This was his intention in extending to Jesus the dinner invitation. He wished to discuss the law with him, for he knew that Jesus understood the law. He hoped that through such conversation, he would discover the place where the law that he loved and the words of the Master could co-exist in his own soul. He desperately wanted to be healed of his inner turmoil.

Simon sat at table, deep in disquieting thought, drumming his fingers nervously. A certain acquaintance of his, a scribe, had also been invited. This man was sitting to Simon's left. Simon had requested that he come to write down all that Jesus might say, and anything else that might transpire at this important meal, for he wanted to study the conversation afterward. Words were very important to Simon. He loved words. And Jesus's use of language was so different. His words had the power to shake the soul to its very foundation. While greatly admiring Jesus's ability to use language in this way, Simon nevertheless found Jesus's vernacular very strange—and this is why he wanted the scribe to record the conversation. Simon had also a few other friends present, as well as his wife, who assisted in serving the meal.

While Simon was thus lost in thought, Jesus appeared suddenly in the room. Because he was in such a state of anticipation and anxiety, and so focused on his inner musings, Simon had not gone to the door to greet him. The servants had earlier opened the front and back doors to allow the evening breezes to waft through the house. Thus the front door had been left standing open, but with no one there to greet the arriving guest.

Jesus stood in the room until finally he was noticed. Simon looked up at him as if seeing something in a dream, and then came to himself. He stood and ushered his guest to the table, seating him to the right, while making profuse apologies. Jesus emanated such love that Simon was soon calmed, and they were able to settle into the meal and engage in light conversation. As the evening progressed, the two spoke together in such a way that Simon felt he was "known" by Jesus—that he was being understood. Simon had never before experienced this with anyone, and it caused his inner conflict to melt gradually away.

Magdalene and the Alabaster Jar

A SUDDEN gust of wind blew through the lower level of the home. The servants rushed to close the back door and restore things to their rightful places. Several tapestries had fallen and some objects near the door had been blown over. While the servants were thus occupied at the back of the house, making some commotion as they tidied up, Simon looked toward the front door and was astonished to now see Magdalene standing in the room! She had entered unseen through the front door. Had the servants been there, they would certainly have stopped her. But there she was, standing in the dining hall, her veil almost completely covering her face, her head bowed in such a way that no eye could meet hers. She wore a deep red dress made of layers of sheer fabric overlaid with a mantle dyed in variegated shades of deep red, with golden borders. She was quite enwrapped in all these layers, leaving exposed only her hands, which held an alabaster ointment jar. Simon looked at her as if she were a ghost. He could not speak, so startled was he. Jesus, his back to her, looked at Simon's dumbfounded face and then slowly turned and saw Magdalene. With a slight nod of his head he gave her permission to approach.

Magdalene felt intense remorse for all she had done in the past, but she nevertheless tried to be still within herself. And truly, it took all her strength to appear even halfway composed. All she knew to do was to beg Jesus for mercy, hoping that perhaps the God he served would cleanse her.

As she looked at Jesus she was overcome by his presence. Words cannot describe what was taking place in her soul, except to say that the wings of her heart opened and her soul was flooded with light. She felt herself to be in the presence of the King of All. In that moment she was able to know that he was the bearer of something beyond the earthly realm. Jesus was no ordinary human being. She knew somehow that he hailed from cosmic spheres.

She was not able to explain this to herself, but she recognized a light emanating from him that few had seen prior to this. Her insight was made possible by the humble state she had entered into after he released her from the demon. This humility stood in stark contrast to the darkness she had known before. Feeling that absolutely nothing within her own self could save her from the snares the evil one had set for her, she had reached the lowest state of her life. There she stood, feeling herself to be the lowest of the low, standing before what she knew to be the highest of the high.

In an act of pure humility, of wanting to offer all she was, she fell to his feet. She removed his sandals, opened the alabaster jar, and anointed his feet with aromatic oil. I saw the being of Christ meet her there at Jesus's feet—through his feet she was touching the Christ. While this was taking place, while she anointed the feet of Jesus, she inwardly experienced the Christ, as if she were being touched by rays of sunlight that illuminated her soul. She was so overcome that she began to weep and kiss his feet, her tears falling freely as she whispered beautiful words of adoration and pressed her face against them.

Some of Simon's friends, also Pharisees, were most uncomfortable with this display. Attracting Simon's attention, one said in a low voice: "You must be rid of her. This is humiliating to behold!" Simon was troubled, for he knew that a part of his own soul really wanted to be in Magdalene's place also. But he was not humble enough. Jealousy rose up in him, confronted by a "sinner" taking the place he himself wished to occupy! If only he could feel such devotion, if only he could lay aside his need to be in the right, to follow the law, to receive approval—if only he could allow himself to enter so humble a state as had Magdalene! For he knew she was receiving something that could only be received through humility. Out of his jealousy he asked Jesus how he could allow a transgressor to make such a show of herself.

Jesus's illuminated face glistened with tears, so touched was he by Magdalene's devotion. Looking directly into Simon's eyes, he quietly said: "Simon, I was called to be a guest in your home, but when I arrived there was no one to greet me, nor was there any vessel of fragrant water set out for me wherewith to wash my feet—and yet this woman has sought me out with all her heart and has found me and has anointed my feet with the most costly of oils. She has washed my feet with her tears."

As he spoke these words, Magdalene lifted her head—and while yet kneeling, wrapped her veil around her face. She did not want Simon to see her and made no eye contact with him. She then bowed her head, waiting to be dismissed.

The scent of the oil filled the room. Jesus placed his right hand upon her head and through his hand power flowed into her body. Magdalene's body softened and relaxed, and she let out a sigh of relief. Jesus said: "Your sins are no more. Take care that you do not return to them. Go in peace." She knelt forward and kissed his feet once more, then picked up her jar and left Simon's house, feeling herself a changed woman.

Simon could no longer eat. He was uncomfortable, reproaching himself for having thought himself above this teacher. For in his heart he had thought he would perhaps be able to assist Jesus in changing his ways enough to please more people, especially the Pharisees.

This intention was not an ill-advised one. He really did want to serve Jesus, but he had not been able to see Jesus in the way this woman of questionable reputation had done. He was in despair over this as he sat at the table.

Jesus, knowing his thoughts, spoke to him of all the things that ail humanity—of the myriad forms of sickness, both mental illness and bodily disease. He spoke of how he had come to heal all types of illness, and then spoke of the greater ills of humanity, of the numberless diseases of the soul that are so much more pernicious than those of the body. Finally, he spoke of evil, of how evil works within the human soul and how subtle are its ways. He gave Simon a picture of how the evil one does his work, using Magdalene as an example. Simon began to feel compassion for Magdalene, for he could see she was like every human being who gives place for the evil one to do his work.

Jesus said, "I look upon the heart and see beyond all outer influences. I see the true spirit."

To this, Simon humbly said: "Oh Master, would you also look into my heart and tell me what you see?"

Tears streamed down Simon's face as Jesus said: "Simon, I see a man who was brought up in the way of his fathers, who was born into the law. The law is deeply inscribed in your heart, for you come from many generations of men who have upheld the law. But many, many generations ago your fathers knew not only the law; they knew also the love of God, for in the law they still heard God's voice. This has been lost through time, and the law alone is all that remains to you. As such was it passed down to you. But you have not been able to hear God's voice in the way your fathers did. This is a source of great sadness within your soul, Simon. For you long to hear God's voice and to feel God's love. This is why you continued to seek me out and why you invited me to your home. Yet when I came it was the law in you that met me. It was the law in you that kept you sitting at your table instead of greeting me at the door. I have come to heal the law. I have come to restore love to the law. I bring the word of God to the law. This is the desire of your own heart, Simon." He paused, smiling kindheartedly at Simon. "And that is what I see as I look upon your heart."

Simon humbly said: "Master, I would lay down the law and follow you."

Jesus replied: "No, Simon, do not lay down the law, but bring your law and follow me, for I have need of disciples like you. You shall serve me well."

From that time forward Simon was a loyal disciple of Jesus, even while remaining in his religious profession; and he was able to influence many others to follow Jesus.

Magdalene remained for many days in a state of pure joy. Lazarus and Martha rejoiced over her changed heart and offered many prayers of gratitude. They felt they had found their sister at last. It was as if they were meeting her for the first time. Magdalene made plans to hear Jesus speak, and thought also that she might travel along with him and his disciples, and, as Martha suggested, perhaps even become a disciple. This was not, however, to be the end of Magdalene's struggle with evil. She would require further healing before she could truly lay down her life and follow the Master.

VIII

Traveling with Jesus

I WAS WALKING down a dusty road, following a small cart pulled by a man. Magdalene was journeying with several women and other disciples of Jesus in a northwesterly direction from Jerusalem. The cart contained supplies for the disciples. Magdalene felt fairly content and peaceful at the moment, but was beginning to wonder what she was getting herself into. She had decided to follow Jesus to hear him teach, but a part of her remained hesitant. The woman to her right was rambling on about the trivial details of her life while Magdalene politely listened, but inwardly she was marveling at the fact that her life had brought her to such an odd pass—trudging along a dusty road behind a cart.

By nightfall the traveling party had reached a small town where an elderly woman who owned an inn offered them sleeping quarters. The large rooms of the inn were open and sparsely furnished. Magdalene was given a pallet on which to sleep, positioned near a window. Gratefully, she removed her sandals and reclined her aching body against the pillows, gazing out the window at the waning crescent moon. So exhausted was she that she fell almost instantly asleep. But her sleep was short-lived. Soon she was awakened by strange whispering, hissing voices.

Demons were attacking her as voices of doubt, urging her to leave behind all this "nonsense" and return to her capacious and comfortable home. Her mind churned with conflicted thoughts: *Why am I here? How could I even belong to this mission? What am I doing?*

She kept thinking about Jesus. She felt unable to be close to him, partly because he was surrounded by such crowds most of the time. She rued the fact that she had come so far, to the point of actually journeying with his followers, walking like a commoner from town to town, the distance separating her from her castle increasing day by day. Yes, Jesus had released her from a demon, but she was now plagued with interminable doubt.

Her pride was unrelenting, however, and she could not bring herself to admit weakness to the others by leaving. She feared that if she left Jesus, she would go back to being the tormented person she had formerly been. She wished a sign would come to her and tell her what to do, thinking that if she were to receive a sign to continue, she could then muster the courage to do so.

Magdalene wrestled for the remainder of the night with such thoughts. When morning broke, she arose and prepared herself to join the others, acting as though she felt fine about everything.

Magdalene prepared for the day. She put on her jewelry—her gold rings, bracelets, armbands, and necklaces. Then she paused. So many bad memories flooded her as she looked down at the rings on her fingers. She tried to set the memories aside, but the emotions lay too close to the surface. Abruptly and resentfully she stripped off the pieces of jewelry and placed them inside a pouch. Just then, Jesus approached and asked her to come with him to the well to draw water. The well, which was used by the community, was only a few paces outside the door of the inn.

As they walked to the well, Magdalene tried to conceal her somber mood, cloaking it in silence—but this gave her instantly away, as she was so rarely silent. Jesus seemed light-hearted. The sun was warming the air, and the day held promise. As he drew water in a vessel, he said to Magdalene, "Where is your jewelry—your rings, your bracelets?"

"I don't want to wear them." Magdalene's voice betrayed her true feelings.

"Perhaps you will want to wear them later?" He smiled, but did not look at her.

She answered tersely, "No, I am done with them." She clasped the vessel in her arms and looked down into its emptiness.

"If you are done with them, let us throw them into the well," Jesus said with some humor. He took the vessel out of her arms and began filling it with the cool water.

Anger flashed across Magdalene's face. She thought, *He is saying that he doesn't trust me to let go of my jewelry! And he is testing me to see if I can!* But in truth, Jesus was only offering to help her unburden herself of the weight of her past.

Magdalene stared into the well, wishing she could throw herself into its depths. She did not know what to do with her anger. Jesus leaned his back against the wellhead and smiled warmly at a few people passing by, going about their morning affairs. Magdalene was angry that he could be so peaceful and happy, smiling as if everything was fine, while beneath the surface of her beautiful face she seethed and boiled.

After a few moments, Jesus quietly took her wrist and said, "Some day you will see that bracelets and rings are not the most beautiful things to adorn your hands. Some day your hands will be beautiful, not because of what man has made, but because you will be bearing something that no man can make."

Some people came to draw water, chatting lightly of the details of their lives. Jesus picked up the vessels and escorted Magdalene back to the house as she struggled to withhold painful, searing tears.

Drawing Water from the Well

69

A Little Boy is Healed

BEFORE they left the small town, the woman who owned the inn came to Jesus and asked if he would visit a young boy stricken with a lame leg. Magdalene and one of the disciples followed Jesus to the boy's home. They found him bedridden and in pain, his right leg malformed and much thinner than his left. Magdalene stood back by the door, not wanting to bring into the room her heavy, doubting heart. Jesus had asked her to come, so she had agreed, even though she did not want to burden others with her darkness.

With no crowd as witness, Jesus entered calmly into the dim room and gazed upon the boy, whose name was Aram. He knelt down to speak with him. He reached into the boy's soul and could see the trauma he had suffered in being born into this life: his mother and her family were indentured servants, and his mother, pregnant with Aram at the time, had been severely beaten by her lord for having made a costly mistake.

The boy experienced this while yet in her womb, and for this reason his soul had pulled back from his process of incarnation. His will had been crippled in such a way that his spirit could not fully enter into his body to take proper hold of it and form his leg. He had, so to say, one foot in and one foot out of his body.

He had also failed to bond closely with his mother as a result of the trauma they had experienced together in the beating, for naturally he had a deep fear of losing her.

Jesus whispered many things to Aram and joined with him at a very profound level. He was able to draw his soul forward—the part of Aram, that is, that had refused to incarnate fully.

The little boy's spirit recognized Christ in Jesus. Jesus sent to Aram a beautiful image of himself holding Aram's mother, cradling her lovingly in brilliant light, speaking to the part of the boy that was discarnate, saying, "I am holding your mother and taking away her pain. I will heal her."

This comforted Aram so that he was able willingly to enter completely into his life; while for her part, his mother was healed of the traumatic wounds she had suffered. The connection between the boy and his spirit was strengthened so that a great measure of love—the love of Christ—poured into his lame leg. The boy's spirit emanated great love. As Aram's leg was brought to life, his family tearfully rejoiced.

Magdalene's eyes again filled with tears, but not such as issue from a softened heart—these were tears of shame. She knew the boy had entered a state of profound *love*, for she had experienced the same when Jesus had healed her. But in this moment she could neither feel the love nor enter into it, so blocked was she in her capacity to open her heart to love. She felt miserable knowing that her feelings were not consistent with the miracle that had just taken place before her eyes. She mistakenly believed she was on the outside—a bystander, unworthy of Jesus's love.

Magdalene's Quandary

AFTER the healing, Jesus and the disciples resumed their journey. That evening they entered a lovely town with palm trees bordering its walls. The layout of the town was very organized and aesthetically pleasing. The travelers retired to another inn, situated on a hill.

Once settled in the inn, Magdalene walked out onto a porch running along its south side. Somewhere below and a few buildings away a party was in progress. Music and laughter rose into the air, seeking out Magdalene's wistful ears. She wished she could join the festivities. That is just what she would have done in her prior life, but instead she returned to her room, where she was again assailed by voices. *This is not you. This is not your path. You belong with the rich and the powerful, not with these strange people who wander from town to town!*

Her thoughts turned then to her time in Egypt and the things she had done there. She tried to tell herself that she really belonged in Egypt, that the Mysteries of Egypt were her proper path; but a feeling nagged at her that she did not belong there either. So frustrated was she, not knowing what her path should be, not knowing what she should do with her life, that she could only wallow in misery, her frustrations mounting through the night as the demons plagued her with illusions.

When morning came she was exhausted. She told the women

who came to wake her that she did not feel well and would stay in bed and rest. Jesus was to speak that day, but Magdalene felt she could not bear to hear him, or even see him. She wanted to avoid everyone.

As soon as she was left alone, she began plotting how she might escape her predicament and return home. But as she sought a solution, she felt more and more ill, and fell at last into a deep melancholy.

After speaking and performing several more healings, Jesus returned to the inn and went to find Magdalene, while she, knowing that he had returned, intentionally avoided him.

At this point I felt I could not go on, for I could not bear that Magdalene did not want to be with Jesus. I saw also that she was something of a problem in the eyes of the disciples, and I knew that if she were to continue on with Jesus, she would need more healing. I did not want to go forward in the vision. I felt hopelessness arise in me, and wondered what was causing it. I felt that the vision was perhaps mirroring something on the horizon for me—the impasse one reaches before being able to say yes to proceeding with one's mission. And so it was a great challenge to watch what happened next to Magdalene.

Magdalene was now so far from home that she could not have left and traveled the distance alone; she did not know what she was going to do.

Behind the inn a walkway zigzagged back and forth down the hill. The path ended at a sort of patio surrounded by beautiful gardens where guests could dine. As the patio faced west, the setting sun provided a beautiful backdrop to the gardens. Servants moved up and down the path presenting the courses and attending to the guests. Magdalene stood at the top of the path behind the inn, watching the sunset, while servants passed by carrying supplies and trays of food. She wore a crimson dress and mantle. Suddenly Jesus was by her side.

"I know this is difficult for you," he said.

"Yes, it is difficult," she agreed, frowning.

After a pause, she fairly erupted, "I do not see how this can work. I do not belong with your people. I cannot pretend to be something I am not. I care about you and about your work, but I

am quite certain this life is not for me. I do not value what everyone else here seems to value. I do not have the right kind of
nature. I do not want to be drab. I am not holy, and I do not want
to act holy. Being with your mother shows me just how unholy I
am. This is just another example of my rash decision-making—
that I do things without thinking. I do not know what I was thinking by coming here!"

Jesus kept his eyes fixed on the sunset, which was radiant in
glowing colors of gold and pink. His eyes were sad. He said to her,
"I will have someone return with you if that is your wish."

Magdalene thought about her castle and the unordered life she
lived there. She thought about how her social life had disinte-
grated after she had been seen with Jesus and his disciples, who
were after all a motley group of fishermen, sinners, innkeepers,
and other such common people. And she wondered what she
would do with herself if she did return. Frustrated, Magdalene
cried, "Return with me to what? I have nowhere to go!" She
paused. "I should have Sarah with me!" She was referring to
Sarah, her Egyptian servant, who felt to her at that moment like
her only friend in the world.

Jesus replied, "I will send someone to bring Sarah."

My heart was aching so at this point that again I did not want
to continue the vision. I saw that Magdalene at first thought she
would try to stay with the disciples. She went to the dining hall
that evening to eat with them. But as she sat down, several of the
disciples looked scornfully in her direction, and she could not
bear it. She rose from the table and left before her tears could
embarrass her.

Shortly thereafter, at Jesus's bidding, one of the men left the
traveling party and journeyed to Magdalene's home to request
that Sarah and another male servant return with him. As soon as
they arrived at the inn, Magdalene packed up her belongings and
prepared to leave. I was so distraught watching her take this decision, watching her look Jesus in the face and say no to what he
had to offer her, and instead return to her former life!

IX

Leaving Jesus

AS MAGDALENE prepared to leave Jesus's traveling party, I saw
her walking down the last few steps of the inn where the disciples
and holy women had been staying. On a ledge at the bottom of
the steps sat John, his wavy, windblown hair framing his sweet,
handsome face. He wore a striped sleeveless tunic in dark colors
over a second, natural-colored tunic.

Blinded by tears, Magdalene hardly noticed him sitting there.
When finally she did see him, she felt even more sorrowful—for
of all the disciples, she felt most accepted by John, and the growing friendship between them would now have to be laid aside.
Magdalene put her hand out to steady herself as John looked at
her with pleading eyes.

In the courtyard, her manservant and Sarah, her Egyptian
maidservant, awaited her, ready to leave. Magdalene was relieved
to see them. She was also disturbed by many difficult and con-
flicting emotions, particularly an irrepressible grief that threatened at any moment to erupt.

"Why must Jesus and I be so completely different? Why must I
care for someone who does not fit into my life? I have never felt
so comfortable and yet so uncomfortable with someone! But
now I have to go—no one wants me here and I cannot remain!"
Such thoughts tormented her. She looked at John—he seemed so
innocent. She wished for such purity! He held up his hand and
said, "Magdalene, wait."

"No. I must go," she choked.

"He wants you here, and so do I." He seemed to have read
Magdalene's mind. John's eyes showed that he was sincere.

She replied in tears, "Some of us want what we cannot have,
and some of us do not know what we want."

"I hope you get what you most want, Magdalene."

74

When John said, "get what you most want," he used a word that meant both "receive" and also "find." He was really saying, "I hope you find and also receive what it is you want." He then said, "May you find peace."

"I hope you keep the peace you have found," she returned. Her words had a somewhat bitter edge, even though she truly wanted peace for John.

Magdalene's Dream

AND SO Magdalene left Jesus, at least physically, though her leaden heart made it so very difficult for her to move from the steps of the inn.

Upon reaching home, she looked up at her castle with dread, feeling abhorrence and regret rather than the welcoming warmth of home after a long journey. As I gazed up at the majestic structure, the very stones seemed to mirror the vanity and self-absorption of its owner. Magdalene at once felt nauseated. She could not shake off the feeling that her castle stood somehow as an imposing monument to her past.

Entering through the courtyard into the main portal, she saw that all was as it had been when she left—except that now, after being with Jesus and his disciples, the interior seemed so chaotic that she could scarcely bear it. Everyone in the castle was doing just as they pleased, and the whole place was in disarray.

As she walked into this confusion, she became angry, but her anger was with herself, for she realized what a mess she herself had been. A sharp realization came to her that she had hardly improved at all, even after listening to the teachings of Jesus!

Her anger quickly mounted. She told everyone to leave, and then stormed through the castle to her bedchamber, fell on the bed, and cried herself to sleep.

In her fitful sleep she entered into a lucid dream. She saw Jesus in a parched vineyard. The vines hanging on the stakes were so lifeless that when touched they turned immediately to dust.

Magdalene was standing before Jesus. She said to him: "Master, the vineyard is dead. Let us go elsewhere."

She was parched with thirst and desperately wanted grapes. She felt that she would die if she did not immediately have some.

Jesus said, "Magdalene, look!"

She turned to look where he was pointing, and saw a tender new vine just beginning to creep up one of the stakes at the end of a row of grapevines.

"How long will I have to wait? That one is just beginning to grow." Magdalene's throat was so dry. She could hardly speak.

He answered, "You will have to wait, Magdalene. Do you trust me to bring forth the fruit? Do you trust that your thirst will be quenched soon enough? And that your hunger will be stilled?"

Magdalene then heard her name called. She looked to the right and saw a stout man dressed in fine robes standing next to a cart brimming over with grapes. Behind him lay field upon field of grapevines as far as the eye could see, vines heavy with grapes ripe for harvest.

He said, "Come to me Magdalene, I can quench your thirst immediately."

Her body felt numb, as though it were being moved by someone else's will, as she walked toward the man offering the grapes. She felt dazed as he held out to her some of the dark violet fruit, the juice dripping through his fingers.

When she reached for one of the grapes, a great snarling dog came bounding out from nowhere and lunged at her hand. She wanted to run to Jesus for help, but when she turned to look back, the field was hewn down, plowed over, and Jesus was nowhere to be seen.

She thought that if only she could find the new little vine and remain by it, then Jesus would find her there and save her. But try as she might, she could not find it.

She dug frantically at the dirt with her fingers as the sky grew dark with heavy storm clouds. Sobbing, she cried over and over, "I'm sorry! Please come to me, Jesus!"

She awoke full of the ominous tenor of the dream, her heart restless and on edge, her thoughts tormenting her with the idea that her life was in danger.

All the following day she brooded over the meaning of the dream, remaining in bed, refusing to eat. Sarah came to her room to check on her from time to time.

After some days, word spread through the region that Magdalene had returned. People came to meet with her, or deliver messages, or invite her to functions; but she remained in her room, declining all invitations and refusing all guests.

Eventually Magdalene revived and began to settle again into her life. At first, she had the desire to make some improvements. She had the castle put into order and dismissed certain residents of questionable character. She abstained from attending parties for some time, and turned down offers from men vying for her affections. She did all these things in a state of depression, which she kept hidden from the eyes of others. She made these changes not out of true self-respect, but from her feelings of inadequacy.

Little by little, however, Magdalene fell back into her old ways. Every so often she would think of Jesus—for she was aware of his activity—and would grow sad. But she would quickly set the memories aside, focusing instead on the business of her life. Because she felt so empty, she sought to fill the void by arranging circumstances in which others would have occasion to admire or even worship her, and so feed her vanity.

She developed a business relationship with a certain merchant who bought and sold the oils she made. This proved lucrative, as she was able to procure highly-prized oils—such as myrrh, spike-nard, and the much-revered frankincense—at greatly reduced prices.

As she went about her business, she grew more and more worldly, her heart hardening and her eyes growing blind again to all but the trappings of the material world.

This merchant supplied her with things no one else could: exotic jewels from distant lands, rare spices, and silken textiles of extraordinary colors. She loved these things for the power they seemed to give her over others. She used them to entice people. Wishing to be worshipped for her beauty, she misused her charms to control or to rise above others. And so did her beauty grow more and more tarnished by avarice.

The Turning Point

THROUGH her association with this merchant, Magdalene was introduced to a dark and powerful Syrian man. Although his father was of Arabic descent, this man referred to himself as a Syrian, based on his mother's lineage.

Magdalene entered coldly into a liaison with him. She led him to believe she loved him, so she could become party to the worldly power he wielded. He would say to her such beguiling things as, "Together, you and I can build an empire!" I felt sick seeing him with her. I saw that this man kept many women merely as possessions. They served him in whatever way he desired, while he cruelly mistreated them. They were jealous of Magdalene and looked for any opportunity to damage her reputation.

Although this Syrian esteemed Magdalene above all the other women, still he did not treat her with respect, but instead used her beauty and charm to attract lucrative business connections. He housed her in a wing of his mansion and provided her with many attendants and servants, who however acted also as spies, watching and reporting her every move.

She was expected to make appearances with him at important events. This appealed to her vanity, while giving her the opportunity to acquaint herself with others in the business of buying and selling oils. But it also gave the Syrian all the more occasion to control and manipulate her. He instilled such fear in Magdalene that she could not muster the strength to abandon the relationship, even when she grew weary of him.

There was a major, well-traveled trade route running from the Mediterranean Sea to the Arabian Peninsula, which for centuries had been plied by merchants. Magdalene's agents, however, had discovered a remote, indigenous people quite removed from the main track, from whom one could procure the much-valued frankincense at a very low price—for these natives did not understand its inherent worth. Magdalene was able also to acquire from them such valuable items as spices, textiles, and certain tree resins used to produce oils.

The Syrian was of course well acquainted with this major trade route, as his family had worked it for generations, but he had no knowledge of Magdalene's source of supply. In a moment of carelessness, Magdalene divulged to the Syrian that she had a secret source for frankincense. He made plans straightaway to plunder the tribes in this remote place, and to exploit them.

Magdalene grew distressed when she overheard one of his other women talking about these plans. She confronted the Syrian, saying she would leave him if he did not reconsider. But he did not do so. He simply took the opportunity to manipulate her further: if she remained, he said, he would be lenient with the indigenous people; but if she tried to leave, he would bring upon them great suffering, and perhaps even seize their lands.

In actuality, he did not have information sufficient to accomplish this, for he did not know precisely where this people lived. But he misled Magdalene into believing he knew, hoping to wrest more information from her at a later time.

As this volatile relationship continued, Magdalene came to realize just how powerless she had become. She was seized with fear at what might happen if she did try to leave him. But she knew also that she must find a way to free herself from his menacing grip. She wanted desperately to liberate herself from the abuse she suffered, and so set out to find a solution to her predicament. She sought answers from different sources and various people, revisiting also what she had learned in Egypt regarding the mastery of evil.

As she faced this terrible plight, Magdalene thought again of Jesus and wished things had gone differently. She wondered if he would ever again wish to see her. She felt she was now so very far from everything he represented that there could be but little hope of ever being with him again. Nevertheless, she clung to the words he had spoken to her in private conversation, and at one point the memory of the exchange at the well on her last journey with him came back to her.

He had said then that one day her hands would be beautiful because they would bear something that no man could create. *What had he meant?* As she pondered this, she looked down at her hands, bejeweled with the heavy rings of greed. She thought about all that her hands had done since she had last seen Jesus, and felt a sickening guilt in the pit of her stomach.

But how easy it is to suppress guilt! And this she did immediately. She was indeed living precisely that lucid dream which had come to her: she was caught between the new vine of promise and the man enticing her with luscious grapes. She wanted still the fruit the world could offer. She wanted immediate satisfaction and the prospect of quenching her desperate thirst for power and recognition. But deep in her heart she wanted Jesus above all, although this truest desire lay yet hidden in the recesses of her mind and heart.

Vases and Vessels of the Time

X

Magdalene Healed of a Soul Sickness

I FOUND MYSELF on a hill overlooking Jerusalem. Magdalene did not want to go down into the city; indeed, she was resisting. She was very ill and had to be supported on either side by one of her maidservants—one of whom was Sarah the Egyptian.

Magdalene had grown weak in face of the boisterous winds that buffeted her. It took some time before I understood why she refused to move. And when I did, I did not want the vision to go forward, for something inside me knew that I would need to pass through difficult things with her.

So we stood there on the hill, resisting whatever the future might hold. I understood then that the two women were taking Magdalene to seek out Jesus, for they thought her inability to recover must be due to some evil force at work in her. It had been some time since Magdalene had last been with Jesus, as this was the period during which she had not wanted to see him. The women had been unable to help her, and felt that only Jesus would know how to cure her. And so they had determined to take her to him, dragging her along if need be, out of sheer desperation. Magdalene was humiliated to be in so helpless a state.

Magdalene could feel almost nothing positive toward Jesus. She did remember, though, that she had felt happy in his presence. She remembered thinking he was a very special teacher. But at this time she felt only confusion: *Is Jesus good, or is he in the wrong?* He was so compelling to listen to, but his ideas were so revolutionary. Her life had been tolerable until she had found him—or so she thought. But now everything she had known was crumbling around her. Struggling along in her maidservants' arms, she could not think with any clarity at all.

On their way toward the city they skirted a great stone wall and found their way to the home of the mother of Mark. Magdalene refused to go inside, not wanting any of the disciples to see her so shamefully disheveled. And so they set her down to wait on a patio in the garden while Sarah inquired within whether Jesus was staying there.

Magdalene's illness had reached a peak just as they arrived—the evil plaguing her soul did not want her to receive the help of Jesus. She was under attack and violently ill, and wished the evil spirits would leave her be. A voice inside her spoke out that she should be permitted to remain just who she was, that these people would try yet again to convince her to change her life. She wondered, would things have been better had she never met Jesus in the first place? Her mind reeled.

It was the Blessed Mother who first stepped out in response to Sarah's plea. Magdalene regarded her with only a brief glance, and through glazed eyes. The evil within her looked out through her eyes at this mother of Jesus, obscuring her ability to feel the Blessed Mother's compassion. Instead, she believed that his mother was judging her, though this was the opposite of the truth. Terrible thoughts entered her mind. The Blessed Mother stood there, looking at Magdalene with loving concern. "Jesus will be here in a moment," she said softly.

Magdalene wanted to say, *But I don't want him! Take me away from here! I am nothing to you people! I don't belong with you—just let me be!*

A feverish shudder arose from deep within her. She trembled violently, as fear and anxiety convulsed her. The heavy, divisive darkness within her felt as though it would split her in two, threatening her very sanity. It held her in its grip and would not let her go.

The Blessed Mother stepped back into the house and said to Jesus, "She is not well."

Jesus smiled and stepped out, following his mother.

Magdalene was a piteous sight. She refused to look upon Jesus even though she could feel him standing beside her.

He called out two demons by name. They rose up from her but still hovered near, writhing in the air. They were in conflict with one another, snarling over Magdalene's soul. Hovering there above Magdalene, they were the very two voices she had been hearing inside her mind, opposing each another yet trying each in its own way, like two quarreling children, to lead her astray.

Jesus spoke to them: "Remember me. Look at me." And they did finally look at him and did indeed remember him. They were able to receive his light, and in his presence they were transformed.

I saw all this spiritually. Magdalene remained unaware of these things. She lay on the ground, estranged from herself.

The departure of the demons left Magdalene very weak, unable at first even to sit. She had no strength. She felt empty to the core. The women helped raise her up when she was finally able. I noticed then that Mark's mother had also been there, though I am not sure just when she joined the group.

The Love of Christ Jesus

SOMEWHAT LATER, when Magdalene had regained more strength, I saw her leaning against a tree. Jesus sat across from her, leaning against a tree also, and smiling at her with the sweetest expression of love on his face.

If only I could lend words to the love I then witnessed emanating from Jesus—the powerful, divine love. He held Magdalene in his loving gaze as she returned to herself. I could experience something of this love, but know not how to describe it. It was so different from human love, so truly ineffable!

If only we each could sit together with Christ Jesus in this way and be healed by his loving gaze. My heart aches for this. I am so sad to say that even though in vision I was *there,* I could not take in the full measure of his love. And I wonder how it would have felt, had I been able to accept that full measure. I wonder, what might have been healed within me? Perhaps it was my unworthiness that held me back, or perhaps it was simply not my time. Magdalene, however, was even more resistant to this love.

The women offered her water, which she was able to sip. They invited her into the house to rest, but seeing that she still did not wish this, they allowed her to tarry in the garden.

Jesus asked to speak with her in private, and led her to a more secluded corner. They sat under an olive tree. He said, "Magdalene, I am your friend. I have been waiting for you to know that I am your friend. You have been unable to trust me because you have suffered so much hurt."

His words were painfully true. It seemed that she could only go to him when she was sick and under attack from evil powers. She felt humiliated. At this moment she was again able to feel his love so directly. Again she wanted to be with him. But she still felt unworthy and unfit to be with his followers. She just could not see any way out from her high life, any way to leave it behind.

Jesus then said to her: "Do you understand why this happened?"

She did not answer. She kept her eyes upon the ground. He gently said: "This happened because you went back to your old ways."

Magdalene was very sad—and troubled. She realized that the door to her former life had to be shut, but she knew not how to shut it. She was anxious and afraid because she had relationships with so many dubious people. And she did not know how to break off those relationships without bringing harsh consequences upon herself. Jesus wanted her to remain with him and his followers, but she was not ready. She felt she had to find a proper way to end those other relationships—especially her alliance with the Syrian, of whom she was much afraid.

When she felt fit enough, she announced that she would return to the estate near Jerusalem where she had been staying (which was, I believe, the Syrian's estate), for she felt she had a fresh and firm perspective and could make some changes to her life. At this time, however, she still did not fully intend to leave everything behind and follow Jesus for good, although a part of her did want to make so drastic a change. She knew clearly, though, that she had to put an end to certain relationships, for she could see now that it was her shame and powerlessness that had made her so ill.

Understanding all this, Jesus warned her to be ever watchful and to pray without ceasing.

"I am afraid to shut that door," she spoke softly, referring to her complicated life.

"Do what you think you must, but remember that with me the door is always open, and that you are welcome to join us whenever you are ready," Jesus said.

He then spoke a beautiful prayer on her behalf, of which I heard just this part:

"Father, I give to you your daughter to watch over and keep. When she returns home she will be tender in her soul. Surround her with thine angels and protect her from the adversary. Let her safely return to me. Bless her with a peaceful heart and a clear mind. Let truth and light guide her through the storms."

He knew that she would still have to weather many storms before she would again come to him.

Magdalene could feel Jesus's love, but she did not accept it into the deepest place of her heart. His love was of a different kind than she had ever known; and although a part of her desired that kind of love, a greater part could not yet receive it. Thus she did not bask in it, but allowed it to touch her only at the periphery of her soul.

When Magdalene left Jesus, she thought about the strangeness of his love. It was indefinable, incomprehensible. She wanted to remain in the light of his love and allow it into her heart. But because she was at that time unable to accept it, and because during this period she spent much time apart from him, she was again plagued by demons. She had not yet learned to feel their subtle work in her soul, and thus could not discern when these evil powers were taking hold of her. As she carried on with her life, these powers continued to skirmish for her soul. She had no one to help her see this. And so she had to suffer yet further through this soul sickness before she could return for her final healing—and fully devote herself, ultimately, to Christ Jesus and his mission.

The love and light of Christ banishes all evil. We are all within his loving gaze; his eyes are ever upon us. He is our friend; he is the door that is always open. When we are ready to leave behind our old life, he welcomes us and heals us. He heals the wounds we have suffered through the storms we have weathered. And when we are then ready to enter into full communion with him, he stands waiting with outstretched arms.

The door is open—all we must do is knock, and then walk through. He seeks out the parts of us that are lost, to reclaim us. He says to us: Bring everything that you are to me, for I love all that you are, even your darkness as well as your light. He smiles upon us; he is always embracing us. We belong to him.

I saw Jesus shining like the Sun; his eyes were piercing beams of light that penetrated my soul. I was able to feel his radiant warmth and his ineffable love.

Saint Christopher then came to bring me back, just as the vision closed.[†] I felt full of Christ's love, as if I were light in my body, weightless, free of the heaviness I so often carry in my daily life.

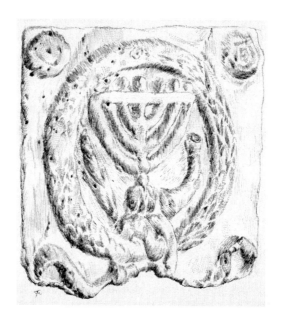

† See Appendix V.

XI

The Stoning

I WAS BEING STONED. I was engulfed in an overpowering fear, feeling every stone bruising my body, as I lay curled into a fetal position. I realized then that I was experiencing this from the viewpoint of Magdalene and wondered what could have brought her into this awful predicament.

I was taken back in time and saw a woman whose name was something like "Nathalia." She was a hateful, spiteful woman, and very jealous of Magdalene. She felt scorned. As soon as Magdalene entered the household, Nathalia had lost her place with her lover (the Syrian). She felt that Magdalene had stolen him from her.

I saw her lurking in the background at a festive dinner being held in a public dining hall in Jerusalem. Her eyes were fixed on Magdalene, watching her every move. Her long, thin face was exposed by her pulled-back hair, which was worn in the style of the Greeks, woven into plaits with tiny golden threads. This wealthy woman appeared garish and wanton, whereas Madgalene, as a lover of high fashion (even if perhaps rather overdone), was quite pleasing to look at.

Nathalia busied herself gossiping with various guests around the perimeter of the room, while vivacious, red-haired Magdalene held court in her usual charming way. Nathalia's crescent-shaped eyes narrowed in disgust as she watched Magdalene gain precedence in the domain where once she had reigned.

The Syrian was there. He wore a formal red robe with black borders. His black hair shone with oil. He was entertaining the guests with theatrical humor and broad displays of affected generosity. Magdalene had tried all evening to keep her distance from him, for she had reached the point of wanting nothing further to do with him. The Syrian was, however, as yet unaware of this, and so continued to act as though they were a couple.

Later, I saw Nathalia standing on some stone steps behind a low wall bordering a walkway that ran just beyond the side entrance to the building where the dinner was in progress. She attracted the attention of the Syrian. He followed her down the steps. Acting as though she felt sympathy for him, she proceeded to tell the Syrian of Magdalene's alleged affairs with other men, warning him that Magdalene was betraying him. She even offered a list of the names of men whose reputations were less than admirable.

As this conversation was taking place, Magdalene was in the hall. As always, she was enjoying the attention she received from the men, often at the expense of their own wives. Once again, she charmed the men with her beauty and her cleverness, while the wives whispered among themselves, shocked by her forward behavior.

At first, Magdalene was oblivious to how she was behaving. But then, suddenly, she looked up. Awareness spread slowly over her face as she realized what she was doing. A feeling of shame washed over her. She felt sick with unease. She wanted to leave immediately, and so arose from the table, making excuses for her early departure.

The Syrian, after his interview with Nathalia, was burning with rage (which, however, he kept well concealed). He intercepted Magdalene at the exit, announcing that he would accompany her home—although she, of course, did not want his company. She wanted to be alone.

"I will walk with my servant, thank you," Magdalene replied, not looking up at him.

But her words had no effect. The servant, who actually belonged to the Syrian, was dismissed. Magdalene's heart was gripped with anxiety. She sensed that something was terribly wrong.

As they walked together, the Syrian acted as though all was well between them. He wrapped his arm around her shoulders possessively and grazed her cheek with his lips. Annoyed, Magdalene pushed him away. She was anxious, wondering how she could possibly end this affair.

Then he grabbed her roughly by the shoulders and kissed her hard on the mouth. Again she pushed him away, crying, "Don't!"

She quickened her pace as he leered at her—but she was no match for him. He was not going to let her go. He grabbed her arm again and spun her around to face him. "Do not think that we are finished with each other! I have plans for us!"

"I want nothing to do with your plans," Magdalene replied, her eyes cast down.

Holding her tight, he said in a menacing voice, "You cannot leave me. I will not allow you to go. You will be very sorry if you do—I will destroy your business!"

At this she laughed in his face and said, "Go ahead and try!"

They had by this time reached a narrow place on the walkway between two buildings, but they were still not many paces from the dining hall. The Syrian lost control of himself and threw Magdalene to the ground. "Adulteress!" he thundered.

In the shadows, Nathalia had been watching the whole scene, a smile spreading over her face.

A group of men came running suddenly to the scene, shouting, "What are you doing?"

"She is a whore!" the Syrian raged. "We must stone her—it is the law!"

Some of the men then called out, "Adulteress!" and picked up stones. They encircled Magdalene, who lay on the ground, her hands held protectively around the back of her head.

Suddenly the men fell silent. Only a few stones had been cast. All was unexpectedly still.

Magdalene opened her eyes without lifting her head and saw a pair of sandaled feet before her. *What was happening now?* Magdalene wondered who this authority could possibly be—who could stop a stoning. *Perhaps I am about to receive an even harsher judgment!* But, she wondered, what kind of judgment could be worse than stoning!

As the silence persisted, Magdalene lifted her eyes. She saw first the shifting feet of her accusers as some stones fell harmlessly to the ground. And then, venturing to look up, she was overwhelmed to see Jesus, his eyes aflame with fury, his lips drawn into a tight line, his gaze penetrating her to the core.

Her first thought was that he was angry with her, that he was judging her. But then, to her astonishment, Jesus scratched a circle in the dirt, encompassing the two of them, and said to the men, "Does the law also allow you to have her for yourself?"

The law taught that it was each person's obligation to condemn those who may be defiling society. Adultery was considered a criminal act, and stoning was the acceptable way of ridding society of those who committed this crime. Most of the men present at this scene were married. Some knew Magdalene and some had even been with her in the past in one way or another and wanted to ensure that the evidence of that history was destroyed. This was why they had been so willing to stone her.

Jesus continued in a strong, level voice, looking boldly into the men's faces: "Which law shall we then abide? Whoever has not sinned against her, or with her, may cast the first stone."

Knowing that he had seen into their hearts, they dropped their stones and fled.

Avoiding Jesus's eyes, Magdalene knelt in shame at his feet and said, "I am again sick, Rabbi."

XII

Martha Comes to Visit

I SAW MAGDALENE standing at the window of her room, looking out over the placid, gray-blue sea stretching beyond the perimeter of her land. The large room was over-decorated. It was
filled with ornate furniture covered in exotic fabrics and cluttered
with expensive trinkets and knick-knacks. Heavy draperies
divided the room and hung also at the window. Silken sheaths of
various hues lay strewn about the floor, discarded like so much
rubbish, several of them having been worn but for a day. Heavy
perfume drifted on the air.

Through the window, a woman could be seen arriving with servants in tow. Magdalene's heart raced with injured pride, her ego
deeply bruised, as she peered past the voluminous drapes, watching the travelers arrive. She was anguished over what the Syrian
had done to her—*having her stoned in public!* An image of him
scorched her mind as she revisited the moment he had laughed so
cruelly as she tried to free herself from his domination—and had
then gone so far as to attempt to have her *killed.*

Magdalene had still been willing to overlook his malicious,
scorpion-like disposition in order to be on close terms with a man
so wealthy and accomplished. And so she had yet clung desperately to the relationship for some weeks. She rubbed the spot on
her arm where the first stone had struck, her mind fleeing then
from the painful memory. Perhaps some other man, she thought,
might ease the agonizing sting left by this one. The faces of possible suitors paraded before her mind. Indeed, there was one man
in particular upon whom she had set her sights. But she wondered, could she ever trust a man again?

As the traveling company drew nearer the gates of her castle,
Magdalene realized to her disappointment that it was Martha,
accompanied by several servants. When Magdalene saw her sister,

a deep sadness came over her. She knew that Martha disapproved of her way of life, and of her excessive display of wealth.

Martha, a woman of comparable means, chose to appear humble and modest. She could hardly rival Magdalene's beauty, although she was not herself unattractive. Her face was thin and

Martha

set, but had also a softness, framed by long, wavy brown hair that she kept modestly covered with a cream-colored veil. Her hazel eyes were close-set and round, and her skin was fair. Although she was serious, there was a touch of lightness to her as well. She wore an unpretentious dress of muted earth-tones, in contrast to the embroidered, gilded gowns that Magdalene preferred.

Martha was genuinely concerned for her sister, but because of her present shameful state, Magdalene could feel only the approach of disapproval. Her pain colored her perception; she did not want to view herself in the mirror of Martha's countenance.

Magdalene's thoughts turned to a memory of her brother Lazarus, in which the two of them had been strolling along the shore of the Sea of Tiberias at the time when her relationship with the Syrian was at its beginning. With great concern he had told her,

Shore of the Sea of Tiberias

"People are starting to talk. This affair could bring dishonor upon our family." She had felt shame at his words, for she respected Lazarus. But she had set that feeling aside and continued to pursue the liaison. Looking back now to Martha, Magdalene knew her sister was ashamed of her. Her heart was filled with dread at the thought of having to face her.

Martha had come for an extended stay, but Magdalene contrived to avoid her most of the time, spending her days in a haze of anguish, hiding in her room, slipping out only late at night to attend social gatherings and lose herself in the frivolities of her wealthy friends.

Martha came to her quarters on some of the mornings-after to try to help her, but Magdalene would not receive her. To face Martha was to face the truth. And the truth was that she was being driven unawares to rely on men as a source of power to boost her waning confidence and to give her a sense of having a place in the world.

At one such soirée she met a wealthy merchantman, whose name was something like "Paulos." He was probably Greek. He was stocky, with tight, curly brown hair and a ruddy face—not at all handsome, but wealthy and very well-connected, and with a winsome enough personality.

Evidently he knew the last man she had been with—the Syrian. Married to a quiet, petite woman who seemed like a shadow, Paulos felt no hesitation beginning a relationship with Magdalene—and this came easily to her as well, since she was available. Paulos was an easy choice, although Magdalene felt she could have had any man she wished, for her beauty and exotic ways were undeniably most captivating.

Paulos was engaged in the merchant business in a nearby town. Magdalene had one of her couriers deliver a message, saying she wanted to arrange a meeting with him. Martha became privy to this nascent affair, and could not bear to see her sister make yet another mistake and suffer yet more pain. So she decided to approach her and beg her to drop the affair.

Through many terse conversations over the following days, Martha persevered and was finally able to convince Magdalene to come and hear Jesus speak. "He truly is your only hope," Martha pressed.

Casting Out the Seven Demons

This vision picks up where the last one left off—with Magdalene and Martha heading off to hear Jesus speak.

MARTHA AND MAGDALENE were sitting in an open field at the outskirts of a town. I felt in myself great resistance to what was coming, although I knew I would be shown just what I needed to see on this particular day. I requested the assistance of an angel to accompany me.

Against the backdrop of some hills, a large crowd was gathered to hear Jesus teach. Right away I noticed Magdalene's dark countenance at the back of the throng. She was fidgeting and was in a state of confused malaise. Her fine tunic and mantle were spread out around her in their glory like a peacock's tail. She was feeling out of place, thinking that only peasants or rebels went to such gatherings.

Intending to break away and go find her merchant friend Paulos, she made excuses to leave, but Martha knew what she was up to and insisted that she stay. As Jesus began to speak, Magdalene languished there at the back of the crowd. Much time had passed since her last contact with Jesus, and during that time she had become even more oppressed by the shadows that plagued her. She was in an even darker state now than she had been before she had anointed Jesus at the house of Simon.

Jesus began to speak about the nature of evil and of all its forms, cautioning those present to avoid even the appearance of evil. He spoke of what opens a person to the influence of evil, saying that if one offers an evil being a place to do its work, many more will then follow, for they will know the door is now ajar. He said, "There are legions and legions that can come against you. It is through love that you become pure, and then these evil beings can no longer take hold of you. Love is the light that transforms evil."

As he continued, a haughty, sarcastic demeanor passed over Magdalene's face. The evil in her was mocking Jesus. She was shaking her head, wagging it back and forth, and looking at the people around her with prideful derision. At the same time she felt something taking hold of her. A sickening feeling of guilt and shame arose in her soul, threatening to make her physically ill.

Ever since the last time Jesus had healed her, she had told herself she was finished with him. She had continued on her former course, unable to let go of her shady associates, unable to let go of her attachment to material possessions, unable to truly change.

Martha believed, however, that it was still possible for Magdalene to change. While she witnessed Magdalene's fall into an ever-worsening state, she had spent many days worrying about her and praying for her. She had seen her make some improvements after her first healing, and knew the light was still there.

Magdalene had not really taken Jesus's words to heart—they had never been allowed to take root, to grow within her. Lacking nourishment, all the good she had felt and all the truth she had heard were withering away. Her soul was like a desert where nothing could grow. As she sat listening to Jesus speak, it was as if his words fell on parched ground.

Martha struggled within as she watched Magdalene. Evil beings tempted her to judge her sister harshly, to be disgusted with her—even to *hate* her. She fought against anger and impatience. She had truly wanted Magdalene to embrace Jesus's words, but as her sister acted with such irreverence, Martha became increasingly resentful of her. She remained silent, however, with nothing of her inner battle showing on her placid face.

Demons separated the two sisters and kept them from loving and accepting each other. This struggle did not abate as Jesus continued to speak—and he was well aware of it.

Looking out over the throng, Jesus could see the darkness hovering around Magdalene, and how it was affecting Martha. He did not go to them immediately, but kept speaking as the conflict within Magdalene's soul continued.

Others in the audience were engaged in similar struggles; indeed, the demons were riled up in that place on account of Jesus's words. Knowing they had been found out, they wielded their black sickles viciously, determined to reap the souls to which they had become attached. They hoped in this way to augment their power to prevent others from receiving Jesus's words. They knew they would be cast out if those words found their way into the hearts of the people.

The demons did all they could to assure their own survival—and many people were overcome by their oppressive darkness. From time to time, Jesus went forth and touched some of them, releasing their demons. But he did not approach Magdalene.

Magdalene was restless, animated with a spirit of sarcasm. Then a sickly feeling of oppression overcame her. A heavy atmosphere enveloped and pressed down upon her. She grew lethargic, trapped in the darkness, seeming even to lose self-awareness.

As Martha looked at her, she thought, "How rude that now, after being such a distraction, she is falling asleep!" She could muster no compassion for Magdalene, nor any clarity regarding what she was going through. This was the work of the demons in Martha's own soul.

And Magdalene was helpless. I saw the murky atmosphere around her begin to affect the people nearby, some of whom were acquainted with her. They fell into a mood of apathy, so that when they glanced at her, they thought, "Who cares? We don't care about her!"

Magdalene felt this apathy also, saying to herself, "I do not care about Jesus. I do not care about his words."

This apathy was a lower emotion even than fear or anger. It was a feeling of powerlessness, of being devoid of light, devoid of hope. With fear or anger there is still a will to act; but in the case of the kind of black apathy to which Magdalene was succumbing, the will forces were all but snuffed out. She had no will to save herself, and no one else present had a will to save her.

Curiously, Jesus allowed this to go on for quite some time. He worked with the crowd, banishing the evil spirits among them, until he had completed this work. Only Magdalene was left.

Then, finally, he strode to her through the crowd. By this time she had been overcome by the evil forces, which tried to speak to Jesus through her. When she saw him coming, she collapsed in agony. I saw the landscape of her soul all black, all her chakras dimmed and shut down, with only scant light flowing among them. Never before had I seen these seven centers of energy in so low a state in any human being, all darkened simultaneously. Jesus had allowed her to descend to this condition, this inner hell (for indeed, this was her experience), so that the glory of God might be manifested in her.

Various levels are encountered in descending to such a state of hell. We might think that a state of abject fear or of violent anger signals arrival at the depths of hell. But no, at the lowest level of hell one is immobilized. One no longer has the capacity to care— as if lost in a void, beyond feeling. At so low a point help is usually needed, for it is very difficult to journey back from this deep and dark place. Very few descend into this pit of apathy, but in our time this descent is becoming more frequent. Unchecked, this condition could bring about a "hell" on Earth. It is through the prayers of the righteous and through divine help that such souls can be saved, that is, resurrected, from their apathy.

Magdalene's soul descended deep into this abyss of darkness so that, in being saved by Christ Jesus, her healing might bring healing also to the Soul of the World. For those with eyes to see, this healing makes clear and gives certainty that all may be saved from the darkness of their own errors, and from the malaise that stems from it.

The healing of all seven chakras was accomplished *first* in the soul of Magdalene. The soul sickness of each of her seven energy centers corresponds to the soul sickness of the energy centers of the Soul of the World, which need cleansing and healing also. This healing will take place over time, as human beings develop spiritually, working more and more consciously toward their own redemption, and that of the Earth. Human beings will do Christ's work, in union with him, and also with the Archangel Michael, toward the eventual liberation and sanctification of the Earth.

The seven chakras are the seven seals spoken of in the Book of Revelation. They are found both in the soul of the human being and in the Soul of the World. There are many deep mysteries concerning these seven seals. They are the repositories of human wisdom and truth, which were sullied and desecrated by human error. Christ, as Lord of Destiny, wields the power to open the seven seals. When the seven seals are opened, the darkness is cast out and there is healing.

This is what Christ Jesus did for Magdalene. He commanded the demons to leave her energy centers. This was much like his cleansing of the temple, where he proclaimed that the temple was his Father's house and cast out all forces that could not abide the Father's presence—for those forces work against the love of God. In this same way did he clear out the temple of Magdalene.

As Jesus stood before Magdalene, the demons within her questioned mockingly: *This is Mary's Son?* Jesus put his hands on Magdalene's shoulders and looked into her eyes. The blackness within her welled up and gathered around her like a thick cloak. With authority, Jesus called out the demons from her body. I saw them detach from her, their great black wings rising up from her back, leaving behind a painful, raw wound in her etheric body, her body of life. The demons cried out in complaint, claiming that Magdalene's life belonged to them, as did everything she possessed. I saw other evil entities gather around her, searching out an opening to enter through as soon as the other demons vacated her soul. But they found no such opportunity, for Jesus repelled them by drawing a circle of etheric protection around her.

In her weakness, Magdalene fell to the ground. When she was able, she looked up at Jesus. He stood above her, his head framed by the sun, so that his countenance was encircled in a halo of light. Only then, in her utter emptiness, could she receive him. In receiving such light, she was herself illuminated. And in this same moment the veil of apathy was lifted from everyone around her. The crowd was healed of all manner of darkness in its myriad forms.

Over the course of the ensuing year, Magdalene would be healed of every level of darkness. This is not to say that she became impervious to the forces of darkness from that time forward. They could, and did, still come against her in an effort to discourage her. It was for this very reason that Jesus told Magdalene, as Martha supported her in her arms, to remain ever vigilant, for until her will could withstand unassisted the temptations that might come her way, she would remain in a most vulnerable condition.

As he spoke, Magdalene was filled with a love she had never before known. At that moment, she resolved to follow Jesus. And from this moment she did indeed forever offer her heart to him and to his ministry. Magdalene was the first individual in human history to receive this kind of healing, this full cleansing of the seven chakras, by Christ Jesus.

That evening, after her healing, Magdalene and Martha talked together far into the night, sitting by the glowing embers in the hearth at the homestead where they were lodging. Magdalene wanted to hear every detail of Martha's experiences with Jesus. Martha told her of many wondrous miracles, and assured her that she belonged with the disciples, inviting her to be present at their next gathering.

Final Healing Through the Blessed Mother

NOT LONG after the foregoing event (I believe it was the next day) Jesus invited Magdalene to accompany him to a room where some of the disciples were assembled. Magdalene did not feel well that morning. A measure of darkness was again making itself known, but although she felt on this account some reluctance, she nonetheless did meekly follow him to the house where the twelve disciples and some of the holy women had gathered.

Great excitement was in the air. They were planning their upcoming journey. Everyone was speaking of the miracles they had witnessed. They looked up when Magdalene entered the

John of Zebedee

room, and some protested her presence. Peter, recalling her strange behavior at the meeting of the previous day, approached Jesus to speak against her presence, saying, "We do not need her to mar our reputations!"

Smiling, Jesus said, "She needs our assistance. And through her I shall do a great work."

To this, Peter emphatically said, "She is not a part of our mission!"

Magdalene wished she could leave, and hung her head in shame. At that moment, the Blessed Mother entered from the left side of the room. She placed an arm around Magdalene, who, weak and shaky, was just then hearing taunting voices in her head. She feared losing herself again to the dark shadows. Jesus pointed to her heart and said in a calm voice,

"Magdalene, your heart is strong enough for this. You can be healed." Sweet-faced young John came to Jesus's side, genuinely concerned. He appeared eager to learn all he could from the Master. He wanted in particular to observe Jesus in every possible situation of healing.

As the Blessed Mother held Magdalene, I saw the "old" Magdalene die in her arms. She was transformed. In this embrace, which I saw as a *Piéta*, the mother of Jesus—so full of compassion—allowed the death of the old to take place, while her son commanded a final demon to come out from Magdalene.

There had been a lack of mother-love in Magdalene's life, and she had never known such profound, unconditional love and acceptance as she did now. It was on account of this lack of mother-love in her youth that she had been driven to seek love in the darkness of the world, in unholy unions.

As the Blessed Mother now poured love into Magdalene, even as the Divine Love anointed her, pure human love quickly filled the void left by the demon that had just quit her. I saw angels all around her.

It was during this final healing with Jesus and the Blessed Mother that Magdalene's seven chakras were finally and completely cleansed. She received at this time a special mission and a special vocation, although she came to understand this only later. Jesus advised her to remain close to the Blessed Mother as a protection against further attacks by the darkness.

With the demon gone, Magdalene was able to look into Jesus's eyes, seeing him in a new way. Her heart came into harmony with his heart. Thus was she made new. Magdalene felt the ecstasy of release and healing as she was liberated, finally, from the bonds of her former nature. Her former self died, transformed by the anointing of Divine Love. The rising of her true self was like a resurrection from the dead.

As this vision ended I received the following inspiration:

May we reconnect to our mothers, and especially to the Divine Mother! May we see ourselves as "mothers" of humanity, and allow love to flow through us to all of God's children.

I wanted to rush from that scene—of Magdalene and the Blessed Mother—and beckon to everyone to heal their relationships with their mothers, to forgive them and to love them. And also to love themselves as mothers, to become the loving mothers they can be to all humanity!

In that moment I knew that this kind of love, the Mother's love, is what "crushes the head of the serpent." It is in drawing from the feminine forces of the heart that we can keep evil at bay. Christ brings us to the Mother and places us in her arms. She will banish the serpent from us. She heals us with the anointing of her love. When we are filled with her love, we become the Balm of Gilead to others. This is what Magdalene became—the Balm of Gilead. As her old self died in Christ, she was made new in him by the Mother's love. Not only was she anointed, but she became also the *Anointer.*

Magdalene began always to carry oils with her. These oils became the means by which she was able to heal others. And she became a healing balm for her Master as well, not only through her use of oils, but also in the unique way she was able to support him with empathy and compassion.

Having experienced the "dying in Christ," she became a guardian of the Death Mysteries, to which she ever afterward holds the key. She is the Priestess of the sacrament of anointing for burial, an initiation we must all undergo to be resurrected—for there is a spiritual anointing that prepares us for our spiritual burial. Just as Mother Mary was able to anoint Magdalene with a divine unction, so Magdalene can pass this anointing on to others who seek her help in giving up the old, through dying in Christ. This divine anointing brings about harmonic changes that prepare us to receive our resurrection bodies—the deeper mystery of which touches the redemption and transformation of the Earth itself. We must die in Christ in order to live in him; Magdalene is the one who holds the keys to this mystery.

PART TWO

Magdalene Becomes a Disciple

Bridge over the Brook Kedron

XIII

A Conversation with Jesus

I FOUND MYSELF near the brook Kedron at the base of the Mount of Olives. It gurgled quietly as it slipped by over stones and reeds, the sunlight glinting off its rushing waters. Although the sun was at its midday zenith, it was quite chilly, and Magdalene, sitting next to the brook, was glad she had remembered to wear her woolen cloak. She smiled ever so slightly as she thought of the drab dress she wore—a grayish-beige tunic with a muted striped mantle over the top—the perfect attire to match her subdued thoughts as she contemplated many things.

Jesus appeared suddenly behind her. He took her by the hand, pulling her to a standing position, and said, "Come, walk with me." Magdalene was happy to see him.

On the east side of the brook rose a hill with a steep, rocky face. Jesus took her arm to help her navigate the uneven terrain. The friendship between them was fresh and new; they were getting to know each other again. Magdalene's conversion was still very present in her mind, leaving her feeling unsure of herself. Having rejoined Jesus's ministry, she chatted about the business side of the disciples' activities, of the doings of the holy women, and of their plans to assist Jesus in his upcoming journeys.

When they reached the top of the hill they came upon an ancient olive tree, under whose spreading branches a woolen blanket was laid. They sat, talking part of the time but sitting in silence also, as sunset approached. These were hours of respite for Jesus—away from the crowds of people and their many demands, which had increased greatly as he became more well-known in the region.

As they talked, they looked out over the valley, over Jerusalem. Jesus felt a great love for the city and its inhabitants. Magdalene now caught a glimpse of the grave responsibility of his mission, as well as that of his disciples. She was surprised, as well as somewhat uncomfortable, that he was sharing such free time alone with her, so she strove to keep the conversation focused on matters of the day—until finally Jesus changed the topic of discussion to a more personal one.

"I see you are struggling with the idea that you must model yourself after my mother. You sense a purity and innocence in her that you desire for yourself. It is good to desire this, but you are also feeling some anxiety in her presence."

As he spoke, Magdalene looked at the ground, avoiding his eyes and playing with the fringe on the blanket. She had indeed

Jerusalem Viewed from the Mount of Olives

been feeling a separation between herself and the Blessed Mother. She did not feel that she could ever come close to being what the Blessed Mother was. After her healing from the demons, Jesus had told her to remain close to his mother. Magdalene had resisted this, feeling unworthy still of the Blessed Mother's love. After all, she had only recently been divested of her chequered past. Magdalene was well aware that everyone knew of her reputation and that they wondered how she could have overcome it. She herself did not know where she fit into the scheme of things, and she realized that some of the other disciples felt the same way about her.

Magdalene thought about her relationships with the women in her life—none of which had been very wholesome. She had not been close to her sister, Martha, and had hardly cared to have close friendships with other women. She was close to some of her female servants, especially Sarah the Egyptian, but not many other women would abide her vanity and self-absorption prior to her conversion.

Her attention had been directed far more toward relationships with men, and these relationships had always been chaotic. In her relationships she sought always power or position. She had a way of influencing people, but this rested entirely upon her irresistible charm and worldly experience. It was not until she had turned her back on her former way of life that she realized how utterly alone she had really been. She became painfully aware that she had never known true affection.

As she reviewed all of this in her mind, it became blindingly clear to her why she felt unworthy of the Blessed Mother's attention, even though they spent so much time together. Such thoughts raced through her mind like wild horses, and gave her no peace.

But Jesus read her thoughts and in answer to Magdalene's resistance, replied, "I hope you will want to know my mother better."

"I know your mother..." Magdalene was surprised by the tension in her voice and immediately resolved to soften it.

At this, Jesus looked into her eyes with a gentle smile. She agreed, then, that she did not truly know the Blessed Mother.

As Jesus again fell silent, Magdalene languished for some time in the uncomfortable awareness of how self-conscious she felt while in his mother's presence. This was because the Blessed Mother, pure vessel that she was, reflected Magdalene's truth back to her. This was not done in a judging way; it was just that whenever Magdalene was around her, she became aware of those parts of herself that needed healing. The Blessed Mother reflected Magdalene's *potential* back to her, but she could not envision becoming this person that the Blessed Mother held up before her.

Magdalene had not yet learned to live independently of the admiration of others. Yes, she had been healed of vanity; but as yet she did not know how to see herself as she was. She wanted to believe that the Blessed Mother would love and accept her just as she was. All of this had flowed as an undercurrent through their early relationship. Outwardly they seemed the closest of friends and were often together, but a constant inner struggle filled Magdalene's heart.

Jesus knew that Magdalene was struggling. He shifted the conversation, allowing her to be more aware of what had arisen between them. He knew she was on a journey to find herself, after having lived for so long with a false sense of herself. Her full healing would take at least another year, and would be an ongoing work.

Note: The remainder of this vision, which addresses the different missions of the Blessed Mother and Magdalene, can be found in Appendix II.

XIV

Jesus Speaks in a Marketplace

I WAS WALKING behind four of the holy women. Several others followed after. One of the women looked back at Magdalene, who was just a few paces back, with a look of compassionate worry coupled with some amusement. She was anxious for Magdalene's sake, but not without some humor regarding her choice of dress. Another woman, to the left of the first, looked back at Magdalene also, but her face betrayed feelings of insecurity regarding Magdalene's presence—she was not so certain she wanted her with them, but was trying to be accepting.

It seemed to me that at this juncture Magdalene was only just deciding to follow Jesus again, and had not yet entirely given up her fashionable apparel. She wore a beautiful deep green tunic and mantle. The fabric was finely woven and very soft. Around the sleeves and hems were golden embroidered bands. It was a showy dress compared to those of the other women, who were clothed in various neutral shades with only touches of color. She was not wearing her usual tinkling jewelry, however, so it appeared she was doing her best to dress down.

A lively wind kicked up the women's robes and twisted their long hair into errant strands as they walked along a path leading to a busy market. Magdalene strode briskly and fervently, her heart going out before her. All she wanted was to see Jesus. And the other women were in just as much of a hurry to hear him teach.

As they entered the marketplace, merchants thrust their wares before them. One man held out in his large hands some small dark grapes, hoping to draw Magdalene's attention. She glanced briefly at the grapes, and it seemed to her in that moment that the man was holding out to her a painful memory, a memory that drew tears of contrition to her eyes. I did not at the time perceive the source of this pain, but felt it had to do with a temptation to which she had succumbed in the not-too-distant past,† for remorse and grief suddenly welled up in the back of her throat, threatening to choke her. She cast her eyes down as she hurried on.

The market was alive with people. It seemed as though every inhabitant of the town was on hand, anxious to buy or sell every-thing from animals to pottery, from spices to cheese. It was set up in a circular space, with booths surrounding a central area pro-vided with a small platform for performers or speakers. On this particular day the crowd was impenetrable around this area. The reason was plain to see: Jesus stood on the platform, his face aglow with an inner fire.

As soon as Magdalene saw him, her anxiety increased. She worried about his choice of topic, knowing that he would be ridi-culed in this place, even hated, for the potentially inflammatory things he might say. Magdalene was worried also that he might be harmed. She pressed forward through the crowd, hoping to attract his attention. She was thinking in his direction, *Please do not put yourself in danger!* She knew of a rumor that had been cir-culating through this town—that the people wanted him to come and speak only so they could catch him in his words and prove him a dissenter and rebel. They were pretending to be open to his teaching, but in truth were lying in wait for him to say something that could fuel their fires of accusation. Knowing this, Magdalene hoped he would speak only of such things as the people were truly ready to receive.

But as she looked at him, Magdalene saw the fire in his face and knew he would do the will of God no matter what might come against him. She stood off to his right and listened with trepidation as he spoke.

Then she noticed a man further around the circle to the right. He was eyeing her with a seductive smile. He was sandy-haired and large-boned and wore a red and brown robe. He was trying to draw Magdalene's attention, but she averted her eyes. She was used to men breaking codes of moral decorum to try to gain her affections, and wanted nothing more of it. Suddenly the man real-

† Refer to Chapter IX: *Magdalene's Dream.*

ized who she was, and became incensed that she did not return his gaze. He sneered gruffly at the men around him, "That whore! What is she doing here?"

The sound of his voice and his accusing words cut like a knife through Magdalene's heart. She wrapped her veil around her head, regretting the red hair that so often gave her away, and withdrew into the crowd. She felt sick with shame and lamented over the person she had been. She felt that the life she had lived was a black mark on Jesus's mission, and that she could not even be near Jesus without attracting scathing judgment.

As Magdalene struggled to remain in the crowd and listen to Jesus's teachings, accusing voices tormented her more and more. She worried also about the derogatory attention she was drawing upon the other women who followed Jesus, knowing that they were trying their best to withhold their judgments of her, allowing her to be who she was.

Torturous thoughts assailed her as she stood hidden in the crowd until, finally, she could bear it no longer; she turned and fled through the back section of the market. Her despair drove her to a hill behind the market, where she fell to the ground between two trees in a thicket.

She wanted to be alone with her grief. Unable to grasp her true self, she felt she was nothing. It seemed to her that if she truly wanted to be a disciple of Jesus, she could not be who she had hitherto been. His mission seemed so great, and was touching so many people—and it seemed to her that she did not fit in with his followers. She felt that everything she had been was for naught, and wondered if she had anything at all to offer. Even her beauty seemed now a curse rather than a blessing, for it had brought her many problems.

Lying between those two trees, she wished she could just leave herself behind and run into the wilderness, so oppressive was her humiliation. But in the back of her mind she knew also that she could not leave Jesus. She had felt called once again to follow him.

"She is Your Mother Now"

AS MAGDALENE wept, she came to realize also how she resented her own mother, who in dying had abandoned her at a tender age. Because of this, Magdalene felt she had never been taught to be "appropriate." Although she was raised by other women, she was unable to feel what it meant to have a mother. She was sure that wherever her mother was, she was ashamed of what Mag-dalene had done with her life.

I thought Jesus healed me! Why am I such a mess? Magdalene wept as remorse pressed upon her heart like a heavy stone. At that moment, a demon appeared beside her and became an onerous weight pressing her down, feeding her mind with the idea that her mother hated her, that her mother had become a ghost and would forever proclaim Magdalene's shame.

The demon tormented her, *You are not worthy to even remember your mother's face!* Magdalene wanted to die. If her own mother could not love her, then neither would the other women—and she so desired their admiration! She felt that the women who followed Jesus did not fully accept her. She was sure they did not want her around, and suspected that some were even a bit afraid of her. And this was partially true. But the women kept these things to themselves, for they knew that Jesus loved Magdalene.

The sun was beginning to set, and the thicket was caught in tangled shadows. Magdalene had not the will to pull herself up from the cold ground. She did not want to face her mother's memory, nor did she want to face her past.

At that moment, Jesus appeared with his mother, just beyond the trees. But Magdalene did not notice them. Jesus's face was peaceful and compassionate as he looked upon the pitiable Magdalene. Remaining at the thicket's edge, he urged his mother to go to her.

Magdalene saw the Blessed Mother's sandals appear by her side, but did not want to look up—she did not want to face her in so shameful a state. Some moments later the Blessed Mother placed her hands on Magdalene's back and said in a voice barely above a whisper, "O, God. O, God. Let her turn to Thee. Let her be Thy handmaiden."

As these words were spoken, Magdalene suddenly fell sick with nausea; she felt that the evil plaguing her would be spewed from her mouth. The demon made her feel that she was a wretched creature. But through the Blessed Mother's compassion, the awful demon was expelled from Magdalene. It was the demon that had been tricking her, pretending to be her mother's voice.

As she was released from its grip she saw with her spiritual eyes the face of her own mother. She was thus able to reach the true spirit of her mother, who came to her on a path of light with outstretched arms. I saw that her mother resembled Martha in appearance. Her mother said, "Magdalene, my beloved daughter! I never left you. I have been with you. I want you to remain with Jesus; never leave him!"

Magdalene was on her knees looking heavenward, where she saw in vision her mother surrounded by rays of golden light, the Blessed Mother standing by her. She saw then her own mother gaze upon the Blessed Mother in adoration, weeping tears of joy, for she could see the light of peace and compassion all around her. Her mother then turned to Magdalene and said, gesturing toward the Holy Mother, "Magdalene, she is your Mother now. Remain with her." She then withdrew, enfolded in wings of light that carried her away.

As the vision of her mother drew to a close, Magdalene fell to the Holy Mother's feet and wept, "I want to live to be worthy of your love!" The Mother placed her hand gently on the back of her head. She said, "Magdalene, I love you. I know you beyond what you know of yourself; and I love you because I know you. You belong with Jesus. You are a part of his mission; he needs you. Let us go forth that we may serve him."

Magdalene arose and wiped away her tears. In so doing she left a part of her former self in the thicket as she set out with new resolve to follow Jesus and to offer him all she was. For he was willing to receive her just as she was. When she met him outside the woods, he put his arms around her and said, in a tone that contained compassionate humor, "Beloved Magdalene, let us go join the others. The meal is set, and they are waiting."

They went to an inn owned by one of the holy women and ate supper with several of the disciples. Magdalene was quiet and subdued. Several of the women acknowledged her with a kindly glance or a tender touch to her hand. They could feel the pain she had experienced. They let her know that all was well, and that they accepted her and loved her.

Saint Christopher then appeared, holding a little banner graced with the face of Magdalene upon it. It looked as though it was woven of light. He told me it was woven by the angels' beholding of Magdalene—that it was their admiring gaze upon her that had called forth this beautiful spiritual tapestry. He said to me, "This was not created without much pain!" He had me carry the banner as we crossed the river, saying, "You carry the banner of Magdalene for others to see."

XV

As the vision began, I found myself in the "world that I am,"[†] where everything was bathed in peach-gold light. I saw the Archangel Michael wielding his flaming sword, his face glowing with radiant fire. He parted the veil to the heavens and allowed me to pass through. I was then in the starry realm, traveling with angels. I passed through certain spheres, until finally I came to the stream of the Akashic Record, where I would do my work.

Magdalene Becomes a Disciple

I FOUND MYSELF in the Holy Land. Jesus was sitting on a stone wall. Magdalene sat before him on the ground, resting her head against his knee. She was in a very talkative mood. She wanted to tell Jesus the whole story of her life. Of course he already knew everything about her and could see her past, but he allowed her to speak nonetheless. No one had ever before listened to her with such compassionate attention. Throughout her adult years she had never been able to open her heart to anyone, to pour herself out to another. Jesus silently ministered to her as she talked on, almost without interruption.

Martha walked through the garden several times, noticing Magdalene sitting at Jesus's feet. She furrowed her brow, worried that Magdalene might be bothering him. "Magdalene, you are tiring the Master with your talk. You should let him rest."

---

† I have often experienced my soul as a world unto itself. This seems to be an experience of many mystics, including Teresa of Avila, who referred to this as the "interior castle." If the soul is imbued with the higher self, and passions and desires have been subdued, the soul is an expansive world wherein there is beauty, light, and movement. I am able to see the spiritual world that the person is building. If the person has only materialistic, worldly interests, and is not forgiving, their soul does not appear like such a "world," but rather as a darkened atmosphere wherein there is little spiritual movement.

"All is well, Martha," Jesus answered with a smile. "I am well enough."

Magdalene was in a peculiar state. She had recently been healed of the seven demons and was still quite raw. She no longer desired her former life, but did not yet know who she really was, or what she might now do. Sitting at Jesus's feet, she felt suddenly an overwhelming need to review her past and to confess all—more to herself than to him. True, he had released her from her past, but there was still a need in her to make sense of it all and to release it by speaking it out. As she spoke, he would from time to time nod his head and say, "Yes… you did that," or "Yes, that hurt you, didn't it?" She looked back on her life, with all its chaos and mistakes, and said, "I have not done so well with the life God gave me." She said this with remorse, and not so much from self-judgment.

"There is a purpose to your life. One day you will see that all you have done is not truly who you are in the eternities. You see one point in time, but I see all time."

Jesus paused and touched her lightly on the head, as if consoling a child, and then returned his hand to his lap. He continued, "Follow me, and you shall see eternity also."

She thought for a moment, then lifted her head and asked in an elated voice, "Master! Are you asking me to be your disciple?"

He bent his head toward hers. "I *am* asking you to be my disciple. Follow me."

She sighed and returned her head to his knee. "I am ready now to leave my former life behind. I have nowhere else to go but to follow you."

"You will leave behind your riches, your wealth?"

"All that I have, if it can be of service to you, is yours. And what is of no use to you, I shall leave behind." She thought of her castle and had no desire to return to it.

Jesus paused and said, "There is more that you will need to leave behind in order to follow me. These things shall be made known later." His voice had a ring of melancholy as he added, "There will be much you will have to let go, if you would follow me to the end."

"Oh, tell me, Master, what else must I leave behind?"

"You will see; you will come to know."

She was quiet for a long time, wondering what he meant. Already she had left her friends, and all the men who adored her, and her castle also, with all its treasures. What more could she give up to follow him?

Then he said, "Magdalene, I love my disciples, and they love me. For the sake of love they will give up all that stands in the way of love."

Magdalene took his words in quietly. Thinking of her past relationships, a question arose in her mind. She did not expect an answer, but asked nonetheless: "What is love, and how can I know it?"

Jesus said, "I will show you the way to love. I love my disciples and they love one another. It is by this love that others shall know that you are my disciple."

Magdalene looked over at the disciples, who were gathered together around a fire pit, eating and talking among themselves. In another group some of the holy women were deep in conversation with the Blessed Mother. Such joy and brightness was in their faces. Magdalene could feel the love weaving among them. She could feel Jesus's love for his disciples.

Jesus placed his hand on her head and closed his eyes, allowing love to stream from him into her. She felt it enter her heart, as if the sun were shining there. She bent over and kissed his feet, then carefully draped her veil around her face and smiled.

"Thank you," she whispered. Her heart was filled with joy.

Reconciliation with Martha

MAGDALENE arose and walked over to Martha, who was busy repairing a basket. Martha looked up and saw instantly the love in Magdalene's countenance. The expression on Martha's face was one of pure joy. Magdalene looked into her eyes for a few moments and felt all the difficulty of the past. She had a sudden, clear knowledge of how Martha had tried over and again to look after her, to protect her, to guide her—while she had only rejected Martha, choosing to pass judgment rather than love. In this clear moment she realized that Martha *had* loved her. There was no need for any of this to be spoken aloud; Martha knew that Magdalene finally felt her love. The love between them had been restored as a gift from Jesus. They embraced, and Martha said, "I see you have become a disciple, for a disciple is one who can love with Jesus's love. I can feel his love in you."

Magdalene cried, "Oh, Martha! I see now that you have always loved me. Forgive me for not accepting it before."

"Have no fear—love will restore all that was lost in the past!" Martha knew this, for she had observed the miracle of forgiveness many times during her travels with the Master.

Magdalene walked through the circle of disciples. She wanted to see each of them now, in her changed state, feeling such boundless love. Some of them looked up at her and smiled a knowing smile. They began then to gather for an evening talk. John sang out in a lively, almost humorous manner, the opening line of a psalm, *The Lord of the field is come, he shall prepare the field!* To which the others sang out in response: *The Lord is good; he sows the seeds!* And so it went on joyously for quite some time—a song about the Sower sowing the seeds and harvesting the Good.

From that time on, Magdalene wanted her work to be the work of love, bringing love to the places where it had not been, helping others to find the love they had lost. She became Jesus's most beloved disciple, because she was willing to lay down all that stood in the way of receiving love. Eventually she took Jesus's love into her very depths.

XVI

I WAS AGAIN in the Holy Land. Before me stood a grove of olive trees, enshrouded in mist. The air was chilly. A path led through the trees, and a few paces ahead I saw Jesus waiting, his breath hanging on the air in small clouds. Magdalene walked briskly down the path toward him, her hands tucked beneath layers of her mantle. Together they walked down the sloping path, coming to a low-lying building.

I had seen this place in a recent vision, in which Jesus had spoken of love and had set the Samaritan boy before the crowd.[†] The twelve disciples and the holy women were gathered together in the warm building. Magdalene still felt unsure of herself and humbly wrapped her veil around her face. I understood that she had decided wholeheartedly to follow the Master after having finally been healed of the seven demons, but was still feeling vulnerable—like a newborn that requires gentleness and nurturing in order to thrive.

The New Covenant of Love

JESUS stood to speak. There was great power in his voice. Holding his arms out to the group as if to gather them all within his embrace, he said, "This is the beginning of my kingdom on Earth, which shall be established under the new covenant, a covenant of love. I did not come to throw down the law, but to bring love into the law."

His words were more eloquent than any I can find to convey his message.

"Those of you who are too rigid in the law may find yourselves in conflict with love; and if you continue to follow me, you will have need of being cleansed of your strong hold upon the law. You

† Refer to Chapter VI.

will have to lay this down and trust in me, for otherwise you can-not follow me to the end. As you trust in me and allow love to work in you, together with the law, you will be able to assist me in

Magdalene Sitting at the Feet of Jesus

bringing forth the kingdom of God and establishing it here upon the Earth at this most important time in the history of the world."

He paused to allow his words to settle into their hearts, and then continued:

The New Covenant of Love

"You will have to face the harshness of the law. Evil will tempt you to question the teachings I shall give you—to comply with the law and to leave me. You may even be tempted to betray me. You have been taught and held within the law, most of you."

With these last words, he looked at Magdalene with a slight smile, because he knew that for most of her life she had lived outside the law. She smiled back at him.

"But I shall bring you into greater understanding of the law and of the Father's love. You will understand and will have a witness of the Father's love. Begin now to think of the Father as a Being of Love. Indeed, He allows judgment to be fulfilled. He allows the law to be fulfilled, but He is a merciful God. Some of you have already experienced His great mercy."

And again he looked at Magdalene. She agreed. She had indeed experienced the great mercy of God. While he was speaking, she could feel God's love descend upon her. She bowed her head and silently wept beneath her veil—so great was the power of God's love pouring through her body, as with her heart she listened to Jesus.

"There is great mercy in everything that happens to you on Earth, although sometimes it is difficult for you to understand or to see or to know this. But after your tribulation is passed—if you contemplate what I am telling you—you will discover that there was mercy present even in your tribulation. And you may ask the angels to show you the mercy I speak of. Not only do I want you to know of the mercy you are constantly receiving from God, but I exhort you also to extend that mercy now to your fellow beings."

This was a new idea for most in the room. After saying this, Jesus paused again to give them time to ponder his words. They imagined many different situations that had arisen in the past; and then they imagined themselves extending mercy into such circumstances and thought how difficult it would be to change.

After allowing them to consider these ideas for a time, Jesus said: "In your society, the balance falls too heavily on the side of the law. Now we together shall even the scales as we bring love and peace. I will show you the way—the way of love—if you will continue to follow me. But the road ahead will be difficult. You will be ridiculed and hated on my account. Some of you will even be killed for my sake."

At this the disciples looked at one another uneasily, while they questioned themselves within as to whether they were strong enough to give their lives to this mission. They thought of the Baptist and how he had been murdered—and a chill ran through their hearts.

Jesus then said: "I will be with you only for a brief while, but together we shall do my work, which is the work of the Father. It is the work of divine love. And it is by love that you shall be saved. Love is the power and the force that saves. He who leaves

Nathaniel Under the Fig Tree

this world full of love is received into a heavenly abode. He who loves not will be cold in the life to come. Do not think that you are incapable of love. As you walk with me you will become more and more capable of love. You will be surprised how much the love will grow within you, until you are able to love even the most unseemly of human beings. For you will see all human beings as your own brothers and sisters; and you will be able to love them, even as I love you. But we must begin with our own circle, which we have gathered together on this evening. As you look around the room, some of you would sit on the side of judgment and some of you would sit on the side of those who would *merit* judgment in the eyes of the culture in which you live—and indeed you have been judging and being judged even as we have sat here."

Magdalene had indeed been feeling the judgment of some in the room. She glanced to the side at the beautiful Dinah,† and felt heartache on her behalf—for Dinah was a known sinner.

Jesus said: "Eventually you will be able to see each other in my light. You will be able to see my light in the other because my light is within each of you. Do not worry that this is not yet so. Be patient while the light grows within you. You have each been chosen—I have chosen you. I have called you to follow me, for your gifts are of great use to me in building the kingdom of God. And although you may not know what gifts you bring, I know them and I see them."

Jesus looked at Nathaniel, sitting at the end of the left side of the table, and smiled. Nathaniel thought about how he had been sitting under the fig tree when Jesus walked up to him and said: *I know you*—and how odd it had been that Jesus had said that to him. But in that moment Nathaniel had felt tremendous love and knew he truly had been *seen*.

Jesus then said to everyone in the circle: "I knew you before you were born." He paused.

Thomas asked: "How can that be, Lord?"

And Jesus answered: "I chose you as my disciples before this life. Even as I chose John, the Baptist, to prepare the way before me, so also I chose each of you as my disciples—and there is a mystery to this, which you will one day know."

---

† Dinah the Samaritan was converted at the time of her conversation with Jesus at Jacob's well (John 4:4–42). Her Jewish mother had married a pagan father and Dinah was an offspring of this marriage. They lived near Damascus, but both parents died while Dinah was young. Later, Dinah had five husbands, one after the other. From these marriages she had two sons and three daughters, who remained with relatives when Dinah had to leave Damascus. At the time of her conversion at Jacob's well, she was living with a man who was a relative of one of her husbands. He was a wealthy merchant in Sychar. The fact that they were not married was not known to the people of Sychar, who held Dinah, on account of her intelligence, beauty, and good nature, in high esteem. After her conversion, she joined the circle of holy women around the Blessed Virgin and was one of the most industrious helpers in the community.

THROUGH THE EYES OF MARY MAGDALENE

And with these words everyone present felt a reverence and awe for everyone else in the group.

Jesus Prays for His Disciples

JESUS SAID then that he wished to pray, and asked everyone to join hands. He knelt in the center of the circle and prayed, saying: "Father, I dedicate these souls to Thee and to Thy work. These are the ones whom I have chosen, and I chose them in Thy name; and they shall lift me up and they shall also lift themselves up. As they come to know Thee and Thy great abiding love, set the angels round about them to protect them until their work is finished. Give unto them the words that they shall utter, bless them with the strength to do Thy will, and bless them also with protection against the adversary. May peace prevail in this community among all members present, that they may love one another as I love them and as Thou hast loved us."

As Jesus prayed, I saw angels all around the men and women, as if they stood in a radiant cylinder of light. After he finished praying, a meal was set out. As the preparations for supper were being finished, Jesus drew Magdalene aside to a corner of the room that was more private. He said to her: "Magdalene, your heart is glad for some things, but troubled in other ways. Do you want to share your thoughts with me?"

She said: "I am happy about the teachings of this new kind of love and I want to feel this love for all mankind; I am ready to follow you wherever this path may lead me. But as you were speaking, I kept seeing something in my mind, something like a dream, though I was not sleeping."

She paused, wondering if she should continue. Jesus seemed open to hearing what she had to say, so she went on.

"I saw that you will be harmed, but I know not under what circumstances or when this is to be. But I fear for you. I fear this path can lead only to the same fate as that of John the Baptist. You could be captured, imprisoned, tortured, and killed. Please tell me my dreaming thoughts are not true! But even if it is to be so, still shall I follow my Master."

Jesus said: "Only God's will may work through me, Magdalene.

You must trust in God's will and remember that the Father is a loving God. And remember also what I have taught you about mercy. Do not fear, Magdalene. Trust in me and remain with me."

She answered: "Yes, my Lord. My heart is with you now, and I will remain with you until the end."

When she went to rejoin the others, the feeling in the room was light; everyone felt a deeper love for one another.

Afterward, as Jesus walked with Magdalene to the road, he said to her: "Magdalene, you have the gift of sight. This will grow in you. Do not fear it. It is a gift from God. You will be able to see and know in a way that is beyond what most can see and know. Go now in peace."

She left him then with a feeling of excitement for what was coming. But the feeling was tempered also by what they might have to face.

Walking side-by-side with Christ is not easy for those who fully give their heart to his work. They may receive the condemnation of others. But it is a path of light; it is a path of love. As we strive to love everyone around us, we receive more and more of his light and love—it grows in our hearts. And when we pass from this life, his light and love shall be our heavenly abode. For his love endures all things. His love transcends time and space. It is an eternal love.

As the vision drew to a close, I saw myself standing in a field. I was working with every kind of person to till the field and was fully enjoying the work. I knew that I was seeing this because my heart wants to remain connected to all humanity and to labor with any and all who work to uplift the Earth.

XVII

Jesus Has Supper with
Martha, Magdalene, and Lazarus

AN ANGEL APPEARED to me just as I entered into vision. We traveled together through brilliant rays of light. Emerging from the light, I found myself in a marketplace in the Holy Land, alongside Magdalene, who was buying spices and herbs, placing them gently into the basket on her arm. She was dressed simply, and her heart was light as she chatted with a merchant. Her spirits were jubilant, for the Master was going to be present for supper that evening at the family homestead in Bethany, where Martha was then living.

Martha had taken upon herself to oversee, with the servants, the preparation of the evening meal. Wanting to be helpful, Magdalene had taken stock of the herbs in the kitchen and had decided they were not good enough, so she had gone to the market to find some that were fresh. Secretly, though, she wanted to go also so that she could calm her heart and recollect herself. The thought of Jesus coming to stay at the house made her heart feel as though it would burst—so full was she of love—but she needed to compose herself. Martha was pleased that she had decided to go to the market.

Upon her return, Magdalene handed the basket of herbs to Martha. Martha noticed that her sister's face was flushed. Not knowing how to manage her feelings, Magdalene begged for time alone and went to her room. She lay upon the bed and gazed at the ceiling. She became aware of her heart. With unrestrained expectancy, she felt her heart as though on the road leading to Lazarus's home—the road Jesus was traveling at that very moment! She wanted nothing more than to see him, and could think of little else.

Before long, Jesus and his traveling companions appeared at

the door. In an alcove just inside, a servant assisted Jesus with his sandals and offered him fragrant water with which to wash his feet.

Magdalene felt his presence the moment he arrived. She had to hold herself back, not wishing to make any bold display. She arose and went calmly to meet Martha and Lazarus, who were greeting Jesus already.

Lazarus escorted Jesus and the disciples to their quarters while Martha returned to the kitchen, where she and the servants were preparing the meal. Magdalene did not know what to do with herself. She stood near the sitting room and watched Jesus retire to his quarters.

An insatiable hunger welled up within Magdalene to hear Jesus's words of wisdom. She entered the beautifully decorated sitting room and sat down to wait. The ceiling was arched and delicately painted. Exquisite textiles lay spread upon the sitting cushions. Finely woven rugs covered the floor. On a small table near Magdalene stood a small golden sculpture. The table was covered with a cream-colored linen cloth, bordered in blue.

As Magdalene focused on the presence of Jesus in the home, a profound peace settled upon her, calming her soul, releasing any anxiety she harbored still.

She felt prepared now to receive him. In a greater way than ever before, she felt open to communion with him. She was entering into a higher state of awareness, more so than any of the others in the household—for she knew of his mighty Presence to the very core of her being. Of course, all in the house felt his love for them, and they in turn felt also a deep reciprocal love for him, along with great respect and admiration. His arrival was a cause for celebration. It was a joyous, momentous occasion! But Magdalene experienced something quite different beyond this: she was filled with a pure knowing and with a childlike faith and innocence.

Martha entered the sitting room and said to Magdalene: "Would you come to the kitchen to oversee the setting of the table? We want it to be pleasing for Jesus and you can make it especially beautiful."

In fact, Martha had noticed that Magdalene seemed to have slipped into a dreamy state, and, anxious that she might tumble further into some overt emotional display, she hoped to divert her by assigning her a stabilizing task. Work in the kitchen would be just the thing, she had thought, and so she had requested her assistance. Magdalene could sense Martha's good intentions, and with perfect understanding and a warm smile told her she would join her in a few moments. Martha retreated to the kitchen, feeling as usual an unnecessary burden of responsibility for Magdalene's emotions, worried about what Magdalene might do. With tense hands she kneaded her frustration into the dough on the breadboard before her.

The Fruit of Eternal Life

FINGERING the tassels of the linen cloth on the table by her side, Magdalene smiled to herself, deep in thought. Suddenly Jesus was standing near, his face radiant with a warm smile. She stood respectfully to greet him. She did so in a formal way, keeping her head bowed and making no eye contact, while gesturing toward a cushion for him to sit upon.

They sat in silence for quite some time. Jesus allowed Magdalene to be in his presence as much as she desired. They were communing with one another on a level very different than that accessible to most people, who for the most part remain closed to each other due to walls set around their hearts. But with Jesus, Magdalene was able to commune freely, simply receiving him while he received her.

In this state, in the silence of his loving presence, many emotions rose to the surface of her soul and were released. Many questions rose also, and many scattered thoughts—but they too were released, until finally her soul was emptied out and silent. As she embraced the silence, her soul stood ready to receive Jesus's words; and it was then that he commenced to speak.

He asked her, "Who do you know that I am?" His eyes saw into the depths of her soul, and she allowed it.

She bowed her head as the knowing entered her awareness, or rather, rose from within her. She was given an image of an exalted, fiery tree—brilliant beyond anything she had ever seen. The tree was laden with luminous fruit. She said to him, "I see that you are the fruit of the tree of eternal life."

He nodded his head, and she continued, "You will bring immortality to all mankind."

She then saw another image: evil men, soldiers upon horses, charged against the tree, hacking it down with dark scythes. The fruit fell to the ground, but the men took no notice of it. Magdalene saw the fruit glowing red and falling like great drops of blood into the ground. Wherever it fell, the Earth was healed and grew lush and verdant.

She looked up at Jesus, and, choosing her words carefully, said, "Oh, my Master, evil men will try to stop you! And although this knowledge brings me much grief, I see that in the end good will come from what is to be done—that the Earth will be healed! But I do not understand all I see."

The image faded from her mind. She opened her eyes and looked at Jesus through her tears. He said to her: "I have revealed to you a great mystery, which you do not yet understand; but you will come to understand the mystery of what I shall do for the children of men."

He was silent then for some moments, and she was also.

It was then that Magdalene felt absolutely sure of her calling to remain with Jesus as a steadfast companion. She knew she was to be with him through all—through whatever might come.

During the following brief time of shared silence, several servants appeared at the entrance of the sitting room, desiring to be in Jesus's presence also. Magdalene looked up, and seeing the pleading looks on their faces, invited them in, motioning them to be seated on the floor. From various parts of the house other servants then arrived, longing also to hear his words. And they too were invited to sit. Lazarus then appeared and sat next to Jesus.

Before long, Martha was left alone in the kitchen, for the servants had all slipped away one by one to hear the Master speak. No one in the house was thinking of supper—they hungered only for Jesus's words. And so Jesus spoke to them.

He spoke of the heavenly kingdom. He taught of the world that was in spirit, speaking to them of the angels, and of the work of the angels. They yearned to know what lay beyond earthly existence. He taught them about his Father's kingdom. He taught them the principle that deeds done on Earth serve to form an abode in the kingdom of spirit. He said to them: "Whatsoever is sown on Earth, whether good or evil, becomes your habitation in the hereafter. As you sow beauty and goodness and compassion and charity, so will you find yourself in a beautiful kingdom after you leave this world. This is according to the justice and mercy of the Father."

His words quenched the thirst of their souls. Some were able to see in their minds images of what he was speaking about. Magdalene sat at his feet as he spoke. She felt a great love for all in the room—a kind of motherly love, so pleased was she that they had stopped whatever they were doing to come to hear him.

Magdalene and Lazarus Receive a Blessing

AFTER some time had passed, Martha appeared at the entrance of the room where Jesus was speaking. She was almost frantic with worry, feeling overwhelmed and abandoned. She wanted everything to be perfect for him, but had been left entirely alone in the kitchen. Resentment had taken hold of her heart, and she felt that Magdalene must be behind it all, that she had somehow drawn everyone in the house away from their duties and had given them permission to listen to Jesus's teaching.

With guarded tension in her voice she said to Magdalene, "Magdalene, did I not request your assistance? You have left me abandoned with all the work!"

Magdalene looked up at her with love in her eyes, for that was all she felt for Martha in that moment. Jesus looked upon Martha also with great love, saying to her: "Have no fear, Martha. All will be well. Magdalene has chosen the better part." And then he said, gesturing toward the others gathered in the room: "All these have come so that their hunger may be filled."

Martha felt sad at these words, for she wanted only to fulfill her desire to please him. Knowing this, Jesus said: "Martha, we shall yet partake of your meal and we shall do so with much gratitude." He said to the servants: "Go now to Martha. Go and assist her."

And so the servants went, leaving Magdalene and Lazarus alone with Jesus.

He said to them, first to Lazarus: "You are my spirit brother"; and then to Magdalene: "You are my spirit sister."

He held his arms out toward them as if to embrace them both.

"I have chosen you out from the world. You have seen me, and you know me, and therefore we are one; and I shall bring about great things through both of you."

Then he put his hands on their heads and blessed them with a sweet blessing, consecrating them to himself and to his work. Thus were their hearts consecrated to his heart.

Afterward, Magdalene and Lazarus looked at each other, feeling themselves to be at one. They were *knowing* each other in the light of Christ and were attuned to each other in a mysterious way. Over time, their brother-sister relationship would deepen into so profound a oneness that they came to feel this relationship as something far beyond a familial relationship. Jesus gave them the ability to commune with one another on a deep soul level, similar to the way he communed with them. This ability only increased with the passage of time.

Afterward there came into Magdalene's heart the question why Martha was not also present with them to receive this blessing. Jesus smiled and said: "I have reserved Martha for another task. She has also a noble path, but a different one from yours."

His words immediately soothed Magdalene's heart.

All were called then to gather for the meal. They went with great joy to the table. The entire household was in good spirits, feeling deep contentment. Martha was at ease and content and peaceful as she directed the servants to present the meal to the Master. The meal was a reverent one. Such love was present that it became a feast of love. All who partook were edified and filled.

After this, Martha sought out opportunities whereby she also might enter into closer rapport with Jesus, to receive him more deeply, just as she had seen Magdalene receive him. But she did this in her own way. Her faith grew, as well as her desire to serve him.

From this time forth Magdalene and Lazarus became the most beloved friends of Jesus, in whom and through whom he could do his work; and much more could be told of their relationship with him.

St. Christopher came for me at the close of the vision. I told him that I had experienced the humility of Magdalene—I knew she now had recognized that she was in the presence of a great Being. As he carried me across the river, I saw the Tree of Life on the other side. I saw that the Tree of Life is eternal and cannot be cut down. Its fruit never withers and never dies. It is there always. I love the Tree of Life!

Jesus Walking in the Hills Near the Castle of Lazarus

XVIII

Magdalene Hungers for the Word

MAGDALENE was in her room. Several sacred texts lay spread about her. She had been poring over them for hours. Some were papyrus scrolls and others little books printed from wax tablets. She had been taught to read her own language at a young age, and was tutored also in Hebrew and Greek. She had been adamant also that she learn Egyptian, and had managed to convince a certain man to teach it to her to a degree far beyond what most Jewish school-age children would have had the opportunity to do. Privately, she spent days in her room striving for spiritual knowledge. She had an intense hunger for the Word.

She wanted especially to understand the Creation and the Fall. Though as yet not entirely aware of her intentions, she was seeking to grasp the Fall of humanity as a way of understanding her own fall, as a way of grasping what could have brought her to such a pass that it took a miracle to save her. Her most pressing question was: *Who is this Jesus Christ?* She could see and know that there was nothing fallen about him, and this caused her to wonder about his origin. *Where had he come from?* He was born of a woman, so how could he not have a fallen nature?

Magdalene's thoughts turned then to the Blessed Mother, whom she knew was also a special kind of human being. *Who is this woman? Why does the Fall seem to have had hardly any effect upon her?*

These were the only two individuals Magdalene had ever encountered who seemed to lack that fallen nature. She thought about her own worldliness, of all the things she had done in her past to draw her further and further from God. She shook her head, marveling how she could have ever been that person she was before the demons were finally cast out of her. She had changed so much. Her passions and desires had left her. She could no longer desire the things of the world, even had she tried. The finery with which she was still surrounded spoke to her no longer. She could hardly fathom feeling the way she used to feel. All she wanted now was to be spiritually fed.

The Chalice of the Tree of Life

LATER, after Jesus had finished speaking to a group of people, Magdalene asked if from time to time she might meet with him in private, to learn from him, if only for a few moments now and then. He told her, "Magdalene, I will teach you the things you should know. I will restore much to your memory, for that which I shall teach you is that which you shall remember."

When he said this, she felt for an instant that she remembered him, though not in all fullness; she felt only that she knew him from some other time, in some other way.

She said, "Lord, I remember you." Gentle tears flowed unabated, which caused Jesus to smile.

"Magdalene, you were healed through being remembered, for I remembered you. And because of this the demons had to leave you. You were possessed by those demons because you had forgotten yourself; and as you lived your life, you forgot yourself ever more. This is why you gave yourself to the demons and allowed them to live in you. I came to you, and remembered you to the very depths of your soul. Because of this the demons had to leave you. Can you remember yourself, Magdalene?"

She replied, "If I can know that the person I am, the person who is standing before you now, is my true self, ever hungering to be filled with your words, then truly I am knowing myself, Lord. I feel holy in your presence, yet at the same time I know I am nothing. I feel my nothingness, yet it causes me no fear. The nothingness I feel is pure. Will you teach me, Lord? Will you be my Rabbi?"

Smiling broadly, he answered, "I see that you are truly hungering, wanting to be filled. As you have asked, so shall you receive. You have become the least, and because of this you shall become great. I have time for you now. Let us begin."

They separated from the rest of the people who had come to

hear him speak. Magdalene followed him to a tree. They sat beneath it. She was in awe that she should deserve so blessed a time with him, knowing he was so busy with all those who sought his attention. He asked her, "Where shall we begin?"

She immediately replied, "I hunger to know—to remember—the creation of this world."

She felt a great love for the Earth and sought to understand how it had come into being. As the two of them talked, it was as if the Earth were held between them, cradled in deep reverence and love. It was because of Magdalene's great love for the Earth that she was able to receive some of its memory as Jesus taught her. She was not fully aware of how the Earth's memory flowed into her at that time. Jesus gave it to her then, to be restored later to her full awareness.

He began by teaching her what the prophets had written concerning the creation of the Earth, expounding not only the words and visions of Moses, but also the teachings of other nations and other peoples: the creation stories of India and Egypt (some of which were already familiar to her) and of other, indigenous groups. He brought all these stories together into one great whole. He revealed something of the role he himself had played in the Creation. This wisdom was given her in a very gentle way, so that it would not be too overwhelming for her to accept. They did not venture into the story of the creation of humankind; their conversation was centered at this time only on how the Earth had come into being.

Jesus gave her an image related to the Creation, something for her to hold in her mind and heart. It was the Tree of Life, shaped like a chalice, its branches rising up, embracing the Earth in the center. He directed her to maintain the image in her mind. She gazed upon it, and then the image vanished, but the after-affect of the image was impressed upon her soul in such a way that she became one with it. It was a life within her, becoming her. Or perhaps better said, she was becoming it through this very profound experience.

A great gift had been given her soul, the fuller understanding of which would come at a later time. She was able to receive this gift because of her soul's *emptiness*; in silence she sat and received the gift, allowing it to work upon her. Afterward, she opened her eyes, sighing in pure joy, and said humbly, "Thank you, Lord, for what I have received."

Before returning to the holy women, she kissed his feet and looked into his eyes, so filled with radiant love. Martha met her as she walked down the hill to the women, and looked at her with disapproval. Taking her by the arm, she chastised, "Magdalene, it is not proper for you to be alone with a man!"

Magdalene bowed her head, hiding the disappointment in her eyes, and whispered, "He is not *just* a man! I only pray that you may receive him also."

She pulled herself away and walked ahead of the other women, wishing to retreat in solitude so that she could absorb all she had learned. Some of the other women also struggled with jealousy, for it seemed to them that Magdalene was taking Jesus's attention away from them, and that Jesus had chosen her over them. Of course this was not so. It was she who had chosen him.

As she went to her solitary place, Magdalene prayed that Martha and the other women would seek to learn from him also—to know him in a higher way. She returned to her studies, gaining light and knowledge, hungering always for the Word.

From this time forward her love for the Earth grew. She loved the Earth even in its fallen state, for the memory of its pre-fallen state lived also within her. She held the Earth in all its greatness within her heart, and this love would continue to grow as she deepened her association with Jesus Christ. For her, the Earth was one of the stars of the heavens. Gazing up at the stars, she knew that the stars loved the Earth, and that the Earth belonged to the stars: that the stars watched over the Earth and all its inhabitants.

Saint Christopher came for me then, speaking of the Earth—of how beautiful it is, and of how much he loves it. At first we were in a boat crossing the river. But then I told him how I wished he would carry me, like he used to do. And this he did. The sun was beginning to rise, and as we reached the further shore, it leapt above the horizon, its rays of light streaming all around.

XIX

A Plea for Healing

I SAW A SMALL GROUP of weary, downcast people. They were following a man pulling a cart into a town that lay just ahead. Someone was in the cart, curled up beneath an old blanket. Dusk was falling, so they moved more quickly as they reached the gates. As the cart made its way through the main street, the travelers paused to inquire of anyone they met where they might find Jesus. They were told that Jesus was in a house nearby, taking supper with his disciples. As they pressed on, some townspeople followed, hoping they might witness a healing by Jesus. By the time they arrived at the house where he was dining, a large crowd had assembled.

A servant came to the door to stave off the intrusion, saying that Jesus was at supper and that they should return the following morning, when he would be speaking at the synagogue. But the owner of the cart, a humble and meek man, was insistent. He pleaded with the servant to allow him to see Jesus right away.

Just then Jesus appeared at the door with several of the holy women and one of the disciples. He walked to the cart and carefully uncovered the face of a young boy who appeared dead, though he had not yet crossed the threshold.

After uncovering the boy's pallid face, Jesus stepped back and looked at the father, who gazed at his son in grief. Jesus paused, taking in the love of the father for his son, fully entering into this love and feeling it to its very depths. He felt how the love *expanded*, reaching beyond normal bounds of human love, for the father stood now at the brink of losing one he held so dear.

Absorbing this love, Jesus leaned over the boy, caressing his sallow cheek. I heard him speak in Aramaic and wished I could have written the words down, but found that the sounds lay beyond my grasp. He said to his Father in Heaven, "Let this boy be made whole." The words he spoke meant also, "According to Thy will, allow this boy to be made whole."

The crowd rejoiced as the boy was restored to life. They entreated Jesus for more healings, calling out their various maladies. He held up his hands as if to calm the waters and said, "Bring your loved ones to me on the morrow before I speak in the synagogue." Pacified by his words, the people left.

Jesus and the disciples went back inside and sat again at table. Jesus was filled with that father's love, a sweet smile upon his face. He said to all in the room, "Who was healed, the father or the son?"

Thomas, who had witnessed the healing, said, "The son was healed of his illness. He was restored to life."

Again Jesus asked, "Who was healed, the father or the son?"

They all wondered to themselves what Jesus meant. Of course, the father had gone from despair and desperation to relief and elation. This was obvious. They knew, then, that he must mean something else. Thomas thoughtfully said, "Lord, I think they were both healed, for the father was ill *with* his child."

Jesus nodded his head. "Yes, the child's illness was also the father's illness, for the child was sick on the father's behalf. This child had taken upon himself some of his father's darkness and so had become very ill. The father could only know his darkness by facing it as an illness in his own child. And what you do not know—what you have not been able to know—is that this father, through his son's long, protracted illness, had repented of the dishonest life he had been living. This is how he came into so humble a state that finally he sought me out for healing. The restoration of his son to health is a gift and a sign to the father that he himself is forgiven. The father's love for his own self was also restored; this was made possible through his repentance, for his heart was opened. He felt the greatest love that a human being can have for another. This love swelled within his heart. And through the healing of his son, he was able to feel the same love for his own soul."

Thomas then asked: "Lord, must children ever bear the sins of their fathers?"

Jesus answered: "There will come a time when the children shall no longer bear the sins of their fathers."

He said this gravely. "A time will come when the children will set their faces against their fathers and turn away. And as the love of their fathers will not be received into the hearts of the children, this shall indeed be a dark time for humanity. There is a Father in Heaven; and I, His begotten Son, have come into this world to bring the love of the Father to the hearts of the children of this world. Some will receive me, but many will not. I am the *love* of the Father. I come to heal the ills of the children, which they take upon themselves for their fathers. *I am the healing.*"

They were silent for a few moments as they pondered his words. Then he said: "As this little one took upon himself the sin of his father, so shall I take upon myself the sins of the world."

The disciples and holy women wondered if he meant that he would become ill like this child. They wondered what would happen to him if he took on the sins of the world. And how could this be possible? How could he possibly take on the sins of the *world*? Although Jesus was so somber, he was also childlike in his demeanor. The disciples and holy women felt suddenly as though they were in the presence of an innocent child. Jesus said to them: "When I do this for the children of men, when I take on the sins of the world, most of you will not be able to remain in my presence." He then looked at each of them with a penetrating gaze.

Peter immediately said: "Master, I will remain with you!"

Jesus turned his head to the side with a sorrowful look, but smiled at Peter and said: "It is easy for you to behold one who is sick with the sin of another, but it is not so easy to behold one who is sick for all mankind." And they all marveled and wondered what he meant.

Questions kept arising in their souls, but they could not seem to bring their questions out. All fell into silence for a time.

Magdalene was thinking of her own sinful past, of how heavy her sins had been. She wondered who in her life had been diseased because of her sins. Who might have been bearing some of her darkness for her? She did not know, but sat in awe of Jesus's words—that he, as the Son of the Father, would take upon himself all sin that the world had ever known! She felt reverence and gratitude in her heart. She wanted to kneel at his feet, to kiss his feet, to show her gratitude. She reflected upon that day of destiny when, burdened with her sins, she had gone to the home of Simon the Pharisee, where Jesus had healed her. She had felt so light and free. And she thought of the even greater healing she had received when he released her from the seven demons. Had he taken away her sins? Had he taken her sins upon himself? The thought of this swiftly brought tears to her eyes. Instinctively she covered her

Dinah the Samaritan Woman with Jesus at Jacob's Well

heart with her hands and looked at Dinah, who sat across from her at table. The two were struggling to not show emotion.

Dinah was engaged in similar thoughts. She remembered how the presence of Jesus at Jacob's well had been as living water to her, cleansing the murky, forbidden waters from her soul. She too was in a state of deep gratitude. She reached out to Magdalene and they clasped hands.

Jesus then said, "I will lay down my life for all of humankind."

Magdalene bowed her head and sobbed. His mother, the Blessed Mary, understood what he was saying, but the rest did not. Surely he would not allow the sicknesses of humanity to *kill* him?

Note: The remainder of this vision, concerning Christ's deeds in Gethsemane and on Golgotha Hill can be found in Appendix III.

XX

The Holy Women Prepare for a Journey

I WAS LOOKING into the great room of an inn. Several of the holy women were present, along with the Blessed Mother. Upon a heavy table were laid out three tunics in desperate need of repair, their hems soiled and torn. Some of the women were at work, taking great care with the badly frayed garments, content to assist the disciples in this way. The Blessed Mother watched over them as they worked. I could feel the excitement and anticipation in the air, and also the strong bond of love among the women. Toward the back of the room a few of the women sang as they prepared food to be packed for the journey: dried figs, dried fish, cheese, and bread.

Magdalene entered lightheartedly and with an engaging smile through the front door. She offered a satchel of coins to the Blessed Mother, saying she would like to donate them for the coming journey, to ensure that the twelve disciples and the holy women and other followers would have ample money for their needs. As she offered her gift, a concern arose in her that some of the women might think her money had been acquired through impure means, through some questionable business dealing. But her anxiety proved unwarranted, for the Blessed Mother smiled warmly at her with no sign of judgment and took the coins gratefully. Magdalene felt nothing but acceptance.

She went to join the women mending and cleaning the tunics. As she ran her fingers along the fabric of one of the tunics, she felt blessed to be a part of the preparations for the disciples' next journey—for she knew these tunics had been worn in holy places and had witnessed miracles. And as she contemplated the disciples' many journeys, she felt wistful in the knowledge that she had missed so many significant moments. The women had told her of the wondrous miracles they had beheld, and Magdalene wished she had been more faithful, so that she could have been with Jesus through all his deeds. She felt remorse at all she had lost by turning away from him. Even so, she was happy to have returned to him and to his mission, and was strong in her faith that she truly belonged with him.

Dinah approached and touched her on the arm. She understood Magdalene's regret. Magdalene looked at her and said, "I have missed so much..."

She was unable to complete her sentence, and looked down. But feeling Dinah's compassion, she said after a pause, "If only I had been true to him from the beginning and followed him as you have done, Dinah. I know it was so difficult for you to lay down your former life and take up his mission. I want to be strong also, strong enough to remain with him through whatever is to come."

Dinah's eyes brimmed with compassion for Magdalene. She nodded her head. "Yes, it was difficult, and yet the peace in my heart is so deep, so infinite, that I cannot think to turn away from him and take up my former life again. And you have this peace now, Magdalene. This peace will be your life. Nothing is truly lost. So much has been found. *You* have been found, Magdalene. He has found you and you have found yourself. I see only the beauty of it all—the beauty of where you have been and the beauty of where you now are. There is no end to the beauty and the miracle of our Jesus! You are a part of this mission!"

One of the women set down a plate of food and a cup of water next to Magdalene. She felt loved, and was especially warmed by Dinah's compassion and understanding.

It was then that John appeared at the door, joyfully acknowledging Magdalene's arrival with a warm smile in her direction. He did nothing to conceal his enthusiasm at seeing her. Magdalene arose and followed him outside, where children were boisterously chasing one another in the street. He told her of the coming journey, that they planned to head north for a few days. Jesus had been invited to speak at a certain synagogue, and the holy women had been invited to accompany him along with the disciples. John told Magdalene that a group of women in this northern town had requested to visit with the holy women, for they wanted to hear of their experiences with the Master.

John knew Magdalene would be excited to hear this news. This meeting between the two groups of women was being facilitated by an acquaintance of Martha's, a woman whom Magdalene did not know. Martha had been preparing the holy women to meet this group. I understood that the gathering of women would be a profound and important meeting because it was not customary for large groups of women to meet together outside of family and religious celebrations. This coming together could be seen as a scandal. The holy women, however, did not feel fear about meeting. Because of Martha's correspondence with her friend, they felt so strong a connection with the women of this northern town that they knew their meeting was destiny. They were beginning to feel a unity knitting their hearts together. The love of Jesus Christ was already at work within them.

John was one who felt the great importance of the role of women in Jesus's mission; he appreciated that the women were generally more spiritually-minded than the men. Thus he had taken it upon himself to oversee this meeting.

Martha Teaches the Women

I WAS taken forward in time to the meeting of the women. It took place upon a little knoll outside the town. John and Andrew were present. Martha stood and addressed the women for some time, speaking in beautiful words of Jesus's message of love. She was an articulate and gifted speaker. I understood that this was the first time Martha had taken on the role of teacher. She spoke from her heart, and her words touched all present.

Martha's words were a great blessing for Magdalene also, for in this way she was able to hear of many events and teachings of Jesus that she had missed during the long weeks she had been away from him. She saw Martha with new eyes and respected her in this capacity as teacher. Her love for her sister grew to new heights.

None of the women cared to eat, so intent were they on hearing what Martha had to share. The wonderful thing about Martha's speaking was that she was able to prepare the women's hearts to receive Jesus without anxiety. Many of these women did indeed harbor fear about his mission, for so many rumors about him were being spread abroad. Martha was able to guide them into a peaceful attitude of understanding and trust. Forty or more women were present at this meeting.

After Martha finished speaking, all fell silent for a time. One voice then broke into song, and others followed, until all in unison were singing a psalm. Martha's friend then requested that they might also hear some words from the Blessed Mother, who graciously arose and stood before the group.

A long silence followed, as she bowed her head. She then described to them some of the miracles she had witnessed Jesus perform, centering her words on the transformations that had taken place in those affected. She spoke of how their lives had changed, of what they had become after the miracles. It was not upon the miracles themselves that she dwelt, but rather upon the changes wrought in the recipients' hearts, how they came to see more than they had seen before, how their voices were opened and they spoke glorious words, whereas formerly they could scarcely speak at all. She spoke of some who were able to touch others' hearts by the miracle they had received, thereby transforming other lives. And there were even some whose lives had been restored to them, who before death had lived shallow lives, but who in being restored to life consecrated and dedicated themselves to God. The Blessed Mother had carefully watched and witnessed all these miracles.

As Magdalene listened, she could identify within herself how much she also had changed, how different she felt. She wondered whither her path would now take her and what results would follow from her own transformation. With all her heart she knew that she was following her destiny. She felt at one with those who had been touched by these miracles, who had been healed by Jesus—for she counted herself among them.

The Blessed Mother said to the women: "Jesus will come to teach you. He will teach you about the power of love. He will show you the power of love. You will see what love can do. And after you see, you will know. You will have the power of love in yourselves also, and will do the things that he does."

Then she humbly bowed her head and said: "I am here in

service to you. Should you have some need, I welcome you to come to me, that I may serve you."

There followed a time when the Blessed Mother sat beneath a tree and received whomever wished to speak with her. She listened with broad compassion, taking them into her heart, and they were nourished by her love. The other women communed together and sang psalms. An immense feeling of love united their hearts as one.

On the next day they would hear Jesus speak and spend time with him. For this reason they were elated, and as they went to their homes that evening they rejoiced and sang praises to God. Their hearts were fully prepared to receive him the following day.

Martha, Magdalene, and Others Listen to Jesus

XXI

Magdalene and the Old Pharisee

I SAW A MULTITUDE gathered to hear Jesus speak. The holy women had set up a place off to the side in which to prepare food for the midday meal. When Jesus indicated it was time to share the meal, the women passed throughout the crowd and made sure all were fed.

Magdalene carried a large leathern vessel strapped around her hip; from this she served water to all who thirsted. She was full of joy in her service. The holy women sang as they worked. They sang of Moses going up to the mountain, of the burning bush— and of how, when he came down, he also was aflame.

I noticed an elderly man in the audience, squatting at the end of the row where Magdalene was just then serving. He was dressed in the robes and hat of the Pharisees, but his clothes were soiled and threadbare, his hat especially. Most of his teeth were missing. When Magdalene came near his place in the row she felt drawn to him. She thought he seemed strange, yet wise, and also somehow lost, though she knew not quite what made her think such things. As she stood before him she felt suddenly speechless. Something about his eyes caught her attention, as they peered out at her through the weathered wrinkles of his face.

"Please sit down," he said, patting the ground beside him.

Magdalene, seeing that she was at the end of the row she was presently serving, replied, "I suppose I can rest for a moment."

The man rubbed his gnarled hands together, trying to ease the arthritic pain. Pointing to Jesus, he asked, "Who is that man?"

Magdalene looked over to where Jesus was sitting upon some large rocks, in conversation with several disciples and others of the audience. She thought he looked younger. He looked so fair in the afternoon sunlight. Her face softened as she watched him for a moment. "He is Jesus, the son of Joseph."

The old man's eyes filled with tears, which were too thick to run down his face. Rubbing his eyes, and blinking back his emotion, he replied almost inaudibly, "Yes... Jesus ben Joseph—the Nazarene." He paused. "I am here because I had a dream. He is the one from my dream." He then told Magdalene the story of how he had come to this hillside to hear the Master teach.

The previous morning he had been praying in the synagogue. He went to the synagogue only during quiet times, because he was somewhat of an outcast among his fellow Pharisees. He had begun to think differently, to speak out ideas that were suspect to them. He followed an ancient thread of teachings that the Pharisees deemed mythological. They suspected he was losing his mind. And so in his old age he had grown lonely.

On this particular day he was alone in the synagogue, studying the scrolls and praying. He heard a voice telling him to go behind the altar, where there was a box called the "tabernacle," and to lay his hands upon it and pray. As he prayed, the voice said to him with irresistible clarity, "Jedidiah, I have heard thy prayer. Thou art sick with the infirmity of the hard-heartedness of thy fellow brothers in the law. I have heard thy prayers and shall heal thee. Thou art a faithful servant, for thou hast borne this infirmity for many years, and the day is coming that thou shalt be healed." As he told this story to Magdalene, the man's hands were laid over his heart, and he wept.

He looked at her in a fatherly way. The holy women were still singing vigorously of Moses. Looking at Magdalene's red hair, he said, with some humor, "You are one of God's flames." Then, growing more somber, he said, "You are very close to this Jesus. You are his messenger, as was Moses for God. I only hope the people will listen to you when the time is come for you to deliver the message."

He looked over at Jesus again, and tears collected in the folds beneath his kind eyes. "After hearing that voice, I withdrew to my house and lay myself down to rest. Then I had a dream."

Mary nodded her head and smiled.

"My dear wife, who died many years ago, came to me. Her name was Maritha. She held an egg in her hand. She said, 'Look!' and held it out to me. The egg broke open and pure gold ran out from it. From this gold was born a black bird, shrewd and clever. The black bird stretched wide its wings. There was gold on its wings and on its feet. I wanted the bird for myself, for I thought it must have secrets to tell me. But the bird did not care for me. It wanted only to merge with the sun. It flew into the sun. The light blinded my eyes as I watched it go. I looked back to where my wife was, and saw the gold absorbed into the earth. I felt all was lost and tried to retrieve the gold, but I could not. It was gone. Then my wife opened her right hand, and another egg appeared. This egg was not special. It was spotted and gray, unlike the pale white of the first egg. It too broke open, and a homely bird, speckled gray-and-brown, emerged. It was not strong. There was nothing magnificent about it. It hopped to the ground and began picking up seeds in its beak. The bird found a good seed and ate it. The seed grew in its belly until it burst forth as a shining tree!

"Maritha said to me, 'Behold the Tree of Life, which is born out of that which is weakest among the greatest! Out of the weak, shall come the mighty! By its fruits you shall know that it is the Tree of Life.' Then she said, 'Look!' And she pointed in another direction. I saw in the distance the synagogue burning to the ground, and the Pharisees and scribes running to and fro, fending for their lives. Scrolls were being consumed in the fire. The Romans were taking over the town. I knew and saw that the Pharisees and scribes had not the power to withstand the attack because their hearts were too hard. I fled and ran to the hills.

"A man appeared to me, who is the same man as your teacher. He said, 'Jedidiah, because your heart is open you will be safe. Follow me. I will heal your heart, for it has been wounded. It has seen too much misuse of doctrine by others for the sake of upholding the law. You long for the unity of hearts.' He put a small golden key into my hand and told me it was the key to unlock the tabernacle, where I would find the scroll of truth. He told me that the true tabernacle was the temple of his body. He said, 'My body is the temple. I will sacrifice my body for you, that you may be in me, and I in you; thus shall you also become a temple of God.'"

Looking at Magdalene again, he said, "I do not know what this means, but I do know that I have found the teacher who will lead me to the true temple."

Magdalene thanked him for sharing his dream. She wondered if the dream was warning of a future attack by the Romans. The inhabitants of Tarichea and Tiberias had feared such an overthrow for years. She said to him, "I will go and bring him to you now."

She went to the boulders where Jesus was resting and asked him to come and meet her friend. Jedidiah's heart felt as though it would burst when he saw the two of them approaching. Unable to speak, he bent over and lightly kissed the Master's feet.

Jesus took Jedidiah's withered hand and said, "You know me because your heart was prepared to receive me. You have been heavily burdened by the law. It has taken your life from you. But follow me, and you will know new life. You will know the love of a new community." He motioned toward the crowd of people communing with each other during the meal. "You will be alone no more." He placed his hands on Jedidiah's head and blessed his heart—that it be healed of its heavy burdens. Jedidiah felt his heart burn within him, its warmth spreading throughout his body. After this, Jesus turned to Magdalene and said, "Make sure that Jedidiah has a place among us for as long as he desires."

Jedidiah became a disciple and followed Jesus for the remainder of his days. He lived for only three months more, serving and loving the other disciples in whatever ways he could. Magdalene grew to adore him and watched over him, listening to his neverending stories and ideas. He died a peaceful, happy man, in the knowledge that he was loved, and that he had found the prophesied Messiah.

XXII

Supper with the Wedding Couple of Cana

I WAS TRAVELING through brilliant light, feeling myself pulled toward its center. As I came to this center, I passed through a tunnel and emerged in the Holy Land. I could hear a newborn child crying in the distance. I did not know where I was as I emerged from the light—it was an unfamiliar place.

I was standing in the doorway of a sort of workshop full of wooden parts, looking out into bright sunlight. Before the building, a road curved to the right, leading to a nearby town. I saw Magdalene, who seemed to be waiting for someone. She paced about outside, shielding her eyes from the bright light. Jesus then came walking up the road, smiling as he saw her, and said, "There you are!"

Magdalene's heart beat more quickly when she saw him. There was no one else with whom Magdalene wished to spend her time. In his presence she felt alive. She felt she was truly known and seen. Through the miraculous healing power of Jesus she had become a new person, and for this she was profoundly grateful. She wondered how she had ever existed without him, and marveled that she could have resisted him so vehemently in the beginning. She rejoiced over her freedom, no longer burdened by the material things of the world.

Jesus and Magdalene walked along the road toward the home of the young man who had been married at Cana. Nathaniel, as I heard him called, was a beautiful young man. Ever since the miracle at the wedding of the changing of water into wine, Nathaniel's marriage had been especially blessed and watched over by Jesus. It was the first wedding Jesus had attended after his baptism, and the wondrous miracle of the changing of water into wine had blessed the lives of all who had partaken of the vivified beverage. It worked a transformation within their hearts. And this inner working continued. For a year or more the healing had worked on in their souls.

Nathaniel and his wife entered into the sacrament of marriage as a profound *work*, that of purifying marriage through striving for sacred unity. This was the subject of conversation between Jesus and Magdalene as they walked to Nathaniel's home. Jesus told her that he had wished to inspire the ideal of true marriage through Nathaniel and his wife, taking them as representatives for humanity. The impulse to seek true marriage, that is, *divine union*, was planted in all who had partaken of the miraculous wine. Such marriages, Jesus said, would become the vehicle to practice and to learn this kind of union. Nathaniel and his wife felt this ideal most profoundly. Because the wedding guests experienced the miracle of the changing of the water into wine, they had direct *gnosis* of a higher power; they knew that they also could be changed in a miraculous way, and they desired this transformation. The changed wine blessed even the people with whom the wedding guests later associated, for one who has undergone such transformation is a great blessing also to others.

What was done with the water can be done also with the human being individually. That is, an individual can pass from one condition of being to another, experiencing a profound transformation, becoming a "new creature in Christ." But it is even *more* powerful when two souls unite themselves in marriage, for there is then a vessel wherein a profound alchemical transformation can take place. If the couple strives transformatively toward sacred union with each other, then true divine union may be born from their marriage. Then their union can bless the union of others. Jesus explained to Magdalene also the difference between false marriage and true marriage as they walked on.

The two were welcomed into Nathaniel's lovely home, where a meal was being set out, and invited to wash their feet and then sit at table. I stood in awe of the purity of the love between Nathaniel and his wife. Their love felt so holy. Their marriage was truly filled with a rare grace. They were each quite childlike and innocent. Just from their presence Magdalene felt the healing balm of love.

I became aware of something occurring in Jesus, something I had not noticed before, and which is not easy to describe. As I listened to Nathaniel speak, I turned at one point to look at Jesus. He was in such a state of unity with the couple that I could experience them *through* him just as much as I could experience them *outside* him. I could enter into empathy with Nathaniel and his wife by being at one with them through Christ.

This experience went beyond what one sees or knows through normal waking consciousness. It was a most powerful feeling of love and peace, and an experience of grace. I felt it throughout my whole being. Spiritually speaking, there was no separateness between them and Christ, and none between them and me; neither was there a feeling of separateness between Christ and me.

Magdalene experienced this oneness also, something she had not felt with others before to such a profound degree. She experienced Nathaniel and his wife in a state of oneness with Christ, while being less aware of the oneness between herself and Christ. Magdalene was only just awakening to this extraordinary bond between the Master and those he loved.

I could not discern to what extent Nathaniel and his wife understood what was happening. But I do know with great certainty how deeply they felt this oneness: they felt tremendous love from the Master and for him, and a deep connection to him—as well as feeling profound unity in their marriage. Because of Christ's interest in their marriage, the two had developed unshakable faith, and their marriage was endowed with a special power.

The meal was blessed and shared with joy and reverence. To outer appearances one might say that they all just sat down and shared a meal together, nothing more than that. Yes, the feast was indeed a modest one, but the love was boundless and shared by all present.

After leaving the couple's home, Jesus and Magdalene took a path flanking a large hill. The countryside was beautiful, and sparsely populated in that region. It was verdant and light-filled, and just now glistening in the early evening sun.

Thinking of the oneness and love she had experienced with the couple during supper, Magdalene said to Jesus: "Never before have I felt this kind of love, never before have I witnessed such a love."

Jesus replied, "This love is for all. I have come to bring this love to the world. My way is the way of love. I shall bring hearts together and unite them in love. My love is the light of the world; and this light rests upon all who are in the world." He smiled as he gazed toward the sun, glowing gold just above the horizon. Everything around them was imbued with resplendent golden light. Turning his face into the light, he smiled blissfully in the pure joy of the sunlight resting upon his face.

As I watched him bask in the sunlight, I felt suddenly his one-ness with all humanity. I could experience all humanity within him in the same way I had experienced the couple of Cana within him. I could feel this oneness just as easily as I could feel the sun-light—the love is there all around us, and is no more inhibited in its reach than are the rays of the sun!

Jesus opened his eyes and turned his face toward Magdalene. He said, still smiling, "I will teach you the way of love and you will know this divine union. I am one with the Father and I am one with you, and I am one with all of humanity."

The setting sun was at his back when he spoke thus to Mag-dalene. It created an aura around him. I saw the rays of sunlight pouring through him, as if piercing his heart and radiating out-ward. Magdalene was standing in the sunlight raying through him, touched by the beams of his love.

In that moment she experienced him becoming like the sun. Her elevated state enabled her to experience this. It lasted for only the briefest of moments. I basked also in the rays of the sunlit love streaming through his heart, giving life to all. I experienced the *life* in his love. I knew that this moment was given to Magdalene as a preparation for her later experience of divine union. After this event, her heart felt different. She felt as though the sunlight had pierced it with warmth, expanding its capacity for love.

As the sun embraced the horizon, Jesus and Magdalene contin-ued on their way toward the house where the Blessed Mother was staying.

XXIII

Anointing the Bride

I FOUND MYSELF in a rounded room on the upper level of Magdalene's castle, where aromatic oils were being prepared. Magdalene was bent over her work, sorting through herbs. Sarah the Egyptian was at her side. Before her conversion, Magdalene's oils had been used mainly toward vain ends, but since her conversion she had turned to the Egyptian practice of employing oils in healing and anointing. She was just now consulting some Egyptian writings to which previously she had not often turned. These ancient writings explained the use of oils in such rituals as burial and marriage.

I am not certain how much time had elapsed since Magdalene's conversion, but the atmosphere in her castle was completely changed. It was quiet, without the usual noisy guests. The castle itself seemed to have let go its vanities. It hardly seemed the same place I had visited during so many prior visions.

As my gaze settled upon Magdalene, I could see that her soul shared fully this new, humble attitude, that it also had let go its vanity and desire for possessions. No longer full of herself, she could now receive from the spiritual world. I sensed a growing light within her—the light of awakening. From time to time she felt bursts of joy and waves of peaceful contentment such as she had never before known. So happy was she to be serving the Master!

Magdalene raised her beautiful face and told Sarah that she wanted to distribute the oils among the holy women so they also could apply them in healing. Many of these oils were very costly. She was offering them a generous gift.

I went forward in time. Magdalene, Sarah, and several other holy women were attending the prenuptial events of the wedding of a beautiful young girl. She was the relative of one of the twelve disciples. With Sarah's assistance, Magdalene anointed the bride for her wedding with special oils that she had blended for that purpose. She was inspired in her work by what she had experienced with the bridal pair of Cana.

Under Jesus's inspiration, she anointed the bride, preparing her to become one with her husband. She did not do this in so many words, but with the intention of enabling the young girl to transform herself through the sacrament of marriage.

Magdalene was inspired by the Egyptian rituals of anointing for marriage, as well as by those of the Judaic tradition for purifying the bride. She employed these together, along with what she had received from Jesus. As she performed this sacred act, she hoped, with some anxiety, that it would not be deemed inappropriate. Although it seemed there was acceptance, openness, and appreciation from those involved, still she felt anxious to be the one anointing. Even so, she was able to merge this ritual with the Judaic tradition in such a way that it caused no offense; and no one realized that it had roots also in ancient Egyptian practice.

In a quiet moment after the ritual cleansing bath, I saw the bride, whose name was "Cheyla," dressed in a plain white tunic that hung loosely from the shoulders. Her head was uncovered for the anointing. Magdalene anointed and consecrated Cheyla's body with fragrant oils. I was not told which oils she employed, but I did see the source of at least one of them—a tree with pinnately compound leaves, possibly a laurel tree. It was a very sacred oil, which induced a state of worshipfulness.

Magdalene imparted blessings of purification and preparation, most of which were not spoken aloud. She used few words. Each blessing was associated with a particular mystery.

Magdalene hoped that through her act of anointing, Cheyla would be inspired to approach her marriage as an archetype of divine union. The bride was being consecrated to become a *gateway* between the spiritual world and the physical world. Her body was being prepared for a number of souls to pass through this gateway, to be born into the physical world.

In the Egyptian ritual, Isis was invoked as the guiding star for the bride. Magdalene did not invoke Isis outwardly, but silently she invoked the Divine Feminine. In Egyptian custom, the bride was blessed to become a vessel for Isis; and sometimes, depend-

Bridal Pair in Cana

ing upon her bloodline, she was even blessed to *become* Isis. Magdalene employed these ideas in a symbolic way in her anointing, weaving the Mysteries of Egypt together with the teachings of Jesus Christ.

In the Egyptian ritual, the marriage anointing—through purifying the physical union on Earth—was believed to assist toward attaining divine union. This was very important, as it was believed that only through divine union could one become immortal.

In performing the ritual of bridal anointing, Magdalene was especially inspired by her experience of the couple miraculously transformed at the wedding in Cana. She was learning that there was a higher level to marriage, that there was a transformative capacity in marriage, that indeed marriage could be used to attain a higher goal. At that time she did not yet understand how this was possible, but she did know that Jesus could work miracles and bring about transformation, and that he had a special interest in the sacrament of marriage.

The marriage of the bridal pair in Cana had been so different from any she had known before. Their marriage radiated the light of divine union. Magdalene could feel that angels were watching over this marriage, sanctioning and inspiring it. She wanted to be a part of that work. It was something living within her, for she ached also for divine union. She would come to deepen this practice of anointing later, when she was given more opportunities to anoint women in preparation for marriage. As she worked with such brides, she would receive healing for herself also, and for her past—for hitherto she had not been able to experience divine union through her relationships, but now she was preparing for her future work.

Magdalene would not have performed this ritual for just any bride. It was possible on this occasion only because the betrothed and her family were more open and accepting than most. Magdalene had come to know the bride and her family during her time of conversion, and had felt a special connection with the young girl.

After this experience of anointing the bride, Magdalene felt her calling even more deeply. She began to fervently study Egyptian writings on the uses of oils, especially in sacred ritual. From that time forward she carried ritual oils with her always, looking for opportunities to serve others.

XXIV

The Healing of the Youth of Tiberias

MAGDALENE WAS SEATED near an open window. She wore a cream-colored linen tunic with a slit opening at the neck, bordered by deep blue silk bands of about a finger's breadth. Next to the borders—adorning the edges of the sleeves and also the square yoke of the bodice—was finely detailed embroidery in red, blue, gold, and green. Around her waist was a blue silk sash. It was not an ostentatious dress, but quite lovely. I examined the embroidery closely because it was so unique and intricate.

Deep in thought, Magdalene kept twisting her hair around her finger. Finally, she tied it up and tossed it behind her back.

From her window she could see lush, green fields leading down to the shore, and fishing boats off in the hazy distance. Magdala was home to several thousand inhabitants and almost entirely supported by the fishing industry. It was known far and wide for the special kind of preserved fish it produced—small, salt-cured fish like those the Master blessed and multiplied at the miracle of the feeding of the five thousand.

In the nearby town of Tiberias there was a critically ill youth who was not expected to live. Magdalene was acquainted with his family. She called Sarah to her and told her of her concern for the youth, saying she would like to visit the family and see what might be done to assist them. She asked Sarah to gather some oils, whereupon the two set out.

Tiberias was crescent-shaped, all its buildings facing the Sea of Galilee. It was a beautiful town, with palm trees and lush foliage. The homes and other buildings were ranged in rows upon a hill, situated rather like an amphitheater. Upon the rooftops were gardens of cascading greenery and vines. It was interesting that none of the buildings faced each other, as though all wanted to look upon the sea.

Having arrived, Sarah and Magdalene climbed some steep, shallow stone steps leading up the side of a hill next to a cluster of houses. There were at least four tiers of houses here, maybe more. The women reached the third tier and turned onto a path. The steps continued above them to more houses. The path led to a gate, beyond which stood a lovely home surrounded by a courtyard. A second gate led to the front door. As Magdalene and Sarah approached this second gate, a gaunt, elderly woman—perhaps the grandmother or great-grandmother of the ill youth—greeted them.

Tiberias

The youth lay in a small room upon a bed set low to the ground. Family members kneeled around him. He appeared to be unconscious, his breath labored and rattling in his chest, which rose and fell as though a great weight were resting upon it.

Magdalene gazed at him. She felt the grief of his impending death and pleaded inwardly, *What can we do?* She knew he stood at death's door.

Timid and unsure of herself, she wished that Jesus could come to heal the boy. She knew, of course, the story of how Jesus had raised a young girl from death. Indeed, there were many other stories she remembered of his saving people on the brink of death, especially that of the healing of the nobleman's son. Surely then, this young lad was also precious in God's sight! Surely he too deserved to be healed!

Some of these accounts of healings she had heard from the twelve disciples; other healings she had herself witnessed. She knew of this power and had faith in Jesus. She breathed deeply and closed her eyes, calming her mind for a moment. All she knew to do was to anoint him with her oils, and pray.

The boy was wrapped in cloth strips, and because he had been shuddering so violently, his arms had been bound tightly against the sides of his body. His legs were also bound together.

As Magdalene opened her oils, the boy's mother loosened the bands so that they could be applied to his chest, arms, and legs. Magdalene took out some oil of myrrh, which sent the mother into a mournful wail, for myrrh was traditionally used in preparing the body for entombment.

The scent of myrrh carried throughout the house, and the entire household wept as death's fragrance seemed to announce the coming tragedy. The mourning had begun—a sort of sing-song wailing—even though the boy had not yet crossed the threshold of death.

With tears in her own eyes, Magdalene said to the mother, "I have brought these oils, not for burial, but for healing. I have great faith in the Master Healer, Jesus."

"But he is not here! I have heard of his miracles also, but he is not here!" The mother cried in desperation.

Magdalene finished her anointing and set down her oils. She went to the mother, and put her arms around her. "I know this boy can be healed through faith; I have faith in Jesus and faith in God. I have seen Jesus perform miracles. It matters not that he is not present with us; his power to heal knows no bounds." She picked up one of the oils. "These oils can restore health—this I know. And our faith can also wax powerful enough to heal even one so sick."

The boy began to stir. His mother thought she detected some improvement in his breathing, which ignited hope in her. Magdalene's words kindled hope in her heart also. She began to think perhaps it was possible that her son *could* overcome this grave illness.

Magdalene arose and went to the boy. She knelt beside him, placed her hands on his right arm, and gazed down at his pale face, framed by matted hair. She looked around at the others in the room, her lovely eyes settling upon each face in turn. Her heart was filled with a boundless love for all present. She felt a growing compassion in her heart for the youth and his family. She closed her eyes and pictured Jesus as if he were kneeling across from her on the other side of the boy. She could see him so clearly. She felt herself enveloped in his peace and filled with his love. As she looked upon this image within, it was as if she were holding the boy in her arms and presenting him to Jesus, as she had so often seen others do—for wherever Jesus was, people were always pleading with him for healing.

With this image in her mind's eye of herself holding the boy, she simply asked that he be healed. She did not know how this could happen. She did not know whether Jesus could somehow be present with this family in Tiberias. She simply asked, knowing that if it were possible, it would come to pass.

I heard, then, the boy's name—something like Bartomaeus.

The peace and love that had enveloped Magdalene settled over all in the room, so that the mourning ceased. Magdalene opened her eyes and looked at Bartomaeus. His chest was rising and falling more regularly. He opened his eyes and began to draw in deep, measured breaths. The tremors ceased.

His mother, kneeling at his left side, laid her hand upon his chest and wept with joy as Magdalene bowed her head and whispered, "Thank you, O God, thank you." Magdalene felt humbled and sought no recognition or attention for this miracle. She said to the family, "This is the will of God. This is His mercy—that your son should be healed. Let us give praise and thanks to God!"

They lifted their hands toward heaven and said: "Praise be to God, for He has come to us in our affliction. He has lifted us up. He is mighty and His works are the works of righteousness!"

Tears of joy were shed as Magdalene and Sarah embraced the family and then took their leave.

As they walked back toward the castle, Magdalene was quiet. Inwardly she was continuously praising God. She was blessing Jesus's name, knowing that he had heard her plea. At the time,

Jesus was away on a journey with the twelve disciples. She could hardly wait to see him again.

I then saw that at the time of the healing of Bartomaeus, Jesus was speaking to a group of men in a small synagogue and had for a moment grown suddenly quiet. With a soft smile upon his radiant face, he had felt virtue go out from him. This was the healing power called forth at that moment by Magdalene. He resumed his teaching then, with no interruption in his theme. John later questioned him why he had stopped speaking mid-sentence, and Jesus answered: "A young boy was healed today." John smiled and bowed his head. Christ was able to be in many places at one time, even as he worked through the body of Jesus of Nazareth. This was not the only time healing was accomplished in this way.

As the two passed through the town, Magdalene felt a great love for all whom she saw, and wondered to herself if this was how Jesus felt, if he always felt love like this for everyone. She wanted to bless everyone! She said to Sarah, "Do you feel this love?" Sarah smiled and nodded her head. The two of them were surrounded with a great light—the light of Christ. Magdalene wanted to feel that way forever.

Saint Christopher then appeared, to bring me back to present time. I asked him to be with me in all the different kinds of journeys I would be making—both inner and outer ones, and in any other transitions. I told him how I often feel that I resist change, as well as moving forward; and he had compassion for me and said he would be with me.

PART THREE

The Raising of Lazarus

Lazarus

XXV

A Conversation Between Lazarus and Magdalene

I SAW LAZARUS in his library. He was sitting at a writing table, his head bent low over a scroll. Above the table hung a grid of boxes containing more scrolls. He was intent on locating a particular passage—a prophecy of one of the prophets of old, which Lazarus now believed referred to the present mission of Jesus. He desperately wanted to locate this passage. The scrolls had been passed down to him through his mother, who had inherited them from her family.

Magdalene stepped into the library. She wanted to know what had been occupying her brother's attention so intently for the past few hours. Lazarus did not look up, but continued scanning the scroll before him. Kneeling on a round cushion near the table, Magdalene said, "I want to speak with you."

"I am trying to find something important," Lazarus replied. He sighed and rolled the scroll back a bit, then set a weight upon it to hold his place. He turned to her, smiling, as a fleeting image of her former self passed through his mind. Whereas she had once been overdressed, boisterous, and vain, the woman before him now was altogether agreeable, sweet, and content. He marveled at the change within her since the time Jesus had healed her. He asked, "How can I serve you, Magdalene?"

She smiled. "Who is he? Who is he, Lazarus? Who is Jesus?"

Lazarus shook his head. "That very question fills my mind, Magdalene. He has told us that he is the Son of God, and that he has come to do his Father's work: to bring love into the world. But there is a great mystery in him that I want to understand. For this reason I have come here to read the old prophecies of the coming of the Messiah."

"And have you found anything?" she asked.

"There are some things that Isaiah said, which I believe point

165

to Jesus." Lazarus stroked his beard. "But I am looking for a certain passage that speaks of one who will come with the power of God to set things right, or to make the path straight... but there is more to it that I cannot remember..." Lazarus drummed his fingers on the table.

"What has he said to you, Lazarus—about who he is?" Magdalene asked.

"He comes to me in dreams, Magdalene. I do not know how he does this. But it seems that when I fall asleep, he comes to me and shows me things, most of which I do not remember. But we are always speaking to one another, heart to heart, in pictures rather than words. And we are always in a place of golden light, like the sun. This has happened many times. He then returns me to my bed, and goes off somewhere—somewhere far away, beyond the realm of the stars. And I want to go with him, Magdalene! But I have never been able to follow him, even though it is my greatest desire. Afterward I am left with an intense hunger to go to his world, wherever it may be. I seem to be losing my appetite for the things of this world—there is nothing here that I desire."

"What do you think is happening to you, Lazarus? What do you think is happening when you are with him?"

"He is teaching me, but I do not know what he is teaching me—I do not remember. I thought perhaps I could find something in these scrolls about the world from which he comes, for it seems to be a world so far removed from our ordinary life."

"Do you think this is the world spoken of in the Egyptian Mysteries? Do you think the initiates ever traveled to this world?"

Lazarus sighed. "I do not know. I have never sought that world, but I do wish I had learned more of such things while I was in Egypt."

"As you know, dear brother, I did study the Mysteries, and I stood watch as others traveled to the spirit worlds and heard their reports upon their return." Magdalene sighed also. "Oh Lazarus, there is so much we do not know. But we must rest content to be with him as he is now—walking with us, eating with us, healing our sick."

She smiled as she thought of how human he was, of how many times they had laughed together—for he did have a rich sense of humor. "Lazarus, I believe he is the Son of God, as he has said he is. And isn't it wonderful—if he truly is the Son of God—that he would be so pleased to sit with us around the fire and listen to us? And talk with us? He has taught us so many things!"

"Magdalene, do you remember when he told us he would take upon himself the sins of the world?"

Magdalene bowed her head. "Yes, but I still do not know what that means."

"Nor do I. But I feel the time is coming when he will do this. He will not always be with us. I feel that his time is coming—"

"Lazarus, I have seen terrible things in dreams and visions—and Jesus told me that I do have the gift of sight. But the things I have seen frighten me. I have seen him being taken... beaten..." Magdalene could not finish her sentence.

"Yes, yes, Magdalene, I have seen the same. But what can we do? We can do nothing to stop him from fulfilling that which he came to do."

Sadness settled over the two as they pondered this matter. Then Lazarus took Magdalene by the hands, saying "Let us pray that we may be strong and may be with him through whatever comes." Lazarus prayed the "Our Father" prayer that had been given them by Jesus. They prayed on Jesus's behalf—for his mission. When they were finished, Lazarus looked into Magdalene's eyes and said, still holding her hands, "He says he is God's Son, Magdalene. And the Father will take care of His Son. We must be willing to let the Father take care of His Son and trust in Him. And you and I have a special assignment to take care of God's Son."

"Lazarus, I have felt that I need him so much—but perhaps he needs us as much as we need him."

Lazarus nodded his head. "I think you are right, Magdalene— he does need us. And I have a feeling that we do not yet know just what he will need from us as his mission unfolds."

Magdalene marveled that the Son of God could need human beings, and yet she knew it was true. She wanted to give to him whatever she could in order to best serve him.

"Magdalene, for a time I want to live a contemplative life. I want to understand this man more deeply. I want to be with him in a more profound way. But I do not know how. I am going to lay aside my business. Choran can take care of it for me—he knows every detail. I want to go away for a time."

"Where will you go, Lazarus?" Magdalene could feel Lazarus's pain.

"I do not know. I need some time alone. I need to somehow satisfy my hunger for the divine. There are so many distractions. Every day people come to my door asking "Where is Jesus?" I have been doing what good I can. I give alms, and as you know, I sent Jeremiah and Lucas to Bethsaida to build a shelter for the homeless. I have gone to the temple to make offerings. And I have brought many to Jesus. I have indeed been busy on his account doing much good, and yet there is something lacking. I hunger for more. I hunger for God. I hunger for heaven. Nothing in this world can assuage my hunger."

"Oh, I think I understand you, Lazarus—but Jesus *is* my solace! When I am with him, I feel that I *am* in heaven!" Magdalene replied. "I feel as if my entire soul is warmed in the sunlight of his spirit. I could kneel at his feet forever. He *is* my heaven. He is here on earth, bringing heaven *to* us! I do not want to go anywhere that he is not! I want to be with him always." She paused, looking at the serious expression on her brother's noble face. "But I understand your desire, Lazarus, and I will pray that your hunger may be filled. I will pray for you while you are gone. How may I serve you as you begin your quest for solitude?"

"Pray for me, Magdalene—that is all I ask."

And so Lazarus went to make arrangements for the solitude he sought, while Magdalene, with a prayer for him ever in her heart, went to meet Jesus and the holy women and disciples.

XXVI

Lazarus Falls Ill

MAGDALENE was at Lazarus's estate in Bethany. She had just arrived with her servant Sarah and a few others. Surprisingly, the estate was dark and still, although it was the middle of the day. No servant greeted her at the door. Bidding her own servants wait in the front portico, Magdalene set about looking for Lazarus. She called his name, but there was no answer. Finding no servants anywhere in the house, she passed through a back door and crossed the outer gardens until she came to a field adjacent to the servants' quarters. She called out to see if anyone was at home, and presently a man emerged from one of the houses. His hair was disheveled and his eyes bleary from a midday rest, but he greeted Magdalene with a smile.

"Good day. Where is Lazarus?"

"He has given us a few days' rest. He said he wants to be completely alone," the servant answered.

"Is he ill?" Magdalene frowned, wondering what could be wrong with Lazarus.

"That is indeed what he told us—that he is not well."

"What is ailing him? He did not answer me when I called," Magdalene replied.

"We do not know. We left him in his room alone. He sent his family away to one of the other properties so he could be on his own without worrying about them."

"If my brother is not well, his servants should not be taking rest. He should not be alone!" Magdalene felt indignant.

"We are simply honoring his request." The servant was by now feeling uncomfortable.

Magdalene shook her head. "Something is not right." She turned and strode back to the manor. As she made her way to Lazarus's wing, she passed through a hallway where her parents' accoutrements still hung about the walls: swords and shields, tap-estries and artifacts. This had been her parents' estate and the walls held many memories.

She tapped on Lazarus's door, straining to hear any sound within. Hearing nothing, she entered the room. Lazarus lay on his bed, a peaceful look on his ashen face. For an instant she thought he was dead. She could detect scarcely any rise or fall of his chest. Touching him lightly on the shoulder, she said, "Laz-arus, wake up. It is I, Magdalene." He stirred and looked at her. "What ails you, my brother?"

Almost inaudibly he replied, "My body is weak."

She began to ply him with questions. "Are you in pain? Have you eaten? Are you thirsty?"

"No," he whispered.

"What ails you?"

He replied that he did not know. She felt his limbs. They were stone cold. She went to a chest and pulled out a woolen blanket, which she spread over him. She rubbed his hands and feet for a few moments. "I am going down to have the servants make you something warm to eat—some broth."

He shook his head, saying that he did not care to eat.

"You must eat something. I will return shortly and help you eat."

She went out and called for two servants to prepare soup for Lazarus. While they worked, she asked them if his illness had been sudden. They replied that he had seemed distant and very quiet for some time, that he had not been as active as usual, and had been spending more and more time alone. She wondered what this could mean. What sort of illness was this? She wanted to find Jesus and ask him to come and heal Lazarus. But she did not want to leave Lazarus just yet.

Magdalene and the two servants took the broth to his room. But he did not want to eat, and asked that they leave it beside the bed, adding that he would try to take some later. Magdalene probed him again with questions, but he refused to talk. Wonder-ing what more she could possibly do, she and the servants finally left the room.

She knew that the Blessed Mother and several of the holy

women were leaving soon to meet Jesus—perhaps they could give him the message that Lazarus was sick. She went to the women and told them about Lazarus. They left the following morning, promising to deliver the message.

After walking for several days (the distance was perhaps thirty miles), the Blessed Mother, Mary Cleophas,† and Mary Salome‡ came to a town in Samaria where Jesus was teaching. When they told him of Lazarus's illness, Jesus smiled and nodded his head.

---

† *Mary Cleophas* was the daughter of *Mary Heli*, the older sister of Mary of Nazareth. Because of the age difference, Mary Heli's second daughter, Mary Cleophas, was only about four years older than Mary of Nazareth, even though she was her niece. In the course of her life Mary Cleophas had three husbands. The first was called Alphaeus, who had been married before and already had a son, who grew up in their home. This son was Matthew, who later became one of the twelve disciples. She bore one daughter, Susanna, and three sons to Alphaeus: Judas Thaddeus, Simon, and James the Less, all three of whom went on to become part of the circle of the twelve disciples of Jesus. Her second marriage was to Sabas, to whom she bore another son, Joses Barsabbas, who also later became a disciple—however, unlike his four brothers, not one of the twelve. Her third husband was a Greek, Jonas, who brought with him a son, Parmenas, from an earlier marriage. Parmenas also became a disciple of Christ. To Jonas, Mary Cleophas bore a son, Simeon Justus, who was about ten years old at the time of Christ's Resurrection. Simeon Justus, after the death of James the Less, became the second bishop of Jerusalem. At the start of Jesus's ministry, Mary Cleophas settled in the neighborhood of Capernaum close to the house of the Blessed Virgin. Later she lived in Cana. Mary Cleophas, when desperately ill with fever at the home of Peter in Bethsaida, was healed by Christ Jesus. She died five years after Christ's Ascension.

‡ *Mary Salome* was a cousin of Mary of Nazareth, and the wife of the fisherman Zebedee. Zebedee and Mary Salome had two sons, James and John, sometimes referred to as the sons of Zebedee. They became disciples of Jesus—John being the only one of the twelve who was present at the death and burial of Christ and who, together with Peter, was in the garden of the holy sepulcher on Easter Sunday morning. Peter, James, and John were the three disciples who witnessed the Transfiguration of Jesus on Mt. Tabor. They were also present with Jesus in the garden of Gethsemane after the Last Supper. Near the beginning of Jesus's ministry, Mary Salome lived in the house that previously had been the home of the holy family in Nazareth. Later she lived near Capernaum. Mary Salome is named in the Gospel of Matthew as one of the holy women at the foot of the cross. She was one of the four Marys directly beneath the cross: the Virgin Mary, Mary Magdalene, Mary Cleophas, and Mary Salome.

"Lazarus is indeed ill, but it is not an illness of this world. I will go to him when it is time."

Curiously, he sent no return message to Magdalene, nor did he send anyone to assist her. Jesus knew that Lazarus was suffering a sickness of the soul that had arisen as a result of their close association with one another since the time of the Baptism. Lazarus wanted desperately to be like Jesus and to do the things he saw Jesus do. Christ Jesus was the highest ideal of what Lazarus wanted to become.

In his hunger to emulate what he saw in the Master, Lazarus had come to more and more resemble him. He had begun to hunger so intensely for the spiritual world that he was losing his desire to be in the physical world, as he had told Magdalene.

He had started to ponder the Ancient Mysteries, trying to find ways of connecting with the spiritual world. He knew no way to reach the spiritual world other than through death or through the Ancient Mysteries.

While the twelve disciples were in general more centered upon the material aspects of Jesus's ministry—such as teaching, handling crowds, managing busy traveling schedules, and seeing to many other logistical details—Lazarus had started to lose interest in the temporal world. Questions began to arise from the depths of his soul. And the more he awakened, the more questions arose. He continued to assist Jesus financially, but withdrew gradually from the daily affairs of the ministry in order to spend time alone with his questions.

Occasionally Lazarus retired to a cave to fast and pray. Nothing remarkable happened on these occasions, however, other than that he emerged even less interested in the physical world than he had been before. Rejecting the physical world in this way, his body soon fell ill.

Magdalene felt her brother slipping away. She knew that without some intervention he would die. She waited for Jesus to come, but after some days, when he did not come, and there was no word from him, she asked Martha to come and see what she could do. Martha tried to convince her brother to accept her help in nursing him back to health. She too was most distressed at his worsening state. The two sisters sent another message to Jesus, through a servant: *Lazarus's state is worsening! Please come!* But still there was no word in return. Jesus did not come.

From time to time, Magdalene would ask Lazarus, "What can I do to help you get better?"

"Nothing. There is nothing, Magdalene. I will be better only when I am in the next world," was always his reply. She had to face the grievous reality that he wanted to die. Sometimes she would weep and beg Lazarus to choose life. "What of Jesus and his mission? Is not that enough for you to remain? Why do you want to leave us?" But he would answer only that he was sick for God.

Then one day the idea came to Magdalene that if Lazarus could *visit* the spiritual world, this might suffice him. She thought that if he could experience the spiritual world in this way, perhaps he would be so strengthened and renewed that he could engage again in life. So one night she suggested to him that she facilitate for him a "temple sleep," pointing out that this could lead him into the spiritual world and help him better understand his purpose in life. He agreed. But the idea, although hers, made Magdalene anxious also, for she knew well from her studies of initiation in Egypt the inherent dangers of such a proceeding. It might however be their only hope.

Still, Magdalene wondered why Jesus had not come to heal his friend. Had he received the message? She knew that Lazarus's soul sought communion with the divine so keenly that he would die to achieve it—and it seemed time was running out.

As preparation, Magdalene began to review what she had learned in Egypt, especially the ancient resurrection rite, and its "temple sleep." This turned her thoughts also to the baptismal rite of John the Baptist. Had he not baptized in such a way that the person receiving the baptism was brought to spiritual vision, and thereby often to a renewed sense of purpose in life? His baptism was also a kind of "death"—a death of the former sinful self, leading to a new, spiritual life. To facilitate such vision, the one baptized was held under water just long enough to loosen the etheric body. This loosening of the etheric body, which is akin to a near-death experience, set up a condition that did indeed open the soul to vision.

John's method of baptism symbolized death and resurrection,

and in this way corresponded to the ancient resurrection mysteries of Egypt. And now, as Magdalene contemplated these two forms of initiation, she understood that the goal of each was to enable the "natural man" to in a certain sense die as a means of attaining communion with the divine, in order thereafter to be resurrected to a new life. Magdalene knew that Lazarus had received John's baptism, but he had never divulged to her what he had then experienced. She did know that something precious and profound had followed from his baptism, but he kept it guarded within his heart. Magdalene believed it was after his baptism that her brother's demeanor had changed, that he had become so much more solemn and reverent. Tears would come more readily to his eyes, and he seemed more introspective. His baptism had set in motion the journey of his soul, and this journey had brought him now to the point where he hungered for the spiritual world alone.

I saw then that Lazarus had been present also at the baptism of Jesus. He had witnessed the descent of the dove and had heard the voice of God saying, *Today I have begotten thee!* He had seen Jesus illuminated with a great light. Humbly he had knelt by the River Jordan, feeling the presence of God. In that moment he had known that Jesus Christ was the Son of God. Later, as time moved on, this knowledge of Jesus would sometimes recede and become for him unfathomable, while at other times he could yet grasp and comprehend it.

Jesus's baptism was indeed a similitude of his approaching death, burial, and resurrection. And this was true also of the baptism of Lazarus. This correlation between the baptism of Jesus and that of Lazarus is a great mystery. But for this mystery to unfold and be revealed, the proper questions must first be asked.

And so, Magdalene made preparations for the initiation, the "temple sleep," of Lazarus. She wished there might be an easier way, something like the baptism of John. But John was gone, and Jesus was not coming. She herself would have to do what she could to save Lazarus.

Another message was sent to Jesus, asking him to come and to assist with the initiation of Lazarus. But as before, no response was received.

XXVII

*The two visions brought together in this
chapter are different accounts of the same events.*

The Home of Lazarus

I STOOD just outside the main entrance of Lazarus's castle. The
front entry had a large, impressive stone arch. The main building
was square, or nearly so, and built after a style foreign to Judea—
reminiscent of Middle-Eastern architecture I have seen. It had
many fine details (which was unusual for the region), with beautiful stonework on the front and running along the edge of the
roof. Off in the distance, beyond the left side of the house, I could
see through the trees a sliver of a lake and a stone path leading
into a garden lined at its back border with a row of short, plump
palm trees. Beyond the row of palms stood another of taller trees
with fine leaves that looked like those of the eucalyptus. All was
bathed in the golden light of early evening. From the angle of the
sunlight glancing down from the western horizon, I judged that
the house faced west and slightly north.

On the left side of the house, just beyond the garden, a path
sloped downward to a gate. Through the gate, another path led
to the family tomb, a stone edifice built into the side of a rounded
hill with stonework similar to that of Lazarus's home.

Preparations for Initiation

I APPROACHED the front door. I was aware that a certain cosmic configuration would be occurring that evening—something
involving the moon—and that Magdalene thought it an auspicious time to perform the ancient Egyptian initiation ritual she
had learned so many years ago.

Lazarus had been preparing for days. He had begun a dietary

regime several days earlier and had also cleansed his body with herbs and oils, using preparations Magdalene had compounded for him. He had continued to spend a good deal of time in seclusion, meditating. As his demeanor became ever more serious and subdued, it was evident to Magdalene that spiritual forces were working upon him.

All who were to play a part prepared themselves by performing certain prayers and rituals invoking protection. The space in which the initiation was to take place had also to be consecrated. This was done with purifying oils and incense, and special prayers. Magdalene, Martha, and several others were to be "handmaidens" in the upcoming rituals. They performed cleansings and various anointings for one another over the three-day preparatory period.

How Jesus and Lazarus Became Good Friends

LAZARUS was a beautiful man. He possessed fine physical features as well as radiant inner beauty. Most of his life he had struggled inwardly despite the fact that he had more than enough of what the world could offer: riches, the esteem of those he admired, comfort, and generally peaceful surroundings. But he was disenchanted with the material world. He could not feel a love for earthly life. In a vague and uncertain way he sought a wholeness that can only be found in the spiritual world.

Then Jesus had become his closest friend, and things began to change for him. He felt a greater purpose for his life and willingly became an advocate of Jesus's work. He was able to influence men in high positions, persuading them to allow Jesus to instruct the large groups of followers he was beginning to attract. At first, the authorities wanted Jesus stopped, but Lazarus was able to assuage their fears, at least for a time.

Jesus was considered quite out of the ordinary when he arrived in Bethany at the beginning of his ministry. He was so different from the people there. Unaffected by the world, it seemed nothing could entice him. At this early stage, people wanted to give him money, or set him up as a kind of ruler, but he could not be led astray by such temptations.

He showed a very deep interest in people, but his interest was not so much in their material, or outer natures, as in their spiritual well-being. This made many uncomfortable.

He was always under scrutiny because of his unusual behavior, especially the way he crossed cultural boundaries, not caring in the least about "rules" of association between different races, or with those considered "unclean."

Many tried to convince Lazarus to discontinue his association with Jesus, wondering what this wealthy and prominent man saw in him; but Lazarus could not be persuaded. He felt that he was known by Jesus more than by any other; and his heart had always yearned to be known in a deep way.

And so Lazarus did all he could to draw audiences to Jesus. It began with small groups, including the Blessed Mother, Martha together with her elderly servant, Mary Mark (the mother of the apostle Mark), Joanna Chusa, several of Mary Salome's sons, and a few others.

They met at first in private, but then the circle grew. Magdalene was not included in these early meetings, for her soul mood at that time was still dark. Martha had tried to persuade Magdalene to come listen to Jesus, but she had emphatically declined. As Jesus's teachings began to spread, Lazarus became very busy, working with men of authority to keep peace in the land, while ensuring that Jesus received the support he needed to be able to reach still more people.

Magdalene Struggles with Doubt

ON THE MORNING of the first day of the initiation proceedings for Lazarus—which would commence at sunset—Magdalene was sitting alone on a bench in Lazarus's garden, listening to the birds. Along with the other participants, she had just finished enacting the "rising of the sun" ritual. There would be three days of such preparatory rituals, followed by the death initiation.

For her role in the proceedings she wore a special dress, which I understood had a significance beyond what I could grasp at the moment. The dress was pure white, and must have been expensive, as it took much in those days to bleach wool to such perfect whiteness. Its style was unusual for the time: the sleeves were drawn tight around the wrists with little cords, and the remainder of the dress hung full and free from pleats gathered across the shoulders. There was a white mantle over the top.

As she sat deep in thought, Magdalene fingered the cords at the ends of her sleeves. The household of Lazarus was immersed in silence and would remain so all day. She began to pray quietly as the birds capered in the trees around her.

Magdalene felt uneasy. She worried about Lazarus's frame of mind. His longing for communion with the spiritual realms seemed too strong, out of balance. As she reflected on this, she became uneasy also that Jesus had sent no answer when they invited him to take part in the initiation. She had received no word from him at all! Magdalene questioned whether he valued what they were doing, whether he though it important.

She had at first felt sure about performing the initiation, but was now flooded with doubt. She had come out into the garden to try to vanquish her fears because she did not want to take this negative feeling into such an important event.

Some of what she was feeling was her own former self-doubt, her worry that perhaps Lazarus did not thoroughly trust her on account of her questionable past. But then the thought came to her that Jesus must be trusting her to do this, for otherwise would he not have come to conduct the initiation himself? She felt overburdened, however, by the responsibility of ensuring that all went well.

For her part, Martha seemed confident about what they were undertaking. Magdalene wanted to speak to her about what she was feeling—but was unsure whether it would do any good.

Struggling with apprehension, Magdalene made the mistake of asking God for a sign that she should continue. It was a mistake because she asked out of doubt rather than out of faith. Receiving no sign, at least for the present, she decided to return to her room to review the prayers and the protocol for the evening's ritual.

Back in her room, Magdalene took down long narrow pieces of papyrus roughly six inches wide and twelve inches long. Prayers were written on them. While saying these prayers, peace settled over her, and reverence for the initiation returned to her.

Her anxiety melted away as she restored in this way her connection to the sacred, magical power of the initiation. For the time being, at least, she knew she could go forward with her plans.

The First Day of Initiation

THE INITIATION had begun at sunset on the evening before, when the ritual of the "setting of the sun," or "burial of the sun," was performed. Those present had been guided to identify, or become one, with the sun as it set, or was "buried," on the horizon. This had both an outer and an inner sense.

As the outer sun set, or was "buried," they stood together in a circle, envisaging the sun also setting in their midst in the initiation chamber—but they envisaged this in a special way, as a *descent* through the chakras of Lazarus.

Lazarus stood in the center of the circle, representing the sun, essentially *becoming* the sun for the purposes of the ritual.

Speaking special words of invocation, the women attendants called prayerfully upon the forces of the sun to "set" through Lazarus's chakras, and for the sun to "bury" itself for the night in his root chakra. They kept vigil through the night as Lazarus slept thus "buried."

Just before dawn the next morning they had performed the ritual of the "rising of the sun," envisioning now the sun rising through Lazarus's chakras into the crown chakra at the top of his head. As the sun rose into the crown chakra, they in some way directed the sunlight of that rising energy as a gift out into the world.

I understood that during the course of each of the three days of the initiation Lazarus was to undergo a specific stage of death.

The first day was devoted to the death of the *ego*, the death of the "natural man."†

When the attendants met with Lazarus the morning of the first

---

† 1 Corinthians 2:14 speaks of the "natural man" which "receives not the things of the Spirit of God."

day, a script was employed. This script was meant to assist Lazarus in entering into his natural man, in becoming aware of his own ego. It consisted of a dialogue between Lazarus and Magdalene. Magdalene spoke and Lazarus responded. In this way the script led Lazarus into a special understanding of his own ego forces.

I cannot disclose the words of this script, but can say more generally that it depicted mythically a journey into the initiate's own ego, and that at the end of this journey the initiate experienced the ego's "death." This "death" experience might vary greatly, according to one's level of soul development; that is, its depth and impact depended greatly on the nature of the particular initiate's own soul forces.

For the purposes of this first day—or degree—of initiation, the *head* was taken to represent the physical location of the ego, and this is why it was the forces of the head that were primarily addressed. At the end of the dramatic action, for example, spikenard oil was applied to the crown of the head to facilitate the release of any negative aspects of the ego that may have been stirred up during the process.

Spikenard has a deep, soul-cleansing quality that can aid the initiate in becoming aware of the natural man, and thereby feeling his or her self as distinct from it, as though observing it from outside.

There was no question of any disregard or contempt for the natural man; rather, the natural man was looked upon with compassion. For after such an experience, if successful, the initiate will have generated greater love for the ego, as well as the ability to face the ego with clarity and mercy. It was thus not a matter of casting off the natural man like an unwanted garment, but of coming to understand it so thoroughly as to *transform* it.

This "releasing of the ego" was undertaken in order to facilitate the overall initiation itself; that is, the ego had to be temporarily sacrificed, or laid aside, in order that the spirit be accorded the required "space" to accomplish its initiatic work.

It was not possible, of course, to release the ego completely, for although human beings may overcome certain immoral behaviors and negative traits, we remain susceptible to temptation by evil beings through the impure nature of the *astral body*—which is the seat of our passions and desires. Only very few have been able to fully release the ego and purify the astral body. One example is that of the Buddha.

With this background, we may now more fully describe the "setting of the sun" ritual on the first night of the initiation.

As Lazarus stood in the center of the circle, he was, by virtue of the script previously described, and the prayers offered for him earlier in the day, fully conscious of his natural man. Another individual stood by Lazarus in the circle, representing his natural man, and wearing a dark gray robe. For his part, Lazarus wore a white robe, symbolizing union with his higher self. The natural man faced Lazarus. Certain words and prayers were again spoken. The heads of both Lazarus and the one standing in for his natural man were anointed with spikenard oil. Each spoke certain words to the other regarding the relinquishing of former ways. This was a deeply healing experience for Lazarus—or for any initiate—to undergo.

During the "setting of the sun" ritual the natural man, wearing the gray robe, was symbolically "buried." As the natural man was laid to rest on a stone bench nearby, the ritual worked upon the chakras in such a way as to loosen the *etheric body.* Everyone in the circle directed their thoughts toward furthering this "setting of the sun" through Lazarus's chakras. And as this descent proceeded down through the chakras, arriving finally at the lowest, or root, chakra, the etheric body arose.

What is being spoken of here represents only the barest outline of this initiation, for I was shown only a small portion thereof.

The Second Day of Initiation

ON THE following morning, just before the dawn, the person acting the part of the natural man, who had the night before worn a dark gray robe, was instead attired in a white robe. This white robe symbolized the purification attained through burial of the passions and desires. Another figure played now the part of an *angel* who took the natural man by the hand, raising him up. The angel then joined the surrounding circle of support for the ritual of the "rising of the sun" through Lazarus's chakras.

I should mention here something of importance that I was given to understand. During the "rising of the sun" ritual on the first two mornings, no exit of the sun through the crown chakra was facilitated; rather, having once risen to the level of the sun crown chakra, the sun remained there, illuminating all the chakras, from the root up to the crown. We could say that the sun was retained in each chakra. In other words, the initiators did *not* allow the sun, as it reached and permeated each chakra in turn during its ascent, to then simply continue on, leaving each in succession behind. Rather, matters were arranged in such a way that the sun remained in some sense present in each chakra even as it continued on in its ascent to the crown.

Just as the sun did not continue its ascent beyond the crown chakra during the "rising of the sun" ritual, but remained present as it were in all the chakras simultaneously, something similar occurred with its "setting." When in its descent through the chakras during the "setting of the sun" ritual the sun reached the lowest, or moon, chakra, it did not descend further and pass out from there, but remained present also in all the chakras, "buried" for the night, as it were, in the root chakra.[†]

When a person dies—that is, truly dies, and not in the sense of initiatic "death"—the sun *does* leave the lower chakras behind on its passage through them, as it progresses up and out through the crown.

We are now prepared to understand something of the purpose of the second stage of the preparatory initiation.

To give up the natural man meant to become an empty vessel. Thus, the second day of the initiate's preparation centered on *emptiness*. This day was spent by all in fasting and silence and solitude.

[†] The practices revealed here should not be attempted. They could be dangerous if done incorrectly. Because of this, the entire mystery regarding what was done will not be given at this time.

As the day again closed with the "burial of the sun" ritual, all present held in view more especially now how the sun descended into an empty vessel, into the silence.

But during this second ritual of the "burial of the sun," the sun was drawn further down. It did not come to rest this time at the root chakra, but continued downward to the feet. Indeed, Magdalene poured oils on the feet of Lazarus and spoke sacred words to facilitate this descent into them of the sun.

This descent of the sun past the root chakra and on down to the feet symbolized bringing the person's *star*, or higher self, not only into the body, but all the way down to the feet. And more than this, it was a request, an appeal, that this actually and truly be accomplished—although again, this would be difficult to achieve in its fullness. For the evolution of humankind has not yet reached the stage where the spirit, or higher self, can so readily manifest itself in the physical body.

This initiation, then, was in truth an enactment of the hope that this embodiment of the individual's star might come to pass in the future. It was meant to create the spiritual space where, in future lifetimes, this could become a reality.

Magdalene Beholds the Star of Lazarus

AS MAGDALENE was performing her role for her brother, anointing his feet with the oils, she saw with her spiritual eyes, just above his head, the "star of Lazarus." She recognized this star. It seemed familiar to her. As she was facilitating the descent of his star, this "setting of the sun," she began to weep. For she so loved Lazarus, and was so ineffably joyous to behold the star that he was. Lazarus was radiant during this time. Everyone in the circle could behold the luminosity of his countenance, and I could see that his light was illuminating them all.

The words spoken during this stage of the preparatory initiation centered on taking one's star into the *Earth's center* to illumine it. The participants positioned around Lazarus in a circle stood for the Earth, and they held the star of Lazarus inwardly while speaking certain words to him. The script used in this scene called on Lazarus to speak and on the "Earth" to respond.

On the next morning—the third morning—the "ascent of the star" from the center of the Earth up through the heavenly realms, was enacted.

The surrounding circle stood now for the heavenly realms. They became "stars" welcoming the star of Lazarus into their midst. Again, a certain script was used. In this script, the "heavenly stars" would speak to Lazarus, and his star would respond. After the "rising of the sun" (the ascension of the star of Lazarus in this case), and following upon the enactment of the conversation between the star of Lazarus and the heavenly stars, there came a time of silence.

During this time of silence, and still surrounded by the "stars," Lazarus was open to receiving a message from the *angelic realm*. This was a carefully planned part of the initiation, set up to facilitate the reception by Lazarus of an angelic blessing in preparation for the approaching culmination of the death initiation. I did not enter into the message he received at this time; perhaps it will be given later.

For three nights and three mornings the "setting" and "rising" rituals had been carefully enacted. Each night, as the sun completed its "setting" within him, Lazarus's etheric body would loosen further. This gradual and gentle three-day process had been necessary in order not to shock his body when the time came for the full death initiation. This final initiation could be accomplished only after much purification, and could only be facilitated by those fully conversant with the use of sacred oils and the very specific words to be spoken to the initiate. These were among the things that took place before the final ritual could be performed. And of course, there is a great deal more that might be given at some later time regarding these important events.

XXVIII

Lazarus in the Angelic Realm

AFTER THE THIRD NIGHT the time had come to perform the final ritual. This was intended to loosen the etheric body of Lazarus, thereby initiating him into the spiritual realm—that is, if all went well. Many questions burned within Lazarus, as has been said before, and he hoped this initiation would provide at least some of the answers he sought.

Lazarus was taken into a small stone room and given a special garment to wear; it was a sort of seamless shroud, and pure white. Both its whiteness and its being without seam were significant, for these two aspects of the garment symbolized, on the one hand, purity of soul, and on the other, remaining always "unbroken"—that is, in a state of wholeness. For it was believed that only in such a state—liberated from the fallen nature of the soul as well as from the physical body—could the spirit stand before God. Only in the spirit, free of its fallen members, could one truly "know" God.

As Magdalene stood before Lazarus, dressed now in his seamless white garment, she felt trepidation. He seemed somehow detached, and this unsettled her. The two were alone together, sitting by a window, just after he had dressed for the initiation ceremony. Magdalene asked, "Lazarus, are you sure you want to go through with the initiation?" Sensing her concern, he said assuringly: "Yes, I am ready. Be at peace." But his words did not go far toward calming her doubts.

Magdalene again lamented that her request that Jesus be present had been met with silence. She had wanted him to perform the ritual, but he had not come. Instead, he remained with the disciples, teaching.

The evening began again with the "setting of the sun" ritual, as had been the case on the previous evenings, except that on this occasion an angelic being was invoked to bear Lazarus's etheric body gently across the threshold—while another such being was summoned to watch over his physical-material body and ensure that no adversarial power might harm it during the absence of the etheric body.

The women again offered prayers throughout the "setting of the sun" ritual. Because Lazarus had been through the three days of preparatory exercises, he knew well how it felt when the etheric body began to loosen. On this particular evening, however, the experience was far more intense.

I was shifted then to the perspective of Lazarus. As the sun began to "set" through his chakras, his etheric body rose up, and an angel came forth to guide him. The angel was of unearthly beauty. Lazarus had never before seen such a being. It hovered over him, its light coalescing in ever-changing forms, like a flickering flame.

The angel took Lazarus by the hand, and rose further. Lazarus beheld stars and spiraling galaxies all around him in space. The atmosphere felt very strange. Lazarus dilated into it, feeling hardly any separation between himself and this stellar world.

The angel said, *Come.* A point of light appeared, and began to grow in radiance. Lazarus was drawn toward this light and taken into its brilliant rays. He seemed to be traveling very fast, the angel by his side.

Time passed, but I do not know how much time, according to "earthly" reckoning. He came at last to an angelic realm where numberless angels were gathered in a circle around him. It was as though he was inside a flaming crown of angels. The angels were singing the sound "Ah," and from their singing, their resounding harmonies, a dome of light was fashioned over Lazarus.

I then saw descending through the dome of light a being whom I recognized as Elijah. Lazarus did not recognize this being immediately. As Elijah descended, his robes swirled around him and his arms were extended outward in a gesture of blessing.

Then I saw the face of John the Baptist emanating from the being of Elijah. Lazarus saw this also, and knew that this being, Elijah, was in truth the spirit of the Baptist, whom he had so loved.

I also was in an elevated state of love, feeling blessed to be in the presence of this being. He was absolutely beautiful. His "heavenly reward" was all around him. This is difficult to describe, for it cannot be pictured in a material way.

As he beheld the being of the Baptist, Lazarus's heart erupted in grief over the brutal way John had been killed. He felt more grief now than he had been able to acknowledge at the time of John's death. For here, in the spiritual realm, his grief was direct and powerful. He understood that a part of himself had died when John was murdered. And as John approached him now in the angelic realm, the part of Lazarus that had died with John returned to him, and he felt healing spread throughout his soul.

The Descent of Lazarus

JOHN THE BAPTIST was one who held the Mysteries of the death initiation. And because of his love for Lazarus, he had been drawn to him as the death initiation commenced. Lazarus's angel turned him over to John the Baptist, who was to guide him now in his descent.

As the descent commenced I saw below us a "lake of light," which I knew to be a "portal" to another realm. This also is difficult to describe.

It was as though we were standing in a light-filled lake; and as we prepared to descend through this lake, light gathered around us at its surface wherever we touched it. Then, as we began our descent, light burst out all around us.

We passed through many spheres of this light, which I understood represented angelic realms, descending further and further until we came at last to the sphere of humanity, of which there were many levels. We descended through each of these levels.

Having reaching the lowest level of the human sphere, we continued down then through the kingdoms of Nature, of which there were also many.

I could hear Nature singing the "One Song of Nature." I do not know how I knew it was the one song of nature, but it was a song of Earth, and very different from anything I have ever heard in the music of the spheres.

We passed through the many levels of Nature, continuing lower and lower until we reached its lowest kingdom. I began to feel a heaviness, intermingled with fear. It became clear to me that I was feeling fallen Nature's pain and sadness.

The Golden Sphere of the Mother

HERE WE PAUSED. We were at the threshold of hell. John the Baptist held his hands over Lazarus's head, whereupon a radiant garment of light spilled from them. It was like water pouring out. The light completely enveloped Lazarus, and the garment of his being grew ever more luminous. Then John told him that he was going to escort him on a further descent, a descent into the Earth, and that he was to experience a "burial" in the Heart of the Mother. The garment of light he was being provided was to protect him as they passed further through the sub-earthly spheres—the realms of darkness.

And so the descent began. As we proceeded through the sub-earthly spheres, Lazarus heard the cries of souls that had become trapped in the bowels of hell. They cried out to him for release. John, however, was not moved by these cries. When Lazarus looked to John for solace, John said, "One who is mightier than both of us shall come to save these souls. Turn your ears away; heed not their cries, lest you lose yourself in the darkness!"

A golden sphere came into view. Peace and warmth emanated from this sphere. We were enveloped in its golden light, light of a different quality than that of the sunlight at the surface of the Earth. This light seemed to have more substance to it. I felt pulled more and more deeply into this light, as if the light wished to receive us into its midst.

Whereas the light of the sun is expansive, offering itself magnanimously to all, touching us wherever we may be, the light at the center of the Earth has a quality of "drawing in," of enfolding. I felt the golden light all through my being as we journeyed into it, drawn toward its center. Lazarus and John appeared completely golden, as though turned to gold.

Then I heard a whispering voice saying, *O My son Lazarus! O My Son!*

Beings in service to the Mother encircled us. They made a sound like delicate chimes and the soft unfolding of wings. They were winged creatures, each with many wings. Upon their faces was the smile of eternity. We were as though enveloped in the sweet smile of the Mother, who smiles into your soul!

I was reminded of how I felt each time I held my newborn babies, of how I could neither turn my gaze from them nor stop smiling. Through these beings the Divine Mother was beaming upon us with unconditional love. They emanated a feeling of reverence for us: they were honored to have us visit their realm.

For three days of earthly time Lazarus remained in the realm of the Mother, and was taught many mysteries that cannot now be given, although some will certainly be revealed in time.

Lost in Hell

WHEN THE THREE DAYS had elapsed, the time was come for Lazarus to ascend, to return to his body. He began his ascent filled with the love of the Mother, which he had absorbed into himself. But as he passed upward through the dark spheres of the sub-earthly world, he forgot to honor John's admonition to turn away his ears from the cries of the fallen souls.

Having felt always a deep concern for humanity, he wanted only to save these lost souls. Poised for a time on the precipice of indecision, wondering how he might aid at least some few of these souls, he was swept away suddenly in a tornado of darkness.

At first, just one soul reached out for him. But as he gave heed to this one soul's cry, others joined in, until Lazarus was overwhelmed and overtaken by their entreaties.

Their cries were strange, as if sounding through mire. It was as if the depths of the Earth swallowed their cries. And yet, Lazarus could not turn his ears away. The souls could perceive his light, and they wanted that light for themselves.

As Lazarus was swept away, I saw John reach out for him. But he reached in vain, for the dark forces had waxed too powerful— Lazarus was enshrouded in the darkness, and John could not retrieve him.

And so was Lazarus lost in hell. He witnessed many horrors, the horrors of all humanity's works of darkness. Holocausts and wars passed before my spiritual eyes, just as they were being projected by the wretched souls at Lazarus. I saw the most degenerate of desires acted out, desires that would moreover remain always unfulfilled.

Lazarus lost touch with the love of the Mother that he had come to know. His memory of Her love was being rapidly snuffed out in the darkness. I saw him grow rigid, lying in a spiritual grave, surrounded by the spiritually dead. His light became as the guttering flame of a candle, about to expire for want of air.

Mourning Begins

MEANWHILE, "up above," Magdalene felt deep despair creep into her heart. She would later come to know that her dear brother was lost in hell, but for now she knew only that it was well past the time when he should have "risen," for the dawn had long since graced the morning sky. Her heart grew heavy, and she felt a downward tug. She began to lose touch with herself. She cried out to Martha, saying, "Martha! Save us!" Then she collapsed, fainting alongside the body of Lazarus, which was growing cold.

In a state of alarm, Martha stood up and called a servant to go find Jesus. "Run to Jesus! Lazarus is dying! We are losing him!" Then she too fell next to his body, as though pinned to the earth.

An angel followed after the servant sent to bring Jesus, and it seemed as though the servant was somehow carried with supernatural speed on his way. Bowing before Jesus, the servant bade him come immediately, crying: "Lazarus is nigh unto death!"

Jesus said calmly to the servant: "All is well."

I saw just at that moment how a vision of John the Baptist appeared before Jesus. John, his head cast down, said: "Lord, I have lost Lazarus in hell. He did not do as I bid. I have not the power to retrieve him. Only you have the power to do this."

Jesus replied, "I see that this is true, and all is well, beloved John."

To the surprise of Martha's servant, Jesus turned back to resume teaching the disciples and others gathered there. Several more days passed before Jesus made preparations to journey to Bethany.

In Bethany, Martha came to herself after some time and was

able to arise. Magdalene still lay next to Lazarus. Servants came and carried Magdalene to a bed. One of the servants caring for Magdalene was her personal servant, the beautiful, diminutive Egyptian Sarah, who was also now in charge of preparing oils. Sarah kept watch over Magdalene while Martha and the others discussed the situation and decided they would have to bury Lazarus in the family tomb.

The women began to prepare the embalming oils, although in their grief it was difficult for them to do so. They covered the body with the special oils, to which they then applied crushed herbs. Then they wrapped Lazarus in linen.

Martha sat in a corner, holding the seamless burial shroud Lazarus had worn for the initiation. She held it to her heart in abject grief. She felt so confused. How could this be? The three days had passed; he should have arisen by dawn of the third morning!

Martha charily approached the body of Lazarus. Her faith was ever constant. She thought this must surely, somehow, be the will of God. She pulled the shroud gently over him, kissing his forehead. Then she wrapped his head in linens.

By this time, Magdalene was able to arise. She was disoriented, and had forgotten what had taken place. She sat up in her bed as Martha came to her, saying: "Magdalene, Lazarus is gone from us. It is well into the fourth day now. He is gone." The two sisters held each other and sobbed. Then Magdalene went to his body. Falling upon his heart, she cried out: "Lazarus, what have you done? Do you not love me?"

After this, the body was carried to the tomb and placed on the stone bench in the center of the vault. Three more days passed. All in the household of Lazarus abstained from food, and no one washed or changed clothing, so great was their grief over the death of the friend and brother all had so loved!

Profound sadness settled over the house. Lazarus was so well-loved that his friends and associates came in great numbers to pay their respects. Word of his death spread rapidly. Mourners were led to the door of the sepulcher one by one to look upon his body. There were so many that a long line formed, passing out through the garden gate and down the road. There were hundreds of mourners.

Jesus Wept

Magdalene was in a state of immeasurable grief. And confused. Why had Jesus not responded to their pleas for help? She wondered even whether he truly was who he said he was. For how could Jesus abandon them, after all Lazarus had done for him?

But Martha remained faithful. Martha was so pious. She, unlike Magdalene, never lost faith in God, and comforted all who came to mourn.

"Lazarus, Come Forth!"

JESUS APPEARED suddenly over the hill. The news carried swiftly all the way to the house. When Martha received the news, her heart swelled full and she ran out of the house. When she saw Jesus, it seemed to her that he was surrounded by a halo. She fell to his feet and cried out: "Master, our brother is dead, and Magdalene is overcome with grief. Come, that you might mourn with us. Magdalene needs you."

And so they went to find Magdalene. When she saw Jesus, Magdalene fell upon the ground and wept bitter tears, crying:

"Master, if you had come, my brother would not have died!" Jesus too began to weep. He drew Magdalene to him and held her in his arms. He took her profound grief into his heart and wept with her.

They walked to the tomb, Jesus holding his arms around Magdalene, upholding her. He said "I love Lazarus!" The crowd followed behind them.

The tomb had been shut, for it was thought the corpse would by now be decomposing. Jesus asked that the door be opened. After some protest, the door was opened. With one hand on his heart, Jesus stretched forth the other and cried out "Lazarus, come forth!"

At that moment I saw into the sub-earthly realm where Lazarus lay trapped among its horrors. A star appeared suddenly above him. No other soul in the underworld could see the star, but Lazarus saw it. It slowly penetrated the darkness. And then he heard his name. But not only this. He heard his true name, which cannot be divulged, for it is the name written on the white stone.[†]

This was how Lazarus was called forth. Only by one's true name may one be called up from the depths of hell. I did not hear the true name of Lazarus, because I cannot. Only the person to whom the name belongs may hear it.

Thus did Lazarus rise up from the grave of fallen humanity, drawn on by the light of the star.

Just at the threshold to the underworld, John the Baptist was waiting to receive him. A part of the being of John then merged with Lazarus.

And as Lazarus traveled on, protected within the light of his own star, he received into himself also the imprint of Christ's star. Thus it was that the star of Christ entered into Lazarus. This imprint of the star of Christ was to work in him throughout his later lifetimes, in the course of which his own star would become ever more resplendent.

In this way did Lazarus come back into his body. And news of the miracle of his raising spread rapidly, arousing awe and wonder throughout the land, but provoking also fear and sharp divisions. This truly was the beginning of the end of Jesus's mortal life.

† Revelations 2:17.

The initiation of Lazarus was the enactment, within the compass of an individual soul, of a primal story that applies equally to the archetypal development of humanity as a whole. When Lazarus went through this initiation--which led to his physical death and then his retrieval from hell by Christ—a seed was planted for all of humanity. This is the story of us all: that we descend and lose ourselves, to be called forth in the end by the One who knows our true name, thereby rising above that which beckons us to death.

St. Christopher came for me as the vision closed. He thanked me for bringing forth this vision of Lazarus. I heard Nature singing the "One Song of Nature" again as I crossed the river. And when later I brought the light of this experience to the nature beings, the golden light of the Mother was all around us. I was praising God. Amen.

The Raising of Lazarus

XXIX

MAGDALENE was lying on a bed in her room at the home of Lazarus. The room had walls of stone and was simply decorated. The bed was made up in natural-colored linens. Magdalene was asleep, but not in a normal way. She was far more removed from her body than is usual when one is only asleep.

Magdalene Taken by an Angel

WITH spiritual sight I could see where she had gone. She was adrift in a dark void, separated from her body. It was as if she had succumbed to nothingness and was drowning, disoriented and unable to tell which way was up; as if she was trapped in a spiritually asphyxiating atmosphere in which she could "inhale" no hope into her soul.

Just then she saw a light coming toward her. An angel approached with hand extended, saying, *Come.* As the angel spoke, Magdalene's soul was awakened and quickened, and she was drawn out from the void.

Then I understood. Magdalene had been watching over Lazarus's body during the part of the initiation in which he entered the death-like sleep, and was awaiting the proper moment to bring him back, to awaken him. As this time approached she had checked his pulse and been alarmed to discover it was slowing down. She felt his face; it was cold. His breathing came fitfully only a few times per minute, and finally ceased. His pulse faded away. She knew something had gone very wrong, that her worst fear had been realized. Panic gripped her heart. All her strength drained away, as though spilling from her heart, and she fainted alongside Lazarus's body.

She found herself in a dark void, and then in a strange place like the murky bottom of a swamp. Trying to move there was like setting out to swim through a quagmire. I saw that she was becoming enmeshed.

195

At first it appeared she was trapped among some reed-like forms, but as I drew nearer I saw she was ensnared by *souls* embedded in the spiritual mire. I heard an awful sound reverberating from those souls! It was a slow wailing, as though through muddy ooze—a rising and falling, horrific, inhuman, siren-like noise. It was the sound of total hopelessness and despair.

Then, in this murkiness of ensnared souls, I detected here and there a tiny flicker of light. Magdalene became aware of this light. She focused on it, and then somehow moved toward it.

Several times she lost her way. She would think she was moving toward the light, but suddenly find she was off the mark and had passed it by.

She had to maintain her focus in order to flow toward it. When she did so, the light acted like a magnet, although her movement still required great effort. But when she did not hold a tight focus, she was drawn away from the light. And this was precisely what was happening now, owing to the powerful and distracting pull exerted on her by the trapped souls.

When finally she came close enough, Magdalene understood that the light she sought was Lazarus. But just then she and he passed by each other in opposing directions, as if falling asunder.

Lazarus did not know Magdalene was there, for just as she had cried out to him, he was pulled quickly away in a whirlwind. As he rushed by, Magdalene felt as though her heart was being torn from her chest, and she spun with even greater force into the scudding rim of the whirlwind that held him in its grip. Caught up in this force, she could not draw closer to him. Soon he was again only a distant spark of light. It was as though he were at the center of a spiral galaxy and she a star on its outer fringe. Only the two of them appeared thus as stars: the other forms in the whirlwind gave out almost no light.

It was the draw and pull of the love between them that kept Magdalene in her place. But the light of Lazarus appeared to be fading. As he slipped away from her sight, Magdalene tried frantically to understand where they were and what was taking place, all the time trying desperately to remain tightly focused on the spark of light she now knew to be her beloved brother. The force of attraction between them was growing weaker. Although sinking in the pool of her fear, she could yet feel her love for him. But she could not feel his love for her, for she was impeded in this by the guilt she felt over his death. Thus did she lose her beloved Lazarus.

It was then, having lost sight of Lazarus, that Magdalene entered the darkness where I had found her at the outset of the vision.

She could feel neither divine nor human love; and since in this infernal region love is the impelling force of movement, she was immobilized. She was aware of the wailing of souls trapped somewhere near, but she was not herself enmeshed in the mire of those captive souls. She knew that if she did not yield to them, she would be protected.

It was her love for Lazarus that had brought her to this place; but, having lost touch with his love, she seemed now as lost as he.

I do not know how long she was caught in this void, but it seemed to her an eternity. Finally, the angel appeared, saying, *Come.* Magdalene did not want to leave; she did not want to abandon Lazarus. But the angel assured her all would be well, and so she followed him.

A Vision of the Cosmic Mother

MAGDALENE was traveling rapidly through the stellar world, the angel by her side, passing stars as they went. They slowed and came to misty veils of green light that worked profound healing upon Magdalene's soul. After passing through these veils, they were drawn into a glowing golden sphere that served as a place of rest.

Immediately, Magdalene felt soothing in her soul. A beautiful Mother radiated golden light in the center of this sphere. She wore a luminous robe. Veils framed Her face. And in Her arms lay an infant. In awe and reverence, Magdalene knelt down next to Her and gazed into the infant's blissful face. The Mother asked her, *Do you know who this is?*

Magdalene answered: "This is the Messiah, the One who will save us." The Mother nodded Her head.

Magdalene watched in wonder as images of the life of Jesus unfurled before her. One image especially captivated her: she saw a great light leave the womb of this Cosmic Mother and enter into Jesus as he reached the age of spiritual maturity.

Seeing from the Cosmic Mother's point of view, I understood that She had had to await the right moment, the proper alignment of the stars, before She could send Christ into the body of Jesus at his baptism by John the Baptist. I watched as John held Jesus under the water, creating an etheric opening through which the Christ could enter into this body.

Magdalene understood from this that a great star had entered into Jesus. She knew that all heaven had been present and in glorious harmony when the destined time for the Christ had come, that all heaven had labored in concord to arrange that he enter into this human body.

Magdalene saw how all was facilitated from *above*, how all things pertaining to this event were accomplished according to the will of the Father.

Then she remembered Lazarus. Images of his death initiation returned to her. The initiation *was* good, but Magdalene saw now that it had been effected through forces from *below*, in such a way that those involved used their *own* will forces, their *own* powers, to facilitate it.

She was shown also that whereas it had been appropriate in previous eras to conduct initiations in this way, the time had now come for this old method of initiation to pass away. Mag-dalene was told that Christ *himself* would henceforth become the new initiation. That he, our Redeemer, would stand between the Above and the Below as the Great Initiator. That he would inaugurate a new initiation—a new way for human beings to know the divine—in which it would be necessary no longer to leave the body in a death-like sleep.

As Magdalene knelt by the Cosmic Mother, she was told that the source of her doubts had come from her own deep awareness that the old initiation must end. The Mother told Magdalene to feel no regret for having conducted the initiation, assuring her that it had been done for a higher good, on behalf of Lazarus's soul, and would in the end serve the purposes of God.

Magdalene was shown how the new initiation would arise through the sacrifice of Christ. As she knelt next to the Cosmic

Mother, images streamed to her from a sphere of light, granting her a vision of what would come to pass.

In this way she experienced his whole Passion from above. But all these images were then enshrouded in a veil of forgetfulness, and placed within her heart, so that when the time came she would have the strength to walk with Jesus through the Passion, even though without a full recollection of the heavenly purpose of his sacrifice. For it was necessary that she enter into the Passion with her *humanness*. She was to pass through the initiation of being fully present with Christ Jesus, in all her humanity, throughout his Passion.

The Cosmic Mother and Magdalene mourned over what was to come. They grieved together in that sphere of light as they watched unfold the events that would bring about Christ's suffering and crucifixion. Magdalene came to see and feel profoundly how all temporal events are held in one great eternal round. Finally, the vision of the Passion receded, leaving Magdalene grieving and weeping.

It was then that she remembered: *Lazarus is dead!*

The Mother assured her that Lazarus's star would be called forth and that he would return to life; that this would be like unto the vision wherein she had seen the star of Christ entering into Jesus. It would be accomplished not through the old initiation, though, but through Christ, through the new initiation he was bringing. And then She said to Magdalene, *Awaken and arise! For you shall see the glory of God's power work upon Lazarus!*

The Star of Lazarus

WITH these words of the Mother, Magdalene returned to herself, traveling with the angel back to her body, lying on the bed. When she awoke she had no recollection of what had happened.

Martha came to her, and, leaning over her, said, "Magdalene, Lazarus is dead. Do you remember?" Thereupon Magdalene remembered how she had been with Lazarus when he crossed the threshold. Martha continued, "We have sent for Jesus. He will come and mourn with us. He will comfort us. Surely this is God's will."

Magdalene wept, while a servant girl washed her face and combed her tangled hair. She could not contain her tears. Everyone in the house, the servants also, wept and mourned—for Lazarus was beloved of all. Magdalene then asked Martha to lead her to his body.

With my inner sight I saw an angel standing at Lazarus's head and another at his feet. The one at his head stood in the heavenly realm, watching over his spirit, while the one at his feet stood upon the Earth. I saw an arc of light joining the angels as they watched over Lazarus.

A heavy weight pressed upon Magdalene's chest as she went to her brother's body. Her hands were clutched to her heart; tears streamed down her cheeks. Finding him wrapped in linen, she knew he truly was dead and wept inconsolably by his body, crying out, "Lazarus! What have you done? Do you not love me?"

Then, after sobbing for awhile into her hands, she lifted her head, pleading, "Remember my love for you when you come into your kingdom, that I may be with you also! Remember me, Lazarus. And forgive me, for I did not know this could be. Never again will I perform this initiation. This work is done—we shall have to find a new way." I felt she said these last words more to those present than for the benefit of Lazarus's spirit.

Lazarus was laid in the family tomb. It was a cave-like chamber dug into the side of a hill, with a carved stone entrance. All who loved him came to see his body.

Magdalene retreated to her room. She took out the papyrus rolls of sacred prayers, and, in tears, held them over the flame of her lantern, burning them to ash. She grieved, not only for her brother's death, but also for the loss of what she had felt to be a deeply significant initiation. She questioned the past few years of her life and the spiritual work she had accomplished. How could it end like this? Her thoughts tormented her as she lay on her bed, lamenting the loss of Lazarus.

Time passed, and then she heard Martha calling, "Magdalene, Jesus has come."

Magdalene was disappointed that he had not come sooner, but even more disheartened by her own powerlessness. She felt it was her fault that Lazarus was gone—and she knew that if Jesus

Jesus Goes in the Evening to Bethany

had been present for the initiation, Lazarus would not have died. She was humiliated.

She did not remember at this time the vision from the occasion of her fainting.

She arose from the bed and with heavy heart went out to meet Jesus. Some of the mourners in the house thought she must be going to the tomb to grieve, so they followed her, intending to mourn with her. But she did not go to the tomb. She separated herself from the small crowd following her and walked down into the garden, where she met Jesus as he came up the road. She broke into bitter tears and fell at his feet, crying, "Master, if you had come, my brother would not have died!"

Jesus raised her up. He looked into her eyes and said, "Magdalene, I love Lazarus. Do not doubt my love for him. Neither doubt my love for you. Take me to him."

They went to the tomb, the crowd following. Jesus asked that the tomb be opened. Martha objected, saying that Lazarus's corpse was surely already decomposing. Others added their objections. But Jesus said that he had come to do his Father's work, that he had come to manifest his Father's glory, and again requested that the tomb be opened.

He stood very straight, his eyes focused on the tomb, tears flowing down his cheeks. He did not look at anyone in the crowd. He was very serious, his attention concentrated. As the tomb was opened, he stepped forward as if into a dream and called out in a loud voice, "Lazarus, come forth!"

His words at once opened Magdalene's spiritual eyes. She was drawn into the depths to the soul of Lazarus, remembering dimly now how she had descended to find him. She understood now that because of the overwhelming grief she had experienced when he died, a part of her had remained with him in the depths. It was as if part of her had died with Lazarus.

And now, as Christ cried, "Lazarus, come forth!" that part of her soul was called forth also. She rose from the depths with Lazarus, feeling herself renewed.

In that moment she was given a wondrous gift: a vision, first, of the star of Lazarus *descending* to summon him from the depths, and then of the light of his star *ascending* to enter into his body in the tomb—all upon the command of Christ Jesus.

A memory of her vision while with the Cosmic Mother flashed now before Magdalene's inner eye. She glimpsed again the star of the Christ entering into the body of Jesus at the Baptism in the Jordan.

As this memory penetrated the eyes of her understanding, she looked at Jesus and saw him in a new way. Her soul was elevated, drawn forth to witness the Christ in Jesus. She understood that she was standing next to him, watching *Christ himself* command the star of Lazarus to enter Lazarus's body.

This was a more profound understanding than she had ever before experienced. It was beyond all the miracles she had seen him perform. She experienced a profound healing: the part of her that had been immobilized with Lazarus in the depths of the loveless spiritual mire was recollected, was "remembered," by the great love and light emanating from Christ.

She was able to see the star of Lazarus within him. She saw Lazarus now also in a new way, and she was in awe of the beauty of his spirit.

"I am the Initiation"

AND SO was Lazarus raised up, fully restored to his body. But it was not only his health and faculties that were restored. He had received also the star of his higher self, the part of himself he had so much desired to find through the death initiation. Of course, a great mystery surrounds *all* the changes that occurred in Lazarus spiritually after he was raised.

Lazarus was resting. The crowds had dissipated. Magdalene and Jesus were in the garden alone. Magdalene recounted to Jesus the story of Lazarus's initiation—how she had experienced such doubt and had wanted to break it off.

She told Jesus how her doubt had increased when no word came from him, but that she had nonetheless felt at the time that she could rely on her own resources—although she now realized she had perhaps gone beyond the limits of what was fitting, trusting more in herself than in God.

She admitted that she knew it was wrong to proceed from a

feeling of doubt, that she had gone against her own intuition, knowing no other way to help Lazarus.

Jesus listened to her with compassion and then said, "Magdalene, it is well. The work of God has been made manifest. And you know now for a certainty who I am; you know I am the Initiation, that I am bringing the new initiation to the Earth. What was accomplished in Lazarus is but a foreshadowing of what I shall do, and of what shall be done by my disciples."

As he spoke, another scene from her vision in the Mother's presence reawakened in her, that of the sacrifice Jesus would accomplish for the sake of all humankind.

She had seen such images before, but always she had pushed them away. She picked up the hand of Jesus and kissed it, tears streaming down her face. He wiped away her tears and said, "Magdalene, this must be so. This is why I have come."

He drew her to his heart, caressing her head in silence.

He said, "Magdalene, I will bring to you the new initiation, which in time you will be able to bring to others. Even as you have worked with the old initiation, so now will you work with the new initiation. You will bring the light of what I shall do to others, that they may know me. And you will have your place in this work. Do not fear what lies ahead in the coming times. Stand by me and you will see what I shall do for the children of men. I shall open the way for all humankind to receive their stars, just as you saw done for Lazarus. I desire that you stand by me through all that takes place. You shall be my witness."

Magdalene replied, "Yes, Master, I will be with you even unto the end!"

Saint Christopher came to carry me across the river. As we traveled, the darkness of doubt left me. I understood how doubt inhibits us in so many ways, and felt the importance of walking in faith. I saw how doubt can lead to pride, and how pride in turn prevents us from receiving guidance. Christopher set me before the Tree of Life in the "world that I am," and told me to rest for awhile. He encouraged me to come to this place when I am in need of rest.

XXX

Restored by the Seven Breaths

I WAS TRAVELING through light, descending finally onto a road in the Holy Land. It was lined on either side by what I think were pomegranate trees. Up ahead stood fig and date trees. I recognized the way leading to Lazarus's estate, for so much had already happened there. Many times Magdalene had gone out to meet Jesus on this road, which he walked so often. As I neared Lazarus's home, I felt how the atmosphere was suffused with holiness and sacred silence.

I became aware that I had arrived at the tomb of Lazarus just moments after he had been raised. As he emerged from the sepulcher, rejoicing and praise broke out from the assembled multitude. Some few fled in fear from the scene, but most fell to their knees, weeping and glorifying God. Jesus wept also.

Knowing that the healing of Lazarus was not yet complete, Jesus held up his hand to the crowd and asked that all return to their homes and leave Lazarus in peace.

The crowds did not want to go. They milled about for a while, waiting to see what else might take place.

Jesus, Magdalene, and Martha took Lazarus, along with the disciples, into the house, leaving the throng behind. The sisters were in shock. They wept into their veils, hardly able to take in the sight of Lazarus walking.

The full restoration of his body was not yet accomplished, and so he moved in a dreamlike way, as one not fully in himself. I experienced his physical revivification as affecting first the densest structural parts, the bones. Then it flowed into the denser tissues, whence it radiated into the organs and the skin. The life-force seemed to move from the inside out. His lungs, heart, and circulatory system were restored last. All that had begun to disintegrate was transformed into glowing life. His skin shone with an unearthly radiance. Magdalene could scarcely cease weeping; it seemed that before her very eyes Lazarus was becoming more and more beautiful.

The resurrection of Lazarus was a *process* rather than an instantaneous restoration, for his being had undergone many changes while in the spiritual world. The physical body needed first to be transformed in order to house his returning spirit.

In a mysterious way Lazarus had become a composite being. He bore the imprint of the etheric body of John the Baptist— from when their souls had merged. And the Christ had given Lazarus also his Life, which I saw as the "star of Christ."

There are many mysteries regarding the spiritual composition of the being of Lazarus after his revivification. When Lazarus was raised, it was indeed a challenge to bring all that he then was—the great being he had become—back into his body.

Once they were safely inside the house, Lazarus knelt on the floor before Jesus. With my spiritual sight I could see the "star of Christ," the Life and Light of Christ, illuminating Lazarus.

Jesus cleared away some residual darkness in Lazarus's soul, darkness adhering to him still from his sojourn in hell, when he had gone lost. As Christ drew forth this darkness, Lazarus expelled it in a sort of outbreath, causing him to gasp. Had Christ not done this, a part of Lazarus's soul would have remained weighed down, or "chained," to the subterranean spheres.

Jesus gave Lazarus then the breath of life—the seven breaths of the angelic spheres. Seven times he breathed upon Lazarus.

Upon receiving the seventh breath, Lazarus became like a *human angel.* His being was raised on high to the level of the angels.

After this Jesus prayed, offering praise and glory, and sealed his deeds through his word to the Father. He then advised Lazarus to rest and be still for at least twelve hours. During this time certain vital cycles and rhythms in the physical body would come into balance, so that Lazarus might then recollect the wondrous mysteries that had transpired in his spirit.

The crowd outside was still in a frenzy, but in the house of Lazarus all was enfolded in the sweetest balm of peace.

Jesus and his disciples and the two sisters shared a meal

together. Lazarus was able to sip some broth. After the meal he retired to rest, and the disciples dispersed also.

Jesus, now alone with Magdalene and Martha, gathered them into his arms and held them for a moment. Magdalene thought he seemed spent. She had never before seen him weep as he had done when he went to the tomb of Lazarus. She also was weak, as she had scarcely touched food during the previous few days.

But she felt comforted now in the arms of Jesus. She could scarcely recall any longer what had taken place after she had fainted. There were fleeting glimpses, but Magdalene was too weary to fathom more, and so she simply allowed Jesus's warmth to soothe her. Questions did flood her mind, for she knew not how to confront the troublesome thought that *it was her fault that Lazarus had died,* but she knew she must wait until things were more settled.

When the crowds finally drifted away, Jesus withdrew alone into the garden to rest. He knelt under a tree. He witnessed in vision the experience of death in humanity. He felt all the grief of humanity from the beginning of time—all the pain that death had wrought. Throughout his life Jesus had observed death and its effects. He had been present with several people as they crossed the threshold of death. His dear father had passed away—and many other loved ones also. And now he had just experienced in a very special way death of his friend Lazarus.

The Angel of Death Appears to Christ

IT MUST be understood that Christ came into the body of Jesus at his baptism in the River Jordan. Prior to his incarnation, Christ had never experienced death in the way human beings do. During his ministry, Christ Jesus had brought several people back from the grave. But now it was his *dearest friend* Lazarus who had died—*Christ himself had lost his beloved friend to the realm of death.* So great was his love for Lazarus, that he *himself* suffered pain over his death! Christ *himself* had entered into a vision of death and felt what it meant to die—absorbing all the attendant pain and grief into the depths of his being. And so, foreshadowing what he would later undergo in Gethsemane, Christ wept over death.

As he was thus engaged in the garden, a great and powerful being appeared to him—a being we could call the "Angel of Death." This is the being who perpetuates death on Earth. The Angel of Death tempted him, saying, "You have suffered the pains of humanity brought on by death. Death is the source of the greatest sorrow and suffering known to humankind. You have borne this suffering. But I am mightier than you! Even you shall not overcome me. Yes, you have brought back a few souls from the grave, but you cannot do this for all. I shall have power over you and claim you in the end!"

This being then sent images to Christ of his own coming death, images that pressed upon him like an unbearable weight, causing him great pain. Christ struggled against these visions until finally he could proclaim: "No! I have come to do my Father's will and shall overcome all trials of humanity—even death!"

To this, the being replied: "You shall become human and you shall be powerless in the end, as all humans are. You came here to become human—how is it, then, that you will be able to overcome death? Can any human being triumph over death? You are descending. You are becoming more and more human. How will you prevail?"

Christ responded, "I can do all things through the strength and power of my Father! I have come into this world to turn the hearts of humanity to the Father, that they may know His power and love. I have come to triumph over darkness, disease, sin, suffering, and death—to transform all of this into love and light, to show the way. I shall not turn from the path before me, for this path is ordained of the Father."

The being then left him, for Christ would no longer grant it audience.

Christ saw now in vision the sacrifice he would make for humanity: he would suffer and offer his life in atonement for all sin. He would die and then be resurrected. He had seen this before, but he now saw his future deeds more clearly.

When Magdalene beheld Jesus again, after his experience in the garden, she thought he looked different. His face carried the burden of pain, and her heart ached for him. She knew he had just passed through something momentous. Since she knew also that her time with him was short (he was leaving the next morning for Galilee), she asked him if she could speak with him about what had happened.†

That evening, Jesus gave a teaching to the household of Lazarus. Later, he spoke to his inner circle, saying that the temple of his body would be destroyed, and that he would raise it up.

But they could not understand his words. Many times during the remainder of his ministry he would repeat these words, but they remained ever dark to the understanding of the disciples.

Jesus Sees Visions of His Coming Passion

† This conversation is recounted in Chapter XXIX.

The Meeting of the Sanhedrin

XXXI

As the vision opened, I first saw Padre Pio[†] greeting me with a glowing smile, his face surrounded by flowers. I was so happy to see him again—my "spiritual father."

I WAS in the Holy Land. I could see Jerusalem in the distance, and noticed an ominous black cloud hovering over the city. As I drew nearer, the cloud of darkness made me feel ill. I wanted to leave. However, I knew there was a reason I was here, so I remained.

The Raising of Lazarus Causes an Uproar

I FOUND MYSELF in a hall where members of the Sanhedrin were meeting together. Within the space of a day they had heard the news that Lazarus of Bethany had been *raised from the dead* by the renowned teacher Jesus! Fear gripped their hearts. They were furious. The atmosphere was dark with dread and anger as they fulminated that this miracle was an act of satan. Ever more darkness moved in as they discussed sinister plans. The angels hid their faces and wept. This was the moment when it was decided that Jesus must be disposed of, that his ministry must come to an end, that the only solution was to arrest him and have him put to death!

My attention was drawn to one particular member of the council. He was short and small-boned. He stood off to the side with his head bowed. Secretly he was in a state of wonder about the curious thing that had happened. I heard his name as something like "Joram."

Joram listened to every word of the council, but the whole time kept his head lowered because his own heart was speaking

† Saint Pio of Pietrelcina (1887–1968) first appeared to the author in the fall of 2009, offering guidance and assistance.

more loudly to him than were the council's voices. His heart was stirred up and in turmoil.

For years he had witnessed demons at work among the people, but never had he heard of anyone being raised from the dead by a demon! He thought, "What would be the motive for a demon to raise someone from the dead?" He shook his head. He had heard of this Jesus casting out demons. But if Jesus were indeed under the influence of a demon, why would he cast demons out of others? It made no sense.

Joram could not gainsay that he stood in awe of this latest miracle, but his solitary voice and low position could not prevail against the consensus of the group. The council moved forward with plans to seize Jesus and have him turned over to the Roman authorities for execution. They strategized also regarding Lazarus, intending to locate and silence him in any way they could—by death, if need be.

After this meeting, anyone overheard speaking of the raising of Lazarus was brought in for interrogation. Most of these were individuals who had been present at Lazarus's interment and subsequent raising. They had mourned with the family and were numbered among the throng that witnessed Christ Jesus call Lazarus forth from the tomb. With exultation and wonder they had left Lazarus's estate and gone directly to Jerusalem, or to other nearby towns, to publish the news. No matter what kind of audience they encountered—whether receptive or antagonistic—all told truly what they had seen and heard.

So strong was their faith after having witnessed such a miracle that they testified with zeal of God's power, even in face of the threat of imprisonment. However, they were not detained at this time, for the Jewish authorities did not want to precipitate an even greater maelstrom. Nor did they want word to get out that they were making plans to stop Jesus once and for all. So such witnesses were simply interrogated and then set free—with the warning to speak of the miracle no more, lest a more serious condemnation come upon them. Despite this threat, however, they went abroad undaunted and spoke of the miracle to any who would listen.

Thus began the plot to stop Jesus of Nazareth.

Magdalene Listens to the Heart of Lazarus

I LEFT the meeting of the Sanhedrin and traveled to Lazarus's estate, where I found him resting in his chamber. It was the day after his raising, and Jesus had left early that morning to resume his teaching, avoiding the region of Jerusalem and traveling north toward Galilee, knowing full well that the authorities would soon be after him. Magdalene remained with Lazarus, glowing with gratitude that her brother was restored to her.

She would lay her head against his heart, hardly able to fathom that his heart was again beating. He allowed her to rest her head there for as long as she desired. I also could hear his heart beating! His holy, holy heart! As Magdalene listened to his heartbeat, she could detect that its tone and rhythm were wholly in accord with the tone and rhythm of the heart of Christ Jesus!

I understood that when Christ raised Lazarus, he gave to him his life. This mystery is contained in Christ's saying, "I am the Resurrection and the Life!" These words can be taken in a literal way—for when we are resurrected, Christ really does become the life within us. He becomes our lifeblood, dwelling fully within us. In the resurrection, we take on his body of life, which then becomes our resurrection body. This is a mystery that was not fully understood at the time of the raising of Lazarus. After his return to life, his body was not simply a revivified physical body, although it appeared to be so. Rather, he had a resurrection body, although it was not at the same level of glory as that of Christ's resurrection body after his resurrection.

As Lazarus lived on in his resurrection body, he found that he had the ability to traverse the boundary between the physical and spiritual realms. His body became a vehicle that enabled him to travel at will into the spiritual world while at the same time remaining physically present in the physical realm, appearing like any other human being. This ability did not present itself immediately, or all at once. It took some time for him to grow accustomed to his changed body, to learn how to work with it so that he could employ it in ever nobler ways. I could see a "star" within him. It was this "star" of his body that was the "vehicle" of such travel. This is quite challenging to explain.

In the beginning, just after his raising, it was necessary that Lazarus adjust to his new way of life. He did not require food, but did eat on occasion for the sake of communion with others, and also simply for the joy of eating. Nor did he require much sleep.

For the first several days after Lazarus returned to life, Magdalene listened to his heart whenever she could. On one such occasion, as she was resting her head against his chest, there came a sudden loud banging at the front entry of the castle. Gripped with fear, Magdalene rose up and went toward the door to Lazarus's chamber, calling for his butler, who appeared immediately, his face flush with fear.

"Gather together whatever servants you can. Then go to the door and tell those without that Lazarus has left!" Magdalene's voice was strained and urgent. The butler turned and rushed down the stairs, calling out names of certain servants as he went.

Magdalene latched the chamber door and turned back to Lazarus. But she saw only empty bedclothes—*where had he gone?*

She could not believe her eyes. Lazarus was gone! A strange peace came over her then, and time seemed to stand still. It was as though she could somehow feel Lazarus within her—her body was tingling, alive with radiance. She could hear his thoughts inside her heart, as if he were saying to her, *All is well, Magdalene. Go and hide. I shall be with you.*

Magdalene left immediately by the back stairs, which led to the butler's quarters. From there she hurried through a passageway leading to the cold storage, and thence out through a back door. As she made her escape, she kept her hand over her heart, for she continued to feel Lazarus within her own heart.

She continued running, through the gardens, and then the stables, coming finally to some small shops. Past all of this she ran, until she came at last to a wooded tract, remote from Bethany.

The voices of the mob had faded into the distance. Magdalene hid herself in the hills behind some rocks, under cover of thick foliage. She was exhausted, but marvelous love filled her entire being—the love of her brother Lazarus. She rested there, in communion with him, until finally she dozed off.

In order to receive Lazarus, Magdalene's being had had to "expand." This was why she needed sleep: so that she could contract and resume her normal state. (This is difficult to explain!) As she slept, the soul of Lazarus separated from hers.

Magdalene awoke several hours later. She sat up, feeling dizzy, and waited for her strength to return. She wondered what she should do and where she should go. While pondering this, Lazarus came walking feebly up the hill. He was still unaccustomed to his new body, and appeared weak. He smiled at her as he sat down beside her on the grass.

"Lazarus, what happened? You were suddenly gone from my sight, but I felt you in my heart!" Magdalene wanted to touch his arm to make sure he was corporeal, but restrained herself.

Lazarus was unaware that he had "disappeared." He knew only that when he had heard the mob, his impulse had been to leap up, grab Magdalene, and run to safety. According to his experience, he had arisen from the bed, gone to Magdalene at the door, and directed her to run with him down the back stairs. He told Magdalene this—that he had experienced himself running out of the house with her.

Magdalene did not know what to say. Finally she said, "Lazarus, I did not see you, but I *felt* you in my heart."

"This is a mystery." Lazarus pursed his lips and closed his eyes. "Perhaps we shall understand this later."

Magdalene was speechless and in awe. They were silent for several moments. Then Lazarus said, "Magdalene, I must go away. They are coming for me. My presence is a danger to the disciples." He held Magdalene's hands to his heart. "Go back and give word that I am gone. By the grace of God, may I dwell in the hearts of the disciples! Perhaps my spirit can remain close, even though I shall go away."

Tears filled Magdalene's eyes as she listened to his words. She looked upon his handsome face, tracing every line closely with her gaze. Something was different about him, but she was not sure what it was. His skin glowed and he seemed ageless; his eyes were clear and bright. "Lazarus, you look different."

He gathered her into his arms and she listened once more to his heart, allowing its rhythm to soothe her. I was in ecstasy, listening to his heartbeat. *This is the heartbeat of the Beloved of Christ!* Lazarus's heart was in perfect attunement with the heart of Christ.

Lazarus had been spiritually reborn through the love of Christ—it was the Savior's love that had brought him back from the grave. Through Christ's love for him, he was able to see that he still had tasks to accomplish in the physical realm. But although it was the will of Christ Jesus that Lazarus return, this alone would not have sufficed to call him back. Imbued with the love of Christ, however, Lazarus's own will was awakened in such degree that he himself then desired to return to the physical world.

Christ would never resurrect a person against that person's will. Resurrection can take place only through the merging of divine will with human will, which, taken together, work true *sacred magic*. Each of us will receive our own resurrection body when we are prepared for it, that is, when our individual will is aligned truly with the divine will.

Christ Jesus loved Lazarus, and Lazarus loved Christ Jesus. Their reunion in the physical realm was indeed sweet—so sweet that Christ wept tears of joy. For Lazarus had chosen *him* over death. Lazarus recognized that Christ *is* the Life and Light of humanity, and he chose *Life*.

Lazarus's initiation fulfilled the purpose of the ancient Death Mysteries. Enacting the Old Mysteries is no longer expedient, for Christ is now the great Initiator, who leads us from the death of our old selves to newly-resurrected life—a life in *him*. As he is the Resurrection and the Life, we may say, *Not I, but Christ in me*.

Every time a part of us dies, such as an old belief, or a part of our lower self, we have the opportunity to be restored to new life. When finally we are able to die fully in Christ, then may we be resurrected.

This is just what happened in the case of Lazarus. He died in Christ. His only desire was to be like Christ, to completely unite himself with Christ, and to dwell in the spirit. When Lazarus was raised to new life, Christ was then in him, in uninterrupted union with his soul.

Magdalene knew that her brother was changed. She did not understand the change, but she knew that something unfathomable had taken place between the two of them; and she kept this in her heart, knowing that she could reveal it to no other.

With a sharp stone she cut off a lock of her hair, braided it into a little keepsake, and presented it to Lazarus as a sign that part of her would remain always with him. She said, "I must go, before it is too dark to find my way." She laid her hand briefly against his heart and then kissed his feet. Then, after gazing into his luminous eyes, she turned and fled back to the castle, entering again by the back passageway.

For a time, Lazarus dwelt in the wilderness. Later he returned to his estate and hid in its underground chambers. Only a few knew he was there. He was however able to live in communion with the disciples in a spiritual way, most often with John of Zebedee, for whom he felt a close and significant rapport, and also with his sister Magdalene.

Bethany Seen Across the Valley of Jehosaphat

XXXII

I BEHELD a beautiful angel clothed in brilliant white light. Together we traveled toward the Holy Land. I hovered above the places where Jesus had walked, and wept as I felt and heard the soft footfall of his steps upon the ground. It was as if the very ground remembered him. I followed the angel through the places of Jesus's final hours and remembered what had happened in each place: the trial, the scourging, and the crowning with thorns; the carrying of the cross, the crucifixion, and the entombment. I felt sorrow for his suffering—and immense gratitude for his deeds, which were eternally imprinted upon my heart.

Then I found Magdalene at another point in time. She was at the castle of Lazarus a few days after he had been raised from the dead. It was shortly after he had gone into hiding. Jesus had gone to Galilee to escape the crowds. Mobs of people, both curious and angry, were still coming to the castle to inquire of the whereabouts of Lazarus and Jesus.

Of all the great and wondrous miracles performed by Jesus, the raising of Lazarus was the greatest, and so it attracted many, all of whom wished to see for themselves the wonder of the man raised from the dead! Magdalene instructed the servants to tell the crowds that Lazarus was gone.

Magdalene's heart was with Jesus and Lazarus. She thought of them unceasingly, and was anxious for their well-being. As Magdalene watched the crowds milling about from a window on the upper floor of Lazarus's estate, she knew that soon she also would have to leave.

Lazarus Appears to Magdalene

ON the night before she was to leave Lazarus's estate, Magdalene lay in bed thinking of her beloved brother and wondering where he might be. Had he found a safe haven? Her soul was warmed by thoughts of him, and she wanted to understand the changes recently wrought in him. Hands over her heart, she smiled to herself as she reviewed the recent, mystifying, events.

Then, suddenly, she saw a light gather itself in the center of the room, whence a human form emerged. She soon realized, with great joy, that it was Lazarus! He appeared as if an angel, in softly glowing light. He could appear this way because he was in his resurrection body—a body of light.

"Lazarus!" Magdalene exclaimed. Then, as if she would be able to converse with him for only a moment, she blurted out her most pressing questions. "What should I do? Where should I go?" She feared for the safety of Lazarus and Jesus—and now she also feared for her own life.

In response to her anxiety, Lazarus said "Magdalene, this was meant to be. It was ordained of God. The Glory of God has been manifested in me. Do not fear the change that has taken place in me. One day you will understand it. I cannot yet explain to you what is happening. I know only that in times past I could not enter the spiritual world, and now I can. I can visit you in this way because I am able to *travel by love*. The love between us, Magdalene, hails from before the Creation. Wherever you are, I can go, because of the love between us. We do not need to be separated."

His words were like a light to her soul, and she rejoiced. Then she asked, "Lazarus, what do you see now? What do you see now that you could not see before? Your hunger for the spiritual world was so great, you nearly died to go there. Can you tell me what you now see?"

"Before, I could feel love, but now I *see* love. Love is a world in and of itself. It is an abode where one can dwell. I can *see* the love between people. I can *see* the love of the angels and the love that surrounds the Earth. Everything is held in the embrace of love.

"Something happened to me when I was baptized—and also when I died—and now what I could remember before only in scattered glimpses is returned to me in bright recollection."

The light around Lazarus shimmered.

He continued, "Mary, he *is* the Son of God! I see it now. Whereas before I could only have *faith* in him, now I *see* and *know! He is the Son of God*, dwelling in a human body!"

He paused to let her take in his words.

Then he said, "I cannot be with him in a physical way. It would be a danger to his mission, and a danger to his disciples. But you can be with him, Magdalene. You can be with him and look after him. He needs you. He will need you with him to the very end—when he undertakes the great deeds he will accomplish for all humankind. I will be with him in spirit, and you will be with him in person."

"Lazarus, what do you mean by this? What is Jesus going to do?"

"I cannot tell you now, Magdalene. Even though he is the Son of God, he will need you—*a human being*—to bear him through what he shall do," Lazarus replied.

Magdalene's voice was resolute. "I shall never leave him, even if they try to send me to the next world!"

Lazarus said, "When things become difficult, I will strengthen you. I can lend you a portion of myself to bear you up. Even so, it will be very difficult. You must pray without ceasing."

She could bear these words because she felt such love from him. Sensing that their conversation was coming to a close, she asked: "When shall I see you again, my brother?"

"You will see me, Magdalene—this I promise. We will meet again." Lazarus was starting to withdraw, the light gathering in closer to his form.

"Thank you, dear Lazarus! I love you!"

As he retreated from her vision, Magdalene held out her hands as if to touch him, tears on her cheeks. "Lazarus!"

His voice was now only a whisper. "Farewell, Magdalene!"

The next day, Magdalene left Lazarus's castle in Bethany and went to join the other holy women. They also were keeping themselves sequestered for the time being, waiting for the tumult to pass. They were anxious to hear what had transpired with Lazarus. Martha and her servant, as well as Joanna were present, along with Mary Cleophas, Susannah, Salome, Dinah, Mary Salome, the widow of Nain, the Blessed Mother, and Magdalene's maid Sarah. Magdalene was comforted by the women's strength. They understood that she, and Martha also, had been through much in a very brief time. Indeed, the two sisters had witnessed

Lazarus become deathly ill, and then *die*; and then, soon there-after, had seen him raised from the dead and returned to life—only to *lose* him again as he went into hiding! Magdalene was nearly overwhelmed by all these things.

The women had received word from Jesus that he was still teaching in Galilee and that he planned to travel soon to foreign lands. Magdalene was glad to hear the news that he was well, but her heart fell when she heard that he would leave Galilee to jour-ney so far away. She hoped that she might somehow see him before he left, although she understood that he must need to go away for a time. She knew that she must trust the Father to take care of him.

Knowing that Magdalene was spent, the women granted her solitude for a while. They took loving care of her, anointing her with oils and then leaving her again to silence. Her heart was full of both joy and grief—joy, because Lazarus was alive again; and grief, because Lazarus was gone and Jesus was in Galilee. And then there was the looming future—the daunting unknown—that occupied her thoughts much of the time.

In the midst of her silent contemplation Magdalene reflected upon Jesus, and was reassured that he was doing what he needed to do. But when night fell she felt alone, and wondered: *Am I too weak to bear what the future might bring? I wish Jesus could explain to me what is happening.*

Suddenly she was utterly overcome with love for him and I heard her thoughts as she wept: *I love him! Should I love him this much? Lazarus told me that he is the Son of God. I know it is true! Oh my Lord!*

The realization that she was the closest companion to the *Son of God* flew to her on swift wings—*I love the Son of God! He is my dearest friend!*

Magdalene's thoughts came rushing through me, causing tears to flow profusely as I felt her immense love for the Master:

I have known all along that he is the Son of God—but I have been afraid to admit it to myself. My heart is wounded by this love. This love is the wound that never heals! And yet, I do not want my heart ever to close again. It must remain open. I will love him for all eternity. He is my hope, and my joy! He restored my brother to me, and he restored to me my soul. He led me out from hell by his own hand. He called seven demons out from me and saved my soul. Oh my Lord! You are my light and my life! Wherever you go, I will follow. Oh my Lord! You are my King. You may never be able to claim your Kingship in this life, but you are my King! I know you now. I know you. You have known me all along, and now I know you.

Conversation Between
Magdalene and the Widow of Nain

THE FOLLOWING DAY Magdalene was resting in the garden, her face turned toward the sun, its warmth bathing her as she thought of how the selfsame sun was shining also upon the face of Jesus... somewhere. Presently, the widow of Nain† came into the garden. Seeing Magdalene, she said, "Magdalene, I have been wanting to speak to you."

Magdalene looked up and smiled, her green eyes reflecting the color of the olive leaves above her head. "Yes, I have been wanting to speak with you also. I have wanted to hear more of your experience—of when your son was raised from the dead by Jesus."

The widow continued, "You and I now have something precious in common, for we have both mourned the loss of a loved one—and then, in some mysterious way, our loved ones have been restored to us."

The widow's eyes danced in the light. "I will never be the same, Magdalene. Before this happened, I had not much faith—but that mattered not to Jesus. He knew I had much *love*, the kind of love that can beckon someone to leave even the grave! It was

---

† This woman, whose name was Maroni, was a wealthy widow from the town of Nain. She was the sister of the wife of the apostle James and the mother of the youth of Nain, who at the age of twelve was raised from the dead by Jesus Christ. This miraculous event, which took place at the entrance to the city of Nain, is described in Luke 7:11–17. The youth's name was Martialis. He later became a disciple and was one of the group of disciples who accompanied the apostle Peter to Rome. Maroni donated generously to the community of disciples and was active as a helper in the circle of holy women. She was also the daughter of the apostle Peter's father-in-law's brother, and so was a cousin of Peter's wife.

enough for Jesus. He told me that it was through my love that he wrought the miracle. From the other side of the veil my son knew and felt my love for him—and it was through this love that Jesus called him forth. And now, my faith in God's power is consummate—for now I *know* God's power, Magdalene. I *feel* God's love, his mighty, majestic love! There is nothing that his love—*in us*—cannot do."

Magdalene nodded her head in agreement as the widow continued. "My son is a changed man. He has a purpose now that he never knew before. You should see him! The way he touches people, and how he loves everyone he meets. He has lifted so many up from the depths and given them such hope. There is a light all around him. All of this I have watched with wonder and awe. He has not told me all that happened to him while he was in the spiritual world, but someday he will. Mary, my son is *alive!* I am so humbled by this blessing!"

Magdalene's face shone as she listened to the widow's words. "I also am in awe. I can hardly grasp all that has happened. I think I have felt every possible emotion in the past few weeks. What great miracles are these—to have my brother, and your son, restored to life! Lazarus is a changed person also, although I cannot yet say in what way this is so. Not only was he raised from the dead through this most unfathomable miracle, but the wonder of resurrection lives on in him. The miracle that he is continues," Magdalene responded, somewhat enigmatically.

The widow nodded her head. "Yes, yes, my son continues as a miracle also."

Then Magdalene said, "There is so much I wish I could say, but for now I must remain silent." The widow nodded her head with understanding. Then Magdalene told her, "Lazarus has gone into hiding."

"Yes, and my son must be very careful also." She paused, studying Magdalene's face. "Magdalene, you are joyous, it is true, but you seem melancholy also, even though so great a miracle has taken place."

Magdalene bowed her head. "Things are changing. I do not know what will happen, but things are changing. That is why I am sad. But I am joyous also, and for many reasons."

The widow put her arms around Magdalene and for a moment held her close. "Oh, Magdalene, I feel that your heart is broken. Is this so?"

"Yes, it is broken. But it is also sound. It is both broken and sound at the same time." Tears slid down her cheeks.

Salome then came to the garden bringing to Magdalene and the widow of Nain the message that the other women wished to gather together to eat and talk, if Magdalene was so inclined. Magdalene agreed, and also thanked the widow for her words.

The three of them joined the other women at table. As Magdalene walked into the room, the Blessed Mother looked at her with compassion. The sweetest expression of love came into her eyes; she could feel and immediately understand Magdalene's heart.

The women wanted to hear of the experiences of Magdalene and Martha surrounding the raising of Lazarus—and of all that had happened over the ensuing several days. Magdalene told them all she could, but there were certain things she could not yet say. These things she kept in her heart.

When Magdalene and Martha finished speaking, the women praised God. They were filled with wonder and awe. They sang a song together. Magdalene's heart grew lighter as she felt the wondrous peace and warmth of their love. She received strength from them to face whatever might happen next.

As she retired that evening, she prayed for each of the holy women. She was truly grateful for them, and for their love.

XXXIII

Under the Stars

AS I TRAVELED back in time, I saw the "colors of the world" fall from my aura as if I were shedding a heavy cloak of burnt-looking, muddied colors. As I continued on, bright colors replaced them: green, rose, violet, blue, and gold. It felt wonderful to slough off the world's cloying impress for a time. I could see before me a point of light in the time I was to visit this day.

Below me lay the sphere of illusions, with its cold inner core of abstraction and death. It undulated with an alluring, sucking force, and within it were a myriad of confusing elements. The further I receded from this sphere, the lighter I felt. Sometimes, in my journey, I paused and hovered among the stars, communing with them in heavenly joy.

Upon arriving in the Holy Land, I found myself gazing at the constellations. That is, I beheld them through Magdalene, who lay on her back staring at the myriad glittering stars spangling the deep-violet night.

Magdalene had come to Galilee to find Jesus. She had to seek him out at night, and meet with him only in the dark, for she also was now being hunted. Her red hair was a telltale sign that she was the sister of the one who had been raised from the dead. For the past several days she had traveled only after sundown.

Under the stars, she had reflected on recent events. She found that her mind was drawn ever and again to that defining moment of all time, when Jesus had restored to life her brother Lazarus, who had been dead for *eight* days!

It was not only Lazarus who had awakened, though, for Magdalene also felt more awake and alive than ever before. There was a rumbling at her core, signaling that something was about to change. Yes, she knew that nothing would ever be the same.

She glanced at the fire, several paces away, where Jesus and

John of Zebedee were deep in conversation. Presently, John arose and motioned to Magdalene that it was her turn to speak with the Master. He then left to join the others camped in a nearby shepherd's field. Wrapping her veil around her head, Magdalene stood up and walked over to Jesus. His eyes sparkled in the firelight.

"How is it with Lazarus, Magdalene?" Jesus wanted to know how *she* was accommodating to the change in Lazarus, rather than wondering about Lazarus's well-being, for he was of course more than privy to the changes in Lazarus. He knew that Magdalene had been deeply and forever affected by the miracle.

"He is well. He is in hiding, but he has... visited me." She knew that Jesus would understand what she meant.

Motioning for her to sit down beside him, Jesus looked into the fire and then laughed gently. "Lazarus has been so interested in the Mysteries—and now he has *become* a mystery!"

Magdalene smiled at Jesus's humor, agreeing that Lazarus was indeed *very* mysterious. Her heart warmed as she thought of the wisdom and light that now emanated from Lazarus. She was indeed filled with the unfathomable mystery that had become one with her brother.

Jesus was happy to be reunited with Magdalene and was in a light-hearted mood. He kissed her on the forehead and said, "The raising of Lazarus is a mystery—but I shall show you an even greater mystery."

"I am not so sure I can bear more mysteries! I am still regaining my balance after this miracle." She breathed in deeply.

Jesus's face took on a serious look. "You will never again be the same, Magdalene. Your greatest work will soon begin." He paused, noticing her pensive expression, knowing she was concerned about the future. "Beloved, do not worry."

Magdalene gazed up at the stars. "Lord, what world do you come from?"

He answered, "I have told you that I and the Father are one. I have come from my Father's house."

"Is your Father's house among the stars?"

Smiling, almost laughing, he responded, "Yes, I come from the stars. But so do you, Magdalene. It is just that I remember myself from before this world, and you do not yet know who you are."

She nodded her head in agreement. "It is true. I do not know who I am. Even in my short lifetime I have lived already through so many false identities. I had to cast them all away, and not without great pain. Now my only identity is to be your disciple—and this path is unsure. The path seems dark before me, unfamiliar and lonely. Even though you are my beloved friend, still I feel quite alone. I no longer enjoy the society of my former friends."

She did not regret the loss of her friends, but her heart did ache for them, and she wished she could share with them Jesus's gospel of love.

She continued, "I do not even know how to serve you. I know only that it is my path to do so."

"And you shall serve me, in ways you cannot now fathom."

The night seemed to sigh in rhythm with the crickets' song and the crackling of the fire. Jesus regarded the night sky, and then said in his endearing way: "The stars are listening to us." Magdalene was filled with joy at the thought.

Jesus took his mantle and wrapped it about her shoulders and then put his arms around her, saying: "Your home is in the stars. No matter what happens, remember this." She leaned her head against his chest. They were silent for a while.

Then Jesus quietly sang a children's song—one that most Jewish children knew. As soon as Magdalene heard the first phrase, a memory came rushing to her. She was perhaps three or four years old. Mary and Joseph of Nazareth were visiting Magdalene's parents at their Bethany estate. A vivid picture of the curious little boy Jesus arose—he was a bit older than Magdalene. The two were playing in the gardens, playing the usual games of the time. And one night, amusing themselves under the stars, they had sung a song they both knew, the very song Jesus was now singing:

> *O there is a bright star in the heavens!*
> *That star is the one I will follow—*
> *I will follow it to the Promised Land.*

> *O there is a bright star in the heavens!*
> *That star is my one true light—*
> *I will follow it to the Promised Land.*

"I remember how we sang that song together once…" Magdalene said as Jesus held her close. "I was so innocent then."

He laughed. "Yes, the fire that you are was only a spark when you were young."

"I remember your mother, too. She was the most beautiful lady I had ever seen—she was so much younger than my mother. I thought she was an angel. Do you remember how she danced with us in the garden? Martha and Lazarus were with us too."

She looked up at Jesus. "I can see her in you. I can feel her love in you." Sighing, she looked down at the ground, and added, "Everything was so simple then." After a few moments she asked, "Have we found the Promised Land?"

"The Promised Land is where all promises are fulfilled."

"I have learned of God's promises to his people; and if there is such a place, it must be glorious—a place where there is no sorrow, pain, or death. And no separation from the ones we love."

Jesus said, "You can live in the Promised Land *now*—in your heart, Magdalene. You can lay hold of the Father's promises and see them fulfilled *within* you. You can help others to do this also. And when you do, there will be a community of hearts living as one. Where this community dwells, there will always be grace and love."

He turned to face her, taking her right hand and placing it over his heart, holding his left hand over her right as he did so. And then she took his right hand and placed it over her heart with her left hand over his.

Their hearts were beating in unison. "I will be with you always as the coming months unfold, and you will see how this can be."

Jesus then held her hands in his lap and looked into her eyes. He beheld all that she was, all the way back to the Creation. He could see her manifold lifetimes and the many facets of her soul.

I also could see her in this way, though not of course to the degree that he could. Magdalene's being was indeed beautiful to behold, and magnificently rich in earthly experience. She is undoubtedly a most royal being. It was as if Jesus traveled back through time in his beholding, recollecting all she was, until, finally, he came to the star of her spirit. As he beheld the pure light of her greater being, Magdalene felt increasingly imbued with that light.

Just then, John quietly and respectfully approached, and when Jesus bid him speak, he said, "Before we retire for the evening, Peter would like to discuss tomorrow's journey."

Jesus nodded. "Yes, I will come now. Tell everyone to gather." John thanked Jesus and Magdalene, and returned to the others.

Jesus said to Magdalene: "We shall journey all together once more, and then I must visit other peoples. I will travel into pagan lands with the three sons of the shepherd. When I return, you and I shall begin our work together." By this he meant a "new work" that they would undertake.

"Thank you, my Lord." Magdalene kissed his hand and then stood to take her leave and join the holy women while he went to join the disciples. As they all gathered together to talk, I beheld a dome of light over the group and knew that angels were protecting them.

Christ then appeared in the Etheric and spoke to me directly, giving me this message for all who come upon this book:

O Child of Light!
I came to Earth to visit my creation.
My heart is filled with compassion and mercy for all.
I see each of you, so precious and unique in your individualities!
I sent you before me to descend to this world to prepare the way
*   for me to come.*
And now I am coming to gather you.
I shall show you the way through the tribulation and bring you to
*   the Promised Land.*
Be true and faithful and watch for me.
I shall fulfill the promises that I have made to humankind.
I am with you always, even to the end of time.
My love is ever around you,
O Child of Light!

Jesus Looking Through a Lattice

PART FOUR

Appendices

Vineyard and Watch Tower Near Bethany

Appendix I

Although the following visions refer only incidentally to Magdalene, they are included here because they offer a background to her childhood and early family life. They are visions of Magdalene's sister "Silent Mary," who remains largely unknown to history. This sister deserves to be brought reverentially into the annals of history in recognition of her importance in the life of Jesus Christ and in the lives of his devoted servants, Magdalene and Lazarus. Full recognition of her destiny, both in life and after her death, remains still a veiled secret. We can be thankful for her presence in the remarkable family to which she belonged, each member of which played an essential role in the unfolding of the ministry of Jesus Christ and in the founding of the early Church.

Dancing for Jesus

I WAS LOOKING upon the lovely face of a golden-haired feminine soul surrounded by peach-gold light. This soul seemed so familiar to me. She gestured downward, to somewhere below us, and I saw immediately that it was to the castle of Lazarus that she was pointing. Then, suddenly, I was there.

In a room at the back of the castle sat a stout woman, a maid, cradling a tightly swaddled infant. She was trying to calm her, for the child was agitated and screaming.

The infant's mother could not endure such crying and so had relegated her, along with her maid, to the further rooms of the castle. She had lost already several children to early death, and could not bear the thought that this little one might follow those others to the same untimely end. And so she had arranged that the infant be tended afar by the maid.

I then saw little Lazarus. He was perhaps four or five years old. I saw also his sister Martha, who seemed about two years old. The sickly baby crying so desperately was their younger sister.

I saw that the father was away from home most of the time.

He was very wealthy, as he was descended from noble blood. He had dark olive skin, whereas his wife was more fair-skinned. Martha and her baby sister had inherited their mother's fair skin. Lazarus took after their father in appearance.

As I came into more intimate connection with the little baby, I saw that her tender soul was unable to abide the harsh reality of the physical world. It was as though her skin was too thin and could not protect her within the boundaries of time and space. For her, awareness of the outer world was like an uninterrupted assault on her senses, such that she had to struggle to thrive.

During her first year of life she wailed most of the time. Eventually the screaming subsided, but when she came to the age when children normally begin to speak, she refused to do so. She had the capacity, but declined to use it.

Although she was present with the rest of the family at certain important events during the year, she avoided their society, preferring to remain alone in the little garden outside her room, where she whispered to unseen beings and rarely spoke aloud to others.

Sometimes she communicated through gestures, but it was difficult to understand her. She grew increasingly estranged from her family, for they could not seem to reach her. She simply could not enter into relation with the physical world, or with anyone living in it.

At age nine or ten her parents passed away. She could see and follow their spirits and would sometimes whisper to them in her garden.

The maid often found her lying on her back, staring at the sky in a catatonic state, not blinking for long periods of time. Or she might find her face-down in the grass and think she was dead. During these interludes, however, the young girl was in fact sojourning in the spiritual world, uninhibited by the coils of mortality. She had visions both wonderful and frightening, but none of these would she convey to her maid or to her family.

Often she ran to and fro, gesturing wildly, acting out what she saw in vision. No matter how many times the maid witnessed this, she was always anxious and overwhelmed by such strange behavior, and would be greatly relieved when the child's face finally softened into a sublime look as her body went limp—spent as it was from the intensity of her experience—and she fell into a deep slumber, a slumber that would sometimes last for days.

The mother of Silent Mary (for so was the child called) had spared no expense seeking out healers for her daughter. But she would not venture beyond the customs and practices of what was considered appropriate by her people, who were strict, law-abiding Jews. The child's father was more open to looking further afield for alternative methods of healing, but the mother would not allow it. Before they died, they had come to wonder whether their child was perhaps possessed, but pride kept them from entertaining such a thought for long. In the end, they had decided there must just be something wrong in the girl's mind, and grieved over their loss.

I heard that the Hebrew name of this child was to have been Miriam bat Zarah (Mary, daughter of Zarah). Her mother had always loved the names Martha and Miriam,[†] and hoped to use them if she had two little girls. But no pair of girls to whom she might have given these two names had yet survived. When her first surviving female child came along, she named her Martha, hoping that another little girl might yet be born to take the name Miriam.

When the child of whom we have been speaking was born, and survived, she was given this name. But later, when it became so sadly evident that this second little girl would never communicate in the normal way, she became known, in Hebrew, as the "Miriam who does not speak," or Silent Mary, as she might be called in English. And when the mother later bore another female child after Silent Mary, she too was given the name Miriam. This latter child would eventually be known as Mary Magdalene, or, more simply, Magdalene.

It was feared that the younger Mary (Magdalene) might acquire "bad" habits from her elder, enigmatic sister, the silent one, so the family made every effort to keep the girls apart. They did not want Magdalene to learn to "throw fits" as Silent Mary did.

---

† "Mary" is the customary English version of the name Miriam, and so will be used hereafter.

It was sad to see Silent Mary living in such isolation, but the family did not know what else to do. They ensured that she had everything she needed, everything they could think of that might make her happy, and they assigned several servants to watch over her.

After the parents' deaths, relatives and servants took over the rearing of the other children, but Silent Mary was left more and more to herself. In later years, Magdalene went off to live in her own castle and rarely saw her strange older sister. Neither did she very often think of her. Silent Mary, left so much alone, came to spend all the more time in visionary states.

As I went ahead in time to just before the baptism of Jesus, I marveled at the great contrast between the two sisters named Mary. Mary Magdalene was at that time deeply entrenched in the material world, caring little for spiritual things, whereas Silent Mary was almost completely detached from the material world, living most of the time in the spirit. Either of these extreme ways of living might with equal justification have been deemed insane. But, given the ways of the world, not many did in fact consider Mary Magdalene insane, whereas most agreed that Silent Mary was so.

Prior to his baptism in the River Jordan, Jesus had gone to meet Lazarus at his castle. I understood that Lazarus and his family had been acquainted with the Holy Family for a long time, even that Lazarus had grown up knowing Jesus.

At this time Jesus had been traveling quite extensively, teaching all who would listen. He was loved by many. Although most thought him somewhat strange, they nonetheless loved to listen to his wise words. He had not done much healing up till now. He was just beginning to feel the unfolding of his true mission, and had come to speak with Lazarus about this.

There had been a few conversations between Jesus and his mother in which he had told her that his time was coming, the time when he would live out the mission for which he had come to Earth. But he was not yet fully aware of just what this would entail, or of precisely what he would undergo.

When Jesus arrived at the castle, Lazarus, Martha, and several of their friends were waiting in one of the many gardens to hear him speak. In the dim light of dusk, he began by recounting some experiences from his recent travels. While he was speaking, he suddenly paused. He thought he heard moaning and sounds of weeping nearby. The moaning stopped, so he continued… but then he heard it again. No one else seemed to notice the anguished sounds.

Now, the garden where they were meeting was on the same side of the property as was the garden of Silent Mary, although the two gardens were set apart by several stone walls.

Jesus felt grief arise in his heart. Every so often he would pause to listen, and then continue speaking. When the talk came to an end, Lazarus came to Jesus to ask why he had seemed distracted. Jesus replied, "I heard a soul weeping from that direction," and pointed toward Silent Mary's garden.

"It is nothing," Lazarus replied, touching the elbow of Jesus, whom he invited to come sit at table, where a beautiful meal was laid out. "Come, let us eat."

As the others walked toward the warmly lit dining hall, Jesus stopped thoughtfully at its entrance. "Go and attend to your guests, Lazarus. I am fasting this evening." He turned from the hall, and while walking toward his quarters heard again the weeping. A servant was standing at attention nearby in the hallway. Jesus asked the servant to show him the way to the wing whence the weeping came. The servant led him to a door in a darkened passageway. By the door hung a cord. The servant pulled the cord, which rang a bell inside the quarters. Slowly, Silent Mary's elderly maid cracked open the door and peered out, very surprised to see Jesus standing before her.

"I heard someone weeping, and would like to see who suffers so," said Jesus.

"Mary does not speak, nor does she receive visitors," was the emphatic reply. The maid dreaded Mary's crying fits and was not about to let the presence of Jesus set her off.

"Go and tell Mary that I, Yeshua ben Yosef (Jesus, son of Joseph), am here, and ask her if she might see me," Jesus persisted, feeling a great urge to see her. He knew that Lazarus and Martha had a mentally unstable sister, but had never seen much of her. They rarely ever brought her up in conversation.

The elderly maid ambled slowly into the garden and beckoned softly to Mary, who did not move from her place by an ancient tree. So she walked over to Mary, and, lifting her face gently, said, "Mary, there is a man named Jesus who wishes to see you. Shall I grant him entrance?"

Mary's tear-streaked face nodded a simple "yes." Shocked, the maid stood up, walked slowly back to the door, and allowed Jesus to enter. She took him through the main room into the garden.

I noticed that the three primary rooms were kept very dark, with curtains drawn. One servant stood ready in the main room, and was hardly ever asked to do anything, while another servant, whose only task was to play music, sat in the shadows of the portico near the garden. These two, together with the maid, were Silent Mary's sole companions. The maid was Mary's primary attendant, for only she would Mary allow to do such things as comb her hair, or dress her.

As Jesus entered the garden, he found Silent Mary at the base of the ancient tree, lying on the ground, her head against one of its gnarled roots. He knelt down a few paces behind her. She was weeping, holding on to the tree, every so often rising up on her knees to look into the branches, her face and hair wet with tears. Then she would fall forward again, clinging to the tree and moaning. The maid looked at Jesus and shrugged her shoulders, as if to say, "Do you see?"

Silent Mary fell to the ground on the right side of the tree and began to tremble. The trembling became more and more violent as the moments passed. She crawled over to a large stone and pressed her cheek against its smooth surface, her tears washing over it. Suddenly she stood up, her face full of wonder and awe and her hands raised in a gesture of cosmic reverence, as if she were seeing a great light in heaven. For several moments she was quite still. Seeing the radiance around her face, Jesus rose and moved a bit closer to her.

When the vision ended, Silent Mary walked over to Jesus and fell at his feet, again weeping. He took her by the hand and drew her petite, gaunt frame to a heavy, sculpted bench near at hand and set her down among the pillows provided there. She drew herself together like a little bird nesting with folded wings.

"I have heard that you do not speak, but if it be the will of the Father, please do speak to me, and tell me what you have seen." Jesus spoke in a gentle, measured voice.

Silent Mary did not speak in full sentences, and could barely articulate what she had seen. In the simplest of phrases, hardly above a whisper, and with her head bowed, she told Jesus what was to become of him.

She told him that God would come to be in him, that the God in him would perform mighty miracles, that he would be both loved and hated, and that he would suffer terrible things. She said that twelve would follow him and carry his message to the world. She told him that he would suffer in a garden and bleed in great anguish, and almost perish from the evil that would strive to hinder him.

And then she told him of his death—what sort of death he would suffer, and that after his death he would be resurrected from his tomb in glorious light.

At the end of all this, she said she would not live to see any of these things come to pass, for she would soon leave this world to be with the angels. Jesus's eyes were closed as he listened intently to all Silent Mary said, a few tears gliding down his cheeks.

Silent Mary fell quiet again, refusing to speak further, her lucid moment flown. Jesus sat in deep contemplation. Suddenly, Silent Mary leapt up and ran into the shadows of the portico, awakening the old musician who had taken his afternoon nap there on an old chaise. She thrust his stringed instrument into his lap. The servant dutifully filled the garden with lilting melodies as Silent Mary, in a state of vision, commenced dancing with rejoicing angels who were just then proclaiming the resurrection.

In her loose and flowing white dress, without sash, mantle, or veil—her hair hanging long and free—she did indeed herself look like an angel. Her arms were raised high in a gesture of awe, as though she wished to receive heaven into her being. She made great circling movements around the garden, sometimes slowly, sometimes with great fervor. I could see the colors of the rainbow stream from every gesture of her dancing.

Jesus's heart was full of wonder. In a mysterious way, this special soul had opened to him the angelic realm, and a deep impression of the dance of the angels was made upon his soul. From this time forward, Jesus sometimes danced this angelic kind of movement with his closest companions.

It was owing to this experience that Jesus shared together with Silent Mary—that is, the witnessing of his own Passion through her, as well as the other words she spoke—that he came to know that the time was come for him to seek out the baptism of John.

I was again taken ahead in time—to the foot of the cross on the hill of Golgotha. I saw Silent Mary's soul present in the spiritual realm. She had witnessed every deed of Jesus's Ministry and Passion from the spiritual realm, and also through the perspectives of Lazarus, Martha, and Magdalene!

I wanted to know more about this soul, and came to understand how important an individuality she is, for she was able to witness the Passion of Christ before it took place. And, as witness from the spiritual realm of *all* he did, she remained intimately connected to him. She is someone who could bring the reality of his deeds for the Earth into future times, either through inspiring others spiritually, or through bringing to remembrance during her own subsequent lives what she saw during the time of Christ. Her work is to bring to light the Mystery of Golgotha. I saw also that she is someone who loves to dance!

Jesus Visits with Silent Mary Again

I SAW a little girl, about six years of age, kneeling on a cold, hard floor. Her hands were clasped to her chest and her head was bowed. She was striving against invisible evil beings, praying silently with all her might, her hair matted and dark against her white nightdress. She frantically wanted her mother, but knew she could not have her. I could feel her pain at being all alone. Her maid was a heavy sleeper and had no notion that the little one was up all night suffering so.

I soon saw that this was the little Silent Mary whom I had seen before. I saw that she struggled with comprehending the difference between past, present, and future, and that sometimes her apparent babblings were about future events she had witnessed, while not herself understanding that she was seeing the future.

She did not enter into conversation with anyone, but would occasionally speak out isolated phrases, all of which was very disconcerting to her parents. On one occasion, for instance, she suddenly pointed toward Lazarus, saying "He... dead." After losing so many young ones to death, Silent Mary's mother could not bear such torment. It seemed to her that an evil spirit was mocking her through her daughter. Silent Mary was insistent that Lazarus was "dead," and would not stop repeating these words. She said other things also that were frightening for her mother. This sort of thing kept happening, until finally her mother could no longer bear having Silent Mary near. And so, as was mentioned before, Silent Mary and her maid were sent to live apart from the rest of the family.

Silent Mary suffered much in her soul. It was hard for such a young girl as she to see things so painful to bear. Often the things she saw in vision were imprinted right down to her physical body: bruises and scratches, for instance, would appear suddenly and with no apparent cause. As I entered into her predicament, I felt such sadness and grief, knowing that it was impossible for her to communicate with her family. Silent Mary was almost completely misunderstood.

I went ahead in time to when Silent Mary was older, and her life was drawing to a close. She was on the ground, lying on her back, staring up at the sky, in vision beholding a circle of angels. Her aura was a soft peach-gold light.[†]

Beholding the angels in this way was nothing strange or novel to her. It was her way of communicating with them. At the same time she harbored a great sadness in her soul, because even while in the presence of the angels she was unable to communicate what she saw to her fellow human beings.

It is hard to describe the nature of her thoughts, for she did not

---

† I often see this color of light around souls that have been conceived but are as yet unborn, and also in conjunction with previous incarnations. When in a therapeutic situation with someone whose soul is revealing an issue stemming from a prior incarnation, this same color frequently appears in the aura. But perhaps there is an altogether different reason why I see this color as the dominant color in Silent Mary's aura.

think as normal people do. She accepted herself and her life for the most part, but lacking the capacity to relate to others and to give them the gift of her visions caused a certain pain in her soul. As I entered into this sadness within her, my own throat was in such great pain that I had difficulty speaking. I think this was because I was feeling her pain at not being able to speak.†

Jesus Visits Silent Mary After His Baptism

AFTER JESUS was baptized he went again to visit Silent Mary. As before, she was in her garden when he came to see her, and when he arrived she again immediately beheld the radiance all around him. She could see Christ in him—the Son of God was not withheld from her sight.

When she saw him she thought, Ah! My only friend! Kneeling before him, she pressed her forehead to the ground in reverence and was so overcome that she could not lift herself up. She was weak, also, because for days she had not eaten. She whispered, "The Begotten One!"

Jesus picked her up tenderly, as if she were a child—and indeed she was not much bigger than a child—and carried her to the great, ancient tree. There he sat and cradled her in his lap. Timidly, she touched his cheek. He entered with her into a profound silence. She kissed his hands, touched his hair, and wept.

As he held her, healing power flowed from him, and the warmth thus streaming into her brought her more into present time. She thought to herself that perhaps, after all, it was admissible to be human—seeing that God wanted to be human also. For she knew that God was now in Jesus. It had always been a great challenge for her to remain in her body; indeed, throughout her life she had struggled with being human.

---

† This throat pain may have been more my own pain, for I know that I struggle with fear of speaking or publishing my visions. I have felt like a grain of sand in an oyster shell, turning into a pearl through great suffering—and what if the oyster is never opened and the pearl never shared? As I entered into Silent Mary's pain, I felt this same pain arise in my own soul.

When Jesus could tell she was more present and aware, he said to her, "Thank you for being here with me."

This was Christ speaking directly to the being that she was, acknowledging that she had come into incarnation with him. This was not simply the man Jesus speaking to Silent Mary, for she could feel Christ himself resonating within her being. He spoke intimate words to her, explaining why she was living as she was, and what her life had to do with his mission.

At this time Silent Mary knew she had not much longer to live, that she would soon be called to work from the other side of the threshold. I saw that after she died she followed Christ everywhere he went, like a ribbon of rainbow light streaming always around him—her sweet, benevolent face appearing like that of a curious child, ever watching him.

After this beautiful time of communion with Silent Mary, on this his second visit with her, Jesus told his mother about her. The two of them then set out together to see her.†

On this occasion Silent Mary could see the baby Jesus with the Blessed Mother. But she could not tell that she saw him only in vision, even though he was bathed in golden light and looked unearthly. She did not realize that she was seeing the baby Jesus as he had appeared when actually a child. A memory of him hovered so strongly around the Holy Mother and Silent Mary that they were able to interact with this memory as though it were a living child.

To Silent Mary, the Blessed Mother—robed in dark blue and burgundy—seemed tall and regal. The little child Jesus, appearing to be about three years old, clung to his mother's skirts, playfully winding himself up in them.

Silent Mary had been resting against a large stone; but upon seeing the Blessed Mother, she had arisen and bowed to her, as if to a queen. She knew this Lady from somewhere else, from a different time or place, perhaps even from a higher and better place; and she knew also that this Lady knew her.

I understood that it was significant that both were named Mary.

---

† The Blessed Mother came again later to see Silent Mary alone.

The Blessed Mother was also a Mary of Silence. These two Marys could both "converse" through Silence. It was because of the Silence of her soul that the Blessed Mother had such towering compassion—for "noisy" souls cannot truly be compassionate. And so it was also with Silent Mary. Her empathy was total. To know and to feel the thoughts and emotions of others—that was her gift.

The Blessed Mother placed Silent Mary's head gently in her lap and washed her face with perfumed water, using her own veil for this purpose. From a basket she took out some pretty carved combs, passing one through Silent Mary's tangled hair, pulling it back from her face, and securing it with others. She did this with slow and graceful movements. She did not speak as she tended her friend. She washed Silent Mary's hands and arranged flowers in her hair, lovingly acknowledging her—not out of pity, but out of a pure and certain knowledge of the being she was. Placing her hands gently over Silent Mary's eyes, she blessed her, asking that for the balance of her sojourn on Earth no evil being might have power over her. And her blessing proved efficacious, for Silent Mary suffered no demons during her final days of life.

The Blessed Mother took some fruit from her basket and squeezed out the juice, which she gave to Silent Mary. When the latter could drink no more, the Blessed Mother gave her pieces of the fruit.

The whole time this was going on, Silent Mary beheld the child Jesus playing nearby. At one point she even thought he had climbed up on her and put his little face right up against hers, smiling at her. Silent Mary could see a halo of light around her two visitors.

The Blessed Mother also gave Silent Mary a little honey on a golden spoon, which brought a smile to her lips, for she had seen honey in heaven. She knew it was the food of the angels, the pure golden light of love, and could not fathom how this Lady had come by the heavenly honey. Upon tasting the honey, she gained a little strength. After this, the Blessed Mother left, though Silent Mary was unaware of the manner in which she did so.

The maid, who had fallen asleep, awoke from her nap, and upon seeing Silent Mary, said, "Oh, Mary, I see you have done your hair. And you are so clean!" She praised Mary, saying that she was like a little queen when she was all cleaned up in that way.

Jesus came one last time to see Silent Mary and was again able to converse with her. She told him more things that would happen to him. Their time together was sweet. Silent Mary would forever cherish the time she had spent with God in her garden.

Silent Mary's Death

ON THE DAY Silent Mary died, the castle of Lazarus was busy with many visitors and much activity. Doctors would have said Silent Mary was dying of an illness, and it was true that she was very ill. But in truth she was dying simply because it was her time to go. Her work in the physical world was complete, and the time was come for her to translate her work to the spiritual world. It was because of this that her body's systems had begun to fail.

When she fell into unconsciousness she was dressed in white and laid upon a little bed in the garden, where a few people came to say farewell and mourn her impending death. Family members she had never met came to see her, as well as the few others she had known. Throughout that day, as people came to see her, Silent Mary witnessed all that transpired from outside her body. Her thoughts went something like this:

They did not know me; they did not know why I was here. I was nothing more than an afterthought, for rarely did anyone visit me or consider me... but I have no resentment. I know I was here as a channel for love, and to prepare Jesus for his path.

I saw that by incarnating with Jesus, and by having so deep a connection with him, Silent Mary was able to follow him intimately as his apostle in the spirit—as one who witnessed everything Jesus did.

When Silent Mary crossed over the threshold, the Blessed Mother was with her, one hand on her head, the other over her heart. She blessed her and prayed for her continuously as Silent Mary stepped out from the physical and into the spiritual realm.

And then everything became so crystal clear to Silent Mary's soul. She rejoiced over the life she had lived. She was taken into the bosom of an angel. Wherever she traveled thereafter, and whatever she saw, she experienced from within the bosom of the angel.

Her soul contains the record of all that Christ Jesus did, for she saw it all.

Mother Mary along with some of the holy women, including Martha, prepared Silent Mary's body for burial. She was laid to rest in the family tomb, the same tomb from which Lazarus would one day emerge from death to life. In spirit, she was "standing" right there, at the entrance of the tomb, at the side of Christ Jesus, when he called Lazarus forth. And it was just as she had seen as a little girl, when she had pointed to Lazarus and said over and over, "he... dead."

Jesus Christ and Silent Mary remained in communion with each other. She brought souls to him, both the departed and the living. She was so happy to be with him, working with him from the other side.

Appendix II

The beginning portion of this vision can be found in Chapter XIII.

Changing Water into Wine

I WAS WALKING down a garden path as the sun was setting. The sky shone dark purple, with a pale orange glow on the horizon. Lanterns hung from the branches of trees along this path, which led on to a trellis heavy with fragrant, flowering vines. There was a festive feeling in the air. Up ahead, music filled the house I was approaching. When I arrived, a wedding celebration was in full progress. The path I had been walking ended at a stone walkway. This led into a sort of patio covered with more trellises, from which, again, there hung flowering vines, garlands, and lanterns.

At the entrance a vessel of perfumed water was provided for washing one's feet. A servant was on duty to assist in removing sandals. I looked through the entrance into the patio area and saw many guests. They were gathered together in joyous dancing and singing. In the center of the crowd the bride and groom were engaged in a traditional wedding dance. They clasped their right hands high in the air as they danced clockwise in a circle. Others surrounded them, also dancing in a circle. The bride had curly dark hair, embellished with ribbons. Her dress was likewise decorated with many ribbons, as well as intricate embroidery. I knew that these people were wealthy—not only because of their beautifully decorated house, but also because of the many ribbons on the bride's dress. Ribbons were very expensive in those days, for it took nearly as long to weave a length of ribbon as it did to weave an entire length of cloth.

A great feast had been prepared—another sign of wealth. I walked to the table and saw a dish that seemed familiar to me. In fact, I craved it: stuffed figs cooked in some kind of fruit sauce, which had been baked in a shallow, clay bowl. The table fairly sagged under the weight of the many dishes laid out upon it.

Then I looked to my left and saw the Blessed Mother. She stood at the edge of the dancing crowd, smiling serenely. She was dressed in blue and white. Jesus approached her, and she quietly told him that the wine was already gone. He said, "Yes, the wine is gone. What is to be done?"

She looked up, her head tilted to one side, and smiled at him.

Jesus wore an expression of joy as he said, "Woman, what have I to do with thee? My hour is not yet come!"

By this he meant, "What shall we *do* together? And what can I do about the fact that people are marrying and being given in marriage, while not yet knowing the true Bridegroom? Although I am here to marry myself to humanity, the hour for this marriage is not yet come. If I perform a miracle here and now, they may know that the true Bridegroom is come." (She understood what he meant even though he did not speak any of this out loud.)

The Baptism in the Jordan had taken place only days before. Christ had only just descended into the earthly body of Jesus. The Blessed Mother knew that a great change had been wrought in her son. She was among the first to know, along with John the Baptist. A small number of disciples had already gathered to him, those whose hearts had awakened to the Presence. Some of these were also present at the wedding.

The Blessed Mother was standing before the vessels that had held the wine. She beckoned one of the servants to come to her. Jesus told the servant to fill the vessels with water. The servant said, "Master, the guests are important people. They will not be pleased with water, for they want wine." But Jesus again told him to fill the vessels with water, and the servant complied.

When this was done, Jesus bowed his head and held out the first two fingers of his right hand, touching each of the vessels as he said, "Be wine for the new covenant." (I am not certain this was spoken aloud, but I nonetheless clearly heard these words.) When he lifted his head, his eyes were luminous and bright, and his face beatific. He asked the servants to serve the water to all the guests. The servants looked perturbed, but one of them went ahead and dipped a ladle into the first vessel. A look of astonishment passed over his face as he saw that it was no longer water. I wanted to laugh, his face looked so comical. They checked the vessels and found that all now contained wine. The wine had certain powers; many of the guests experienced a wondrous state of heightened joy and were healed of various maladies.

Marriage at Cana: Changing Water into Wine

The Blessed Mother witnessed this miracle, and she kept it in her heart. In fact, this miracle was *accomplished* in her heart also, for *she* became a vessel for transformation—she became the receptacle for All Possibility. She was then able to know the great potential within everyone for change.

She knew that Jesus Christ could touch water and change it

into wine, and that so also could his touch change a person forever. Under the new covenant that Jesus was bringing forward, all could be transformed. Mary's heart became a great vessel of compassion, a reservoir containing and encompassing for all humankind its potential for transformation.

Whenever Mary appears to us, she holds in her heart our wonderful God-given potential. And when Christ Jesus appears, he holds for us that which stands in the way of our transformation, that which prevents us from reaching our potential. He holds for us our sin and darkness, until we are ready to change.

While Christ was in the flesh, he would walk and talk with human beings. He would drink wine in communion with them. In truth, he came here to wed himself to us.

The wine represents his blood, which would be spilled for us. It also would "run out" in his sacrifice as our beloved Bridegroom. His blood is living water. He *is* life, and he gives us life.

He said to his disciples that a time would come when he would no longer drink the wine with them, but that he would then "drink it in his Father's kingdom." And so, while he was in the process of incarnating more and more deeply into the body of Jesus, he would drink the wine, which was to symbolize that he would take in the Earth in its fallen state, and also humanity in its fallen state, and be in communion with us.

And there are many more mysteries to be revealed regarding the miracle of the changing of the water into wine.

Returning now to Magdalene,[†] it can be said that she mistakenly thought the Blessed Mother was judging her for her past. But actually she looked only to Magdalene's potential. The truth is that Magdalene was judging herself, and could not see her own potential.

I realized that I was in the same condition: while in vision, my feelings of unworthiness were as a pain in my chest. I said to the Blessed Mother, "I am only common water compared to you!"

---

† Referring to the conversation with Jesus in Chapter XIII.

But the moment I thought this, I heard her reply, "No, my daughter, I know only that you are the most precious wine."

The Chalice of Miracles

I WAS TAKEN then to the cross, where the Blessed Mother and Magdalene, along with some few others, were grieving over the death of Jesus. To my left, I saw the centurion bearing his lance toward Jesus's side. Jesus's head was bowed. He had just crossed the threshold of death. Magdalene's head was bowed also, the weight of her tears inclining her toward the Earth. The Blessed Mother embraced her as the centurion moved closer on his horse, his face set like stone. He was carrying out the orders of his superiors, making sure that Jesus was indeed dead. As he lanced the heart of Jesus, blood and water ran out from the wound and rained down upon him. Just then Magdalene lifted her head. She held up her mantle to catch the fluids as they fell.

As the purifying water and the divine love of Christ's blood fell upon him, the centurion was immediately converted. This was the final gift of the body of Christ Jesus—the water of purification and the blood of his love miraculously transforming the centurion's heart.

Magdalene was the human being Christ had loved the most. This is not to say that he loved her in an exclusive way, or that he loved her more than any other, but that he was able to love her to the utmost because she accepted his redeeming love to a greater degree than did anyone else. For she had been purified by his love. *She was water that had been turned to wine.* Whereas the centurion's heart was changed in a miraculous instant, Magdalene's heart was changed over time. She worked to transform her soul through Christ's help. For her, the miracle of transformation took its course over several years. But both these ways can be called miraculous. For some of us, our entire life is an ongoing miracle, though perhaps we will not realize this until we have passed through the threshold of death and can look back from a higher perspective at the life we lived. And for others, grace rains down upon them and they are immediately transformed.

The Strike of the Centurion's Lance

The Blessed Mother was already a pure vessel. Her soul did not require the work that Magdalene's soul required. She is the vessel that holds the living miracle. Her grace is the *essence* of the miracle, we could say. She *is* the love that is the fermenting agent which brings about the miracle of transformation. Magdalene was the water that needed to be held within a vessel of love in order to be transformed into wine.

Magdalene compared herself to the Blessed Mother, wishing she could be like her and thinking she was always falling short. She did not realize that there were no grounds for comparison, for although they both came to be with Jesus as he fulfilled his mission, they did so to serve very different purposes. When Magdalene stood under the cross, catching the blood and water from Jesus in her mantle, she became herself truly a vessel—a chalice of miracles. It was not until she had suffered with her Lord under the cross, and then witnessed his glorious resurrection, that her miraculous transformation was accomplished. Only then could she fully contain within herself the love and the power of the miracle she had thereby become. And she now holds this key for others as they go through the process of deep soul transformation.

Thus is the Holy Mother a chalice of the original *Divine Love*— the Love by which we all were spiritually begotten. Inspired by the Mother, Magdalene became the chalice of *human love* transformed. Her chalice is filled symbolically with the living water of purification, which fell to her from Christ. And this is mixed also with the water of the tears she shed out of pure love for her Savior. The Blessed Mother's chalice, on the other hand, is filled symbolically with the blood of Christ's Love, for his blood contained both the pure—yet earthly—human love given him by his Mother, and the Divine Love he himself brought from the heavenly spheres.

We must bring the two together—the Divine Love and the transformative mercy—by praying that the water of our untransformed souls be changed into the wine of Divine Love. Magdalene will be present throughout Earth's evolution, holding up the chalice of transformation, reservoir of our potential to transform our own souls. Whereas the Blessed Mother holds up the chalice of original Divine Love, inspiring us to continue onward even through our many trials, Magdalene is the guiding

star leading us ever forward to the performance of our own miracle of transfiguration. To know the Blessed Mother is to know
Original Love. To know Magdalene is to know transformed
human love.

May we all accept pure love, so that our souls may be illuminated as we do our work here upon the Earth!

You Could Not Watch with Me for One Hour

Appendix III

The beginning portion of this vision may be found in Chapter XIX.

The Sin of the World

I WAS TAKEN forward in time, to the agony of Christ Jesus in the Garden of Gethsemane. This was the moment when the sins of the world began to enter into him, to be taken on by him.

He had foretold that the twelve disciples would prove unable to withstand the presence of the darkness drawing toward their Master, and I saw that his words did indeed come to pass. Peter, James, and John fell into unconsciousness because they could not endure the depth and breadth of the world's sin. More than this, neither could they endure the unfathomable suffering of their Lord, who was taking on this sin in its full measure. Scarcely could they even have borne their *own* darkness and yet survived. How much the less, then, could they bear the collective darkness of all humanity!

This is one reason they swooned. As for the other disciples, they fled when Jesus was betrayed at the hands of Judas. All save John were unable to remain with Jesus to the end.

At this point I began to feel Christ's agony as he came to know the sins of the world. Of course, I could never have experienced even a feather's weight of what he was experiencing. I could fathom his agony only in the remotest sense. But even so, this vastly unknowable deed of Christ will be forever etched upon my soul!

Throughout this time of Christ's assumption of such terrible darkness, the Father's love expanded, reaching out further and further in its "descent." Never before had the Father's love been amplified to such a degree! The love of the Father poured out to the Son, who in unutterable agony was taking on the sins of the world. Never before had the Father's love reached into such depths. His love was drawn forth toward humanity through the Son's sacrifice.

Magdalene, witnessing the disciples' flight from Jesus, knew that his words had been fulfilled, for she remembered indelibly his prophecy that, save for John of Zebedee, the disciples would prove unable to remain by him throughout his Passion.

The disciples themselves were not fully aware that they were experiencing the utter darkness surrounding the Master—they knew only that they felt so great a fear and so terrible an oppression that they could do no other than flee. The Blessed Mother was able to remain with her Son only because of her great purity. She could remain conscious of the great burden he was carrying, and through her open heart share his unfathomable compassion for humanity and its darkness. It was because of this great compassion that she could remain by him.

As for Magdalene, she was strengthened inwardly in a special and profound way (as shall be described in Book II of this trilogy) so that she also was able to remain and behold in full the sacrifice of Christ Jesus.

John also was able—for a specific purpose—to remain with him till the end. He was sustained in such a way that he could remain.

The holy women also were able to follow him to the cross and remain with him, although they had to keep a greater distance than those who could stay by the cross. It was through the compassion of the Blessed Mother and their deep heart connection to Magdalene that they were able to remain present throughout much of the Passion. The angel of Magdalene was able to strengthen them. All the holy women witnessed the final sacrifice of Christ Jesus. They understood full well that in taking upon himself the sins of humanity, he became the great healing for all, establishing redemption for all through his divine love.

As Magdalene remained by Jesus at the cross, a part of her took on the imprint of his sacrifice, so that during the remaining years of her life following the crucifixion, as well as during her later lives, she carried also the gift of bearing the sins of others, of taking on the sicknesses of humanity. This was, and is, her way of serving her Lord. She was imprinted with the great healing gift

Only John and the Holy Women Stay by the Cross
(Along with the Centurion who Pierced Christ's Side)

of divine love. Because of this, she became a healing balm for others and for the world, and she continues, now and always, at this healing task. She knows the suffering and the darkness, and channels the Father's healing love to those in need.

It was she who in her soul first experienced this healing in its full measure, for she was healed of her darkness by the Master himself. In great faith she had given over all she was and had allowed her darkness to be taken from her, as she received with love the great redemption offered by Christ. This is why she now serves humanity by awakening souls to their inner darkness and to their need for healing, bringing them in this way to Christ.

I felt the great love Magdalene cherishes for humanity. All who awaken and strive to heal their darkness bring her such joy that she would fall to their feet and kiss them, even as she did so many times with Jesus—so great is her joy when even *one* soul comes to Christ.

This is her work: to remain with humanity and watch over all souls, bringing them to Christ. She has no fear of the darkness of humanity, for she was willing to remain with her Master and experience the greatest darkness of all. She bears great hope for all souls on Earth. And she calls out to the world: *His Word is a lamp unto thy feet! He is the Word. He is the light that will bring us out of the darkness!*

Appendix IV

A Message from the Holy Women

During Holy Week, a group of friends came together to commune with the holy women who followed Jesus Christ, and they received this message: "The holy women are spiritually drawn to you and desire that you become further acquainted with them and their mission in serving Christ Jesus."

MANY OF the holy women knew each other before they knew Jesus. Some were related by family ties. Some were followers of John the Baptist and had been prepared and initiated by him so that they might recognize the mantle that rested upon Jesus.

The first official gathering of these women took place, with about half of them present, at the home of Lazarus. Magdalene was not present. She had not yet been healed of the demons that plagued her. Her relationship with Martha was still not a healthy one. She was estranged from her sister. Magdalene was still very much entrenched in her life of luxury and had no use for Martha's "mundane" ways. She thought nothing of Martha's piety.

Present at the home of Lazarus on this occasion were Martha and a few others, including her friends Joanna Chusa and Mary the mother of Mark. These women had watched as Jesus gathered followers, sometimes attracting considerable audiences. Because it was becoming necessary that he travel almost continually, the women wished to set up a support plan to assist him and the disciples as they traveled.

Some of these women were wealthy. A few even possessed more than one home. Several owned inns, and these latter decided to establish accommodations where Jesus and his disciples could stay. They knew others also who owned fitting places that might serve to house the travelers.

The holy women's temporal service to Jesus and the disciples was thus to provide them food and rest. But the more closely they worked with Jesus, the more did their need for inner, spiritual healing grow. It became needful for them to be unburdened of any darkness within so that their gifts could be made manifest, especially their spiritual gifts—gifts that would prove of such worth to Jesus and his mission.

As time passed, other women touched in a certain way by Jesus came into the circle. One such was Dinah, the "woman at the well." Dinah owned an inn, and after the incident at the well, where Jesus had brought before her all she had done in her unseemly past, she became a close follower. There was also the woman usually called Veronica, although that was not her real name.† I heard her being called something like "Sarah," but I think this may have been a shortened form of her true name. She hailed from a family that owned vineyards and pressed the vintage.

---

† Veronica's real name was Seraphia. She lived in Jerusalem and was the daughter of a brother of Zacharias of Hebron, who was the father of John the Baptist. Thus, Seraphia was a cousin of John the Baptist. She was also related to the old priest Simeon and knew his sons. Veronica was already an adult when the 12-year old Jesus was teaching in the temple. At that time she was not yet married. Later, Veronica married Sirach, who was a member of the Sanhedrin. To begin with he was hostile toward Christ and his followers; and often, when he noticed that she was helping Jesus and the disciples, he would keep Veronica locked up at home. Sirach received instruction from Joseph of Arimathea and Nicodemus—both members of the Sanhedrin also—and on this account his attitude toward Jesus Christ changed. He then allowed Seraphia to follow Jesus and serve the community of the disciples. They had three children, two of whom later became disciples. In fact, her son Amandor was one of the first disciples of Jesus. Seraphia was a tall, beautiful, and courageous woman. It was she who purchased the holy vessel from the temple and gave it to be used at the Last Supper. This vessel was the Grail cup, which was given originally by Melchizedek to Abraham, when Melchizedek gave Abraham bread and wine. It was handed down through the ages as a most holy and sacred artifact, eventually—through Veronica (Seraphia)—to come into the hands of Jesus Christ for the institution of the Eucharist at the Last Supper. Seraphia, after her death, received the Latin name Veronica, that is, *vera icon*, meaning "true icon," because of her veil, which on Good Friday received an imprint of the face of Christ. It was not so much a veil as a linen neck scarf, which she had hanging around her shoulders at the time when Jesus Christ on

Veronica Presents Her Veil to Jesus

that Friday was carrying the cross through the streets of Jerusalem. When she beheld his battered and bloody face, she offered her veil, reaching out with it toward Christ's face, as a sign of her empathy for his suffering. He pressed it to his face and the veil miraculously received an imprint thereof. The veil was subsequently given to the Virgin Mary. From her, it came into the hands of the apostles and was brought to Rome. At the time when the persecution of the Christians started, about three years after Christ's Ascension, Seraphia was imprisoned, where she died of hunger.

And of course, we know Magdalene's story: that she was healed of a terrible demon by Jesus, but shortly thereafter fell away again into even deeper darkness, only to undergo further healing by Christ. Magdalene brought many gifts forward after her healings. She had traveled to Egypt and other places, in search both of wisdom and of the things she required to fabricate special oils. Before her demons were finally cast out, she had employed such oils primarily to selfish ends. She had not yet awakened to the spiritual power of these oils. Only after the seventh demon had been cast out from her did she come to know the true power of anointing with oils. The beings connected with her healing oils were then able to work through her, and she became a great healer.

The other holy women also used oils in healing. Christ gave them this healing gift, which is essentially *love*—the gift of love. Each kind of oil embodies an aspect of love, a frequency of love. These oils were thus vessels or carriers of love and became highly sacred as the women, in their healing practice, added to the oils their love.

Many gifts of the Spirit were manifest among the holy women. It was a fateful time. At first they kept these gifts to themselves. But Jesus, who presided over the receiving and opening of these gifts, gave them leave to utilize their gifts in ministering unto others. To this end, he would bring the holy women together and instruct them. Here are some of the words he addressed to the assembled women:

"I have requested your presence in order that I might teach you. In truth, it is the Divine Mother who has brought you together. But She is as yet unable to work upon the Earth, for She had first to sacrifice Herself. When the time is come, I shall set Her in Her rightful place. The world, however, is not yet ripe for this. But this you know already, for women have not yet their rightful place as equals of men.

"And so, despite the great gifts that have been made manifest in each of you, fear stalks among you, for you no longer know your rightful place in society. For this reason you have asked, 'What shall we do?'

"Your hearts desire to serve me and all of humanity, and you have received the gifts necessary to do so. But you harbor fear of what men might do were you to show forth your power. Yes, even some of your husbands are much against what you have brought forth, for it frightens them also. They would cling to the old ways, for they fear priests and scribes and authorities. Their love for you bids them admonish you to be silent and remain veiled, to keep to the shadows.

Jesus with the Holy Women

"Know that I have unveiled you for a purpose, but that you are to be unveiled only to me and to one another. Not even the twelve disciples shall know you as I know you. They are not yet able to understand the beauty and goodness and wisdom gestating within you. But at a later time they will indeed accept you. They will learn from you and draw upon your strength.

"You will be made pure through me. O divine sisters, you have each undergone your own miracle. I have raised you up and you are beautiful to me.

"I set my Blessed Mother before you as an emulation of the Divine Mother. Look to her, my beautiful sisters, for she will lead you and serve you with her compassionate heart. She is the woman of all women. She is of royal birth and you are her ladies of the court.

"On her right hand is Mary Magdalene, whom I set also before you. I do this because she has known the deepest depths. She descended further than any of the disciples, and I raised her up.

"And on her left hand I give you Mary Cleophas.

"These three shall go before you and prepare your way.

"For the remaining twelve, you shall be set apart in threes, and each three shall receive into their midst a higher being who will work through them. These higher beings will collaborate in facilitating the work I would have you accomplish for the sake of my mission, work that must yet be done in secret.

"To outer appearance you will be serving my temporal needs only. But we shall meet together in secret and I will initiate you. I will teach you the Higher Mysteries, for you have ears to hear and eyes to see. Through the men also shall I work a mighty work, but it will be a different work.

"Through you, my sisters, I shall plant seeds that in the far future will grow and flourish into the community of Sophia, where all spiritual gifts will be present. Each of you will be given a gift to carry throughout your lives on Earth. In each life this gift will grow and flourish as you touch others with it. And those so touched by you shall receive this gift also, until all these gifts become a *City*—the Holy City, the New Jerusalem, the heavenly community of Christ and Sophia.

"And within the New Jerusalem there shall be twelve communities, each nurturing a particular spiritual gift. The twelve communities will be open to receive all whose hearts are pure and who wish to come and partake. Certain great beings are stewards of each gift, and these will govern each community. And each community will have also its own precious stone, one for each of the holy women.

"I set before you this trinity of the three Marys. They will work in all the communities and with every being, and with each of the twelve spiritual gifts. They will oversee the great work of building the community of Sophia, in order that I, the Son of God, even Christ, may reign there forever.

"But much work must first be accomplished, both now and in the coming times. You will be instructed and come to know your particular gift."

Such are the things Jesus taught the holy women. As he did so, angels witnessed and recorded his words in the Book of Life. Some of these words can now be given, for it is time. But some cannot now be given, for their time has not yet come.

Among the words that can be given are these, regarding the holy women's question, "What can we do?"

"Those of you in the present time who desire to join in the work of the holy women must first face your own inner darkness and work to heal it. For this darkness obscures your access to the spiritual realm. You must face the guardian of the threshold, whose task it is to reveal to you your own darkness before you can enter that realm. Only in this way can you come to know your spiritual gifts.

"You have several such gifts, but there is one particular gift that each of you is specially charged to bear. It is this gift that will bring you to the Holy City when it is prepared. For that *is* your home. But again, first there is the needed healing.

"In this quest you may come together to assist one another and thereby take courage and draw strength. You will come to discover also, as you progress, that there is work you can do together. This may give rise to great excitement. But do not rush headlong into the future, even though you may sometimes have a sense of the great work you shall in time jointly accomplish.

"Try not to mark out and define this work while you are yet in the process of healing. Do not adopt identities for yourselves before you *know* yourselves. And do not presume to assign each other such identities until all veils have been removed and you can truly say, *I know you.*

"Let go of assumptions and inclinations. What you are to do will be made clear to you when the time comes. You know well enough how drawn you feel to particular spiritual activities, but do not fail to remain open also to new experience, for only in this way will you come to know what you are truly called to do.

"Remember always that you will be enlightened by Christ as he walks with you. At times you will feel this illumination, but at other times you will face your darkness. This is your opportunity to overcome the dark forces within you. You may choose to face these dark forces and overcome them, or you may choose to slumber, turning your backs upon your darkness, as does the greater part of humankind.

"Yes, the world sleeps on while the evil ones marshall their forces. The time ahead will be one of a great confrontation between good and evil. Even so, as you face what is approaching, you will witness miracles. Your gifts will indeed be opened.

"No matter how dark things become or how alone you may feel, know that this is foreseen in order that your highest good may come to you. Know that you yourselves wanted to come to Earth at this time in order to manifest certain gifts, to bring them forth while you are in the physical realm. Know also that it may even be that some of these gifts can be opened only against a background of darkness such as will allow the light to manifest. And know also that the gift you open in this life will be available to you for the remainder of your life, and for lifetimes to come, until finally you receive your glory. And then you shall *become* a gift.

"The holy women are with you and will serve you and will bring to you words of Christ that will lead you on. They bestow these words even now upon your hearts in the names of Christ and Sophia. Amen."

Appendix V

Saint Christopher

SOON AFTER I began to have visions, I realized that it was a challenge for me to return to present time. Sometimes it seemed that I was in an expanded state, and had difficulty contracting back to my normal state. This struggle to contract 'back to size' often lasted for hours, during which time I was in great pain, with dizziness and nausea. Frequently I was also attacked by evil beings on my return journey.

Because of the struggle to return, I prayed for assistance and guidance regarding how this could be done in a manner that would be safer for me. One night I had a dream in which a medieval woman handed me a card upon which the image of a saint was printed. I did not at first know who this saint was—but even so, the woman told me to ask him for help. I soon came to know that he was St. Christopher.

The next time I traveled back in time I had a very intense vision of Christ's descent from the Cross. Afterward, when trying to return, I simply could not get back. Then I remembered the dream and starting calling for St. Christopher to assist me. He appeared immediately and showed me that there was an awful "river" that needed crossing in order to fully return.

The terrible thing about this river was that it was full of all manner of evil creatures that wanted to prevent me from doing this work with the Mystery of Golgotha. They would leap up at me, tear at me, and try to pull me down. But all St. Christopher had to do was put his staff into the "water," and the beings were instantly repelled. He carried me safely across and told me that with his assistance I would always be safe traversing time. He has come to carry me back ever since. I am truly grateful for my strong and fearless traveling companion!

Palestine and Egypt

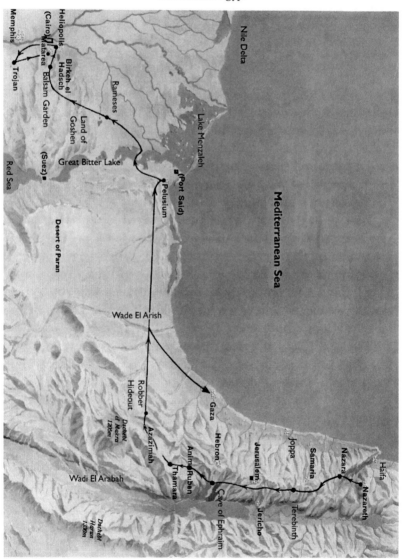

(Showing Travels of the Holy Family to Egypt, according to A.C. Emmerich)

Region of Capernaum and Bethany

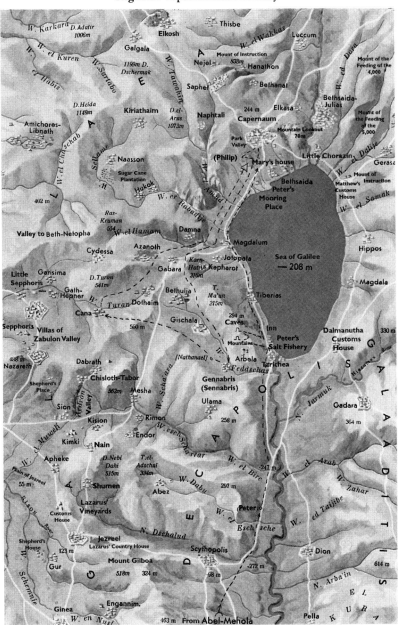

(Showing Travels of Jesus at the Marriage of Cana, according to A.C. Emmerich)

Area Around Capernaum During the Time of Christ

CPSIA information can be obtained at www.ICGtesting.com
Printed in the USA
LVOW121035141012

302782LV00006B/17/P